M000251117

REFORMING NEW ORLEANS

REFORMING NEW ORLEANS

The Contentious Politics of Change in the Big Easy

Peter F. Burns and Matthew O. Thomas

Cornell University Press
Ithaca and London

Copyright © 2015 by Cornell University

All rights reserved. Except for brief quotations in a review, this book, or parts thereof, must not be reproduced in any form without permission in writing from the publisher. For information, address Cornell University Press, Sage House, 512 East State Street, Ithaca, New York 14850.

First published 2015 by Cornell University Press
First printing, Cornell Paperbacks, 2015

Printed in the United States of America

Library of Congress Cataloging-in-Publication Data
Burns, Peter F., author.
   Reforming New Orleans : the contentious politics of change in the Big Easy / Peter F. Burns and Matthew O. Thomas.
      pages cm
   Includes bibliographical references and index.
   ISBN 978-0-8014-5385-4 (cloth : alk. paper) —
   ISBN 978-1-5017-0044-6 (pbk. : alk. paper)
   1. New Orleans (La.)—Politics and government. 2. Political culture—Louisiana—New Orleans. 3. Hurricane Katrina, 2005—Political aspects. I. Thomas, Matthew O., author. II. Title.
   JS1202.A2B87 2015
   320.9763'35—dc23   2015018962

Cornell University Press strives to use environmentally responsible suppliers and materials to the fullest extent possible in the publishing of its books. Such materials include vegetable-based, low-VOC inks and acid-free papers that are recycled, totally chlorine-free, or partly composed of nonwood fibers. For further information, visit our website at www.cornellpress.cornell.edu.

Cloth printing   10 9 8 7 6 5 4 3 2 1
Paperback printing   10 9 8 7 6 5 4 3 2 1

To Clarence N. Stone:
Scholar, teacher, mentor, and friend

And it is worth noting that nothing is harder to manage, more risky in the undertaking, or more doubtful of success than to set up as the introducer of a new order. Such an innovator has as enemies all the people who were doing well under the old order, and only halfhearted defenders in those who hope to profit from the new. This halfheartedness derives partly from fear of opponents who have the law on their side, and partly from human skepticism, since men don't really believe in anything new till they have solid experience of it.

–Machiavelli, *The Prince*

Contents

Acknowledgments

Many scholars have taken the time to provide feedback and advice during the course of this project. First and foremost Clarence Stone, to whom we dedicate the book, continued in his role as mentor to both of us. Clarence's constant willingness to supply insightful critiques played a critical role in this work. His kindness, generosity, and intellect make him a true pleasure, and we thank him both for his efforts in this research and, more important, for his friendship.

Several other scholars made substantial contributions to the direction and content of the book. We thank George Capowich, Susan Clarke, Robert Collins, Peter Eisinger, Steven Erie, and Robert Whelan for their significant assistance. J. Celeste Lay and Chris Fettweis are the best of friends and colleagues. They read earlier versions of the book and made it a lot better. Thank you.

Colleagues attending the annual meetings of both the American Political Science Association and the Urban Affairs Association offered guidance and support, especially Matthew Crenson, Emily Farris, Mirya Holman, Cynthia Horan, Paul Kantor, Mickey Lauria, Paul Lewis, Stephen McGovern, Karen Mossberger, Robert Montjoy, Karen Orren, Joel Rast, Joshua Sapotichne, Hank Savitch, Todd Swanstrom, Jessica Trounstine, Linda Faye Williams, and Margaret Weir. We also thank Michael McGandy of Cornell University Press. Michael saw the promise in this book well before its completion and has supported us throughout the process.

We wish to thank all of the people we interviewed; they spent many hours educating us about the governance, politics, and policy of pre- and post-Katrina New Orleans.

Peter Burns thanks his colleagues at Loyola University New Orleans and Dartmouth College for their encouragement and feedback throughout the project. They include Natasha Bingham, Sean Cain, Michael Cowan, Phil Dynia, Mark Fernandez, Phil Frady, Eric Gorham, Mary Troy Johnston, Sam Joel, Young Soo Kim, Gerardo Lopez, Larry Lorenz, Will O'Neill, Luis Miron, Conrad Raabe, Andrew Samwick, Tommy Screen, Ron Shaiko, Roger White, and Kevin Wildes. Special thanks to Wendy Porche and Chris Wiseman for all their help. The book would not have been possible without the love, support, and guidance provided by Ed Renwick. Loyola students who helped with the project include Helena Buchmann, Allison Cormier, and Ellie Diaz. Many people read earlier versions of the book. They include Renia Ehrenfeucht, David Marcello, Robert Montjoy, Marla Nelson, and Bob Whelan. Thank you. Mike Berner, Adria N. Buchanan, Jessica Cantave, Brittany Dapremont, John Erlingheuser, Sean Gorman, and Elise LeMelle are great friends who supported me during this project. Matt Thomas is the best friend and co-author I could ever hope for in life.

My parents, Peter and Pat Burns, provided me with all the support I needed (and more) to succeed throughout my life. Patty Burns, Ed Thorndike, and Holly Thorndike make up the best family a brother, brother-in-law, and uncle could ever dream of.

Matt Thomas thanks his colleagues in the political science department at California State University, Chico. For their constant encouragement during the duration, I am especially grateful to Sharon Barrios, Jon Caudill, Alan Gibson, Ryan Patten, Robert Stanley, Charles Turner, and Lori Weber.

My coauthor, Peter Burns, is both a colleague and a dear friend. Working with him lends credence to the adage that two heads are better than one. Thank you for everything, Pete.

I owe a debt of gratitude to my parents, John and Jill Thomas, who instilled a love of reading and learning in me; my path to academia is easily traced to their influence. My sons, Zachary and Liam, are sources of pride and wonderment, and even on the toughest days, spending a few minutes with them brings joy to my heart. Most important, my wife, Kristen, was there every step of the way, with an infinite supply of patience as I returned to the office night after night to write (and perhaps more important, when I headed to New Orleans each summer for research trips). Her love and support mean the world to me. Thanks H.B.

REFORMING NEW ORLEANS

Introduction

Rebuilding Governance, Politics, and Policy in New Orleans

New Orleans was different after Hurricane Katrina, but it was not new. On February 12, 2014, a federal court convicted former mayor C. Ray Nagin on twenty counts of conspiracy, bribery, wire fraud, money-laundering conspiracy, and filing false tax returns.[1] That a New Orleans public official used his position of authority to enrich himself and his family was not new, but Nagin's case was different. He was the first mayor in the history of New Orleans to be convicted on corruption charges. The sustained attack by the federal government against public corruption in post-Katrina New Orleans and the citizens' lack of tolerance for corruption were not new, but they were different.

The governance, politics, and policy of post-Katrina New Orleans differed from their pre-Katrina predecessors, but in many instances change began before the storm. Of all of the facets of Hurricane Katrina and its consequences, the ways in which the disaster changed governance, politics, and policy are the least understood. Government leaders at all levels, scholars, and the media use a variety of indicators to gauge the recovery: repopulation, the number of buildings and homes repaired or rebuilt, infrastructure restored, and the number of jobs regained.[2] These measures do not tell us much about the decision-making process or which groups won or lost as a result of Katrina.

After Hurricane Katrina, several questions resounded for people who were considering a return to New Orleans: Where will I work? Where will my children go to school? Where will I live? Will I be safe? Each of these questions is tied to a particular public policy arena: economic development, public education, housing, and public safety. In the chapters that follow, we examine each of these policy areas to provide the details of what has changed and who benefited.

Unlike most other books about disaster recovery, this one explores the dynamics of governmental and political reconstruction. To what degree would the storm affect this struggle between the city's embedded interests on one side and extralocal actors and reform-minded locals on the other? One aspect of our analytical framework places change on a continuum. At one extreme, the status quo prevails after disaster; those who held advantaged positions continue to defend their vested interests and resist large-scale change. Other disaster-stricken cities have also struggled to make significant changes to governance. San Francisco had created a new city plan prior to the earthquake and fires of 1906, but except for the construction of a civic center, it ignored that plan in its rebuilding efforts. The governing coalition in Waco, Texas, resisted governmental intervention of all kinds before a tornado hit the city in 1953. The city's antigovernment ethos dominated recovery decisions and resisted change. Citizens' deep-seated beliefs are baked into a city and its institutions over time. Disasters do not wipe these beliefs away, in spite of rhetoric about a new day or opportunities to start afresh. Post-disaster periods can experience a resurgence of past patterns because people, institutions, and the ethos persist.[3]

At the other end of the change continuum, new interests emerge, entrenched interests weaken, and government, politics, and policy change. At this extreme, disaster expands the scale of change that people are willing to consider. It heightens a sense of interdependence and shared fate among residents, who think, "We're in this together." Charitable acts and altruism rise in the immediate aftermath of disaster.

Disasters are thought to create a window of opportunity to alter political relationships and outcomes and to enable existing leaders to push through changes that failed to find support prior to the catastrophe. They can weaken current arrangements and expose the inadequacies of those in charge. After the Mexico City earthquake in 1985, citizen protests created a social movement that produced a democratic transition in that city. The 1900 hurricane in Galveston, Texas, led to a new, reformed local government structure. Disasters made way for a peace process in Aceh, Indonesia, and organizational and legal reform in Sri Lanka.[4]

Post-Katrina New Orleans provides a test of where New Orleans sits on this continuum. Is it closer to the extreme where entrenched interests prevent meaningful change, or has the city experienced significant and effective changes in its governance structure, policy process, and political outcomes? The mix of old and entrenched relations with newly formed and possibly more equity-minded relationships allows for an examination of who gains and who pays the cost of change.

In some cases, disasters lead to fundamental governmental change. In others, those who ruled before the sudden shock grow stronger afterwards. This book uses the New Orleans case to understand conditions under which emerging interests have supplanted embedded ones.

Sociologists find that disaster recovery reveals where power lies in society. Social conflict drives disaster recovery, which produces winners and losers. Pre-disaster development decisions tend to locate the poor and racial and ethnic minorities in dangerous or disaster-prone areas. As a result, those groups experience greater physical damage from natural disasters than whites. The long-term standard of living declines for communities of color after disasters in part because racial and ethnic minorities are less likely than whites to hold comprehensive insurance before a catastrophe and more likely to rely on governmental aid afterwards.[5]

When the Chicago heat wave of 2005 killed more than seven hundred people, the city's black residents were more vulnerable than whites. In *Heat Wave*, Eric Klinenberg claims that Chicago officials responded too slowly to this disaster, and "that an emerging population of poor, old, and isolated residents makes extreme summer weather especially dangerous."[6] The effects of the 2003 French heat wave also depended on location of residence, level of poverty, and extent of isolation.[7]

Some scholars argue that local elected officials respond to those who exerted power before the disaster and powerful interest groups, particularly from the business community, pressure government to rebuild in the manner they dictate. The poor lack these advantages and so experience a slower rebuilding than those with resources. In the United States, racial and ethnic minorities, regardless of class, bear the burden of disasters because of language, housing patterns, building construction, community and realtor racism, isolation, and cultural insensitivities.[8]

Middle-class homeowners with full insurance coverage are in the best position to receive public and private funding after disasters. When Hurricane Hugo devastated Charleston, South Carolina, many people used their insurance and government money to install luxuries such as hot tubs, leading some observers to call this phenomenon the Jacuzzi Effect.[9] After a disaster, people with money buy or rent the viable housing that remains in the affected area, while those without these resources move from place to place.

Political Arrangements and the Study of Political Change after Disaster

In this book we develop the concept of a political arrangement as a way to analyze change and address the policy process and outcomes. A political arrangement distinguishes actual governance from the formal institutions of government. It identifies how various sectors of society interact to set and support an agenda, endorse and challenge strategic policy options, enact policy, and produce winners and losers. The political arrangement constitutes a body of relationships that gives a city its policy-making character.

To better understand the dynamics of New Orleans's political landscape, we examine the city in two general dimensions: its political arrangements and its fidelity to policy agendas. All cities have some form of political arrangements. Some have a single overarching political arrangement, categorized as a unified political arrangement. In others there are multiple sets of political arrangements, and these typically align with policy arenas. For example, a city may have one political arrangement that exerts influence and decision making over economic development and another political arrangement that exerts influence over public education. When a city has multiple political arrangements, we call it diffuse.

Agenda fidelity represents the degree to which a political arrangement is able to promote and execute an agenda over time. When a political arrangement can sustain a cohesive agenda for a lengthy period of time, the agenda is considered strong. Conversely, when the agenda is loose, intermittent, or even nonexistent, the agenda is considered weak. These two dimensions allow us to categorize a city according to a comparative matrix depicting a variety of city types (see table 1).

TABLE 1

City variation comparison, by political arrangements and policy agenda

		Policy agenda fidelity	
		Strong	Weak
Political arrangement(s)	Concentrated	• Concentrated & strong • Single arrangement	• Concentrated & weak • Single arrangement
	Diffuse	• Diffuse & strong • Multiple arrangements	• Diffuse & weak • Multiple arrangements

Pre-Katrina New Orleans had multiple political arrangements with little agenda fidelity (lower-right quadrant) and was beset with patronage and corruption. But cities can range from the highly cohesive, whereby unified political arrangements exercise strong agenda fidelity (upper-left quadrant), to the dysfunctional space filled by New Orleans. The other quadrants represent stages between these two extremes and may suggest that a city is experiencing transition. One way to approach our investigation about change in the city is to compare this pre-storm starting point with where New Orleans now falls on this matrix.

A political arrangement can be visualized as a series of concentric circles (see figure 1). At the inner core sit those who can set the agenda and who command the resources and authority to fulfill it. Those in the outer core enact policy, and they support and benefit from that agenda and those policies. The third ring from the center contains those who support agenda alternatives but do not currently command the tools necessary to change the agenda. The farther from the center of the political arrangement a group or set of actors is, the less likely they are to set the agenda, implement policies, have their policy options enacted, and benefit from the agenda. Those in the outermost ring of a political arrangement pay the highest costs and enjoy the fewest benefits.

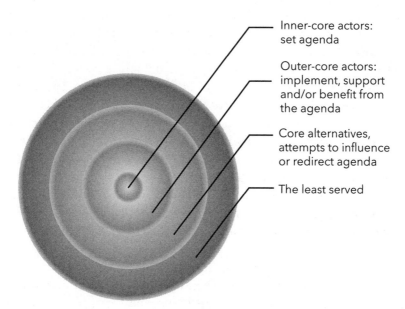

Inner-core actors: set agenda

Outer-core actors: implement, support and/or benefit from the agenda

Core alternatives, attempts to influence or redirect agenda

The least served

Figure 1. Example of a generic political arrangement.

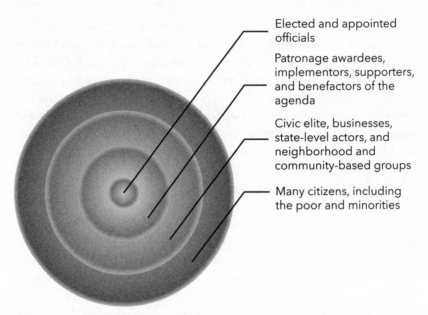

Elected and appointed officials

Patronage awardees, implementors, supporters, and benefactors of the agenda

Civic elite, businesses, state-level actors, and neighborhood and community-based groups

Many citizens, including the poor and minorities

Figure 2. The political arrangement in pre-Katrina New Orleans.

The groups' positions in the political arrangement determine the kinds of policies a city pursues and which groups are likely to win or lose. As the next chapter demonstrates, a dysfunctional political arrangement operated in pre-Katrina New Orleans. It was characterized by corruption at the center, a lack of engagement among those in the middle, and significant racial and economic divisions among the entire population (see figure 2). Elected and appointed officials and their allies ruled this arrangement, which produced substandard services and patronage across a spectrum of policies.

Reformers attempted to achieve change in pre-Katrina New Orleans. They sat outside the political machine in the city's arrangement in that they made, enacted, supported, and benefited from politics, policy, and governance only some of the time. These actors did not rule the arrangement. The civic elite, businesses, and neighborhood and community-based groups played minimal roles in governance and sat outside the core of the arrangement. The poor sat in the outer ring of the New Orleans arrangement. They paid high costs and benefited minimally at best from the arrangement.

In chapter 1 we describe New Orleans's persistent political dysfunction and the inability of reformers to create new political arrangements before the storm. The discussion illustrates the myriad divisions inside and outside New Orleans and explains why those schisms matter to the city's political arrangements. We show how business leaders and civic elites chose not to engage with the city's problems. The chapter concludes with an overview of the destruction wrought by Hurricane Katrina and the subsequent flooding of the city.

The second chapter introduces the four policy case studies that are addressed in this book. For each policy we compare the pre-Katrina political arrangement to the one that existed after the storm. We identify the public agenda for each policy in each period. The strategic choices among policy alternatives are the second lens through which to view the political arrangement. Identifying the options that are selected and those that are neglected also allows us to place groups and individuals within a political arrangement. Actors, institutions, groups, and others who implement dominant policies occupy top spots in the arrangement. A comparison of the public agendas, option choices, and policy enactment in the pre- and post-Katrina periods enables us to gauge whether change occurred, who turned the opportunity for change into reality, who gained benefits, and who paid the costs.[10]

In chapter 2 we explain economic development in the city, especially as it relates to the intersection of the private and public sectors. Chapter 3, the first of two on public education, describes how state-level actors laid the groundwork for significant change in public education prior to the storm. In chapter 4 we delineate the nature of change in public education and highlight the role of extra-local actors. Chapter 5 investigates housing policy, including the massive Road Home program, and chapter 6 looks at the least reformed policy area, public safety, through the lens of policing in the city. In the conclusion we compare all four policy areas to explain how agendas were set, who set them, and which resources were brought to bear during implementation. This offers the opportunity to review who benefited and who did not, both in each policy area and as a whole, and to show how the rebuilding of New Orleans provides lessons for all cities.

The Importance of Resources and Authority

This book explores major themes and lessons regarding the relationship between disaster and political change. We highlight some of them here.

A coalition of those who possess resources and/or authority can change political arrangements after a disaster. Resources include money, organization, human capital, voting power, and leadership. In this context, authority consists of the formal powers granted to an entity by a charter or constitution. Resources and authority are not synonymous, but they are highly interdependent in the urban arena. When both resources and authority are present, the potential for policy enactment is strengthened. Scholars of urban politics have long understood that the right to rule (authority) is often insufficient to implement policy agendas.[11] If those with the right to rule partner with actors willing to supply relevant resources, then the resulting coalition can govern.

New actors who combined resources and authority displaced the established order in New Orleans. External forces—including national foundations—provided resources enabling the city's political arrangements to change. State and federal actors supplied resources but also stripped local institutions of their authority. They were able to take control in part because the city needed those resources to operate city services. Reform dominated the new arrangements.

Katrina evoked multiple responses, some at cross-purposes with others. A top-down agenda prevailed because resource providers and authority holders supported it. The bottom-up agenda failed to take hold because its backers lacked the power to guide a remaking effort. Social capital and increased civic engagement helped determine the extent to which neighborhoods and areas of the city recovered, but they did not set the post-Katrina public agenda.

Hurricane Katrina did not create a new direction for New Orleans so much as it sped up change already in motion. Reform-oriented actors expanded piecemeal reforms that they and others had started before the disaster.

Political recovery from sudden shocks is intergovernmental. The federal and state governments often attempt to take advantage of a disaster and use their resources and authority to occupy a prominent and permanent place in a city's political arrangement. While in that position, they set the public agenda and enact policies they, but not necessarily local residents, favor.

1

Pre-Katrina New Orleans

Cities operate in a context of scarce resources; within that setting, resource providers rule. The pro-growth regime has been the most common type of political arrangement in American cities during the postwar period. In cities operated under this kind of arrangement, businesses provide human and financial capital to elected officials, who make land-use decisions favorable for business leaders. When middle-class homeowners rule, they limit growth.[1]

The existence of a political arrangement does not mean that governance is functional. Some arrangements operate through patronage and corruption and are characterized by mismanagement, substandard services, and poor living conditions for residents. This dysfunctional arrangement leads to a suboptimal city, especially for the poor and most racial and ethnic minorities. Dysfunction typified New Orleans even before Hurricane Katrina struck.

Prior to Katrina, New Orleans lacked a unified force in development or anything else. The business and civic elites played passive policy roles. In the 1960s, Atlanta's corporate leaders supported desegregation of schools because they felt that tenuous race relations were bad for business. In New Orleans in the 1960s, school desegregation was characterized by violence and resistance. The elites cared more about the social order than about development. They did not endorse school desegregation but instead stood for the status quo and refused to be part of a positive political arrangement. According to one longtime member of the black political community: "When public schools integrated, white business walked away and did not come back. They relied on Catholic and private schools. This was a critical decision. New Orleans couldn't be successful without good public schools, and without business, you have a bad educational system."[2]

In 2001, Edward F. Renwick, an expert on New Orleans politics, noted that New Orleans did not have a healthy corporate sector and that the number of business leaders in the city declined each year. The city lacked big corporations with chief executive officers, senior vice presidents, and vice presidents. At the time, Entergy, the city's energy company, was the only Fortune 500 company in New Orleans. As Renwick put it, "The business elite in New Orleans can be put into a phone booth." In contrast to Dallas, New Orleans was a "totally political city." The corporate elite helped solve and frame many problems in Dallas, but in New Orleans, the mayor's office served as the epicenter of city politics. According to Renwick, "The mayor's office rings all the time in New Orleans."[3]

Several social movement–type organizations, which used protests or service provision to represent traditionally excluded groups, existed before Katrina. ACORN, which housed its national headquarters in New Orleans, was most prominent among what Rachel E. Luft calls the first generation of New Orleans's social movement organizations. Wade Rathke, who founded ACORN in 1970, was a graduate of Ben Franklin High School in New Orleans.[4]

Corruption

The arrangement that governed pre-Katrina New Orleans benefited those who held elected and appointed positions. And it favored those who paid to play and had connections with elected and appointed officials. Some residents—the wealthy and middle class, business owners who secured government contracts, government employees, and relatives of those in power—supported these arrangements. These beneficiaries of the dysfunctional arrangement promoted the status quo.

How do we, as social scientists, know that pervasive corruption exists, even when it is patently obvious to just about any observer of New Orleans politics? Scholars find it difficult to quantify corruption. Most use surveys of knowledgeable informants to gauge perceptions of corruption. According to Fahim Al-Marhubi: "Ideally, measures of corruption would consist of objective evaluations that are comparable across countries and over time. Ideal measures such as these do not as yet exist. In their absence, indicators have been developed that are based on foreign businessmen and international correspondents' perceptions of corruption."[5]

New Orleans has ranked high among the most corrupt cities in the United States. In her study of corruption in fifteen large American cities over more than one hundred years, Rebecca Menes concluded that New Orleans ranked fourth among cities for corruption from 1850 to 1880; in the next thirty-year period it ranked third; and from 1931 to 1980, New Orleans was second only to Chicago as the most corrupt city in the United States.[6]

A team of researchers at the University of Illinois at Chicago used the number of public corruption convictions in federal courts from 1976 to 2010 to determine the most corrupt cities in the country. They ranked New Orleans fifteenth on the basis of the 545 public corruption convictions in the Eastern Federal District Court of Louisiana. A similar analysis of convictions for crimes that involved abuses of the public trust by government officials between 2002 and 2013 rated Louisiana the most corrupt state in the country. Louisiana's Eastern Federal District Court, which includes New Orleans, had the largest number of public corruption convictions (247) in the state.[7]

From June 2003 until the end of 2006, the federal government indicted 190 people on corruption charges in the New Orleans metropolitan area. In that period the FBI convicted sixteen people involved in municipal corruption during the administration of Mayor Marc Morial. It also secured twenty-six convictions against employees of the New Orleans public school system for kickbacks, bribery, fraud, and theft, among other abuses. Mayor Morial's uncle by marriage, Glenn Haydel, was convicted for stealing $550,000 from the Regional Transit Authority and spent a year in prison. Lillian Smith-Haydel, Haydel's wife and Morial's aunt, pleaded guilty to insurance contract bribery conspiracy charges. She received five years' probation and four months of home confinement.[8]

By March 2004, the FBI had established two public corruption squads in New Orleans. At a news conference following a guilty plea on federal bribery charges by the New Orleans city council's most senior member, the FBI's special agent in charge of the New Orleans field office said: "It's just brazen down here. In Louisiana, they skim the cream, steal the milk, highjack the bottle, and look for the cow." In response to one of the convictions, U.S. Attorney Jim Letten commented: "Corruption in New Orleans is endemic. I think this simply tells us there is corruption on many levels, large scale and small scale."[9]

The number of corruption cases and convictions does not include that of nine-term U.S. congressman William Jefferson, who represented New Orleans and was convicted by a federal court in Virginia for bribery, money laundering, and use of his office for racketeering. Jefferson received a thirteen-year sentence in federal prison, the longest given any member of Congress to date for acts committed while in office.

Those who benefited from corruption and patronage represented embedded interests in the New Orleans city government. The dysfunctional arrangements were headed by both black and white political leaders, who dispensed patronage to their supporters. They won; the city's services, public policies, and residents lost. Wealthy white reformers and extra-local actors instituted piecemeal reform from time to time before Katrina but struggled to gain a foothold. Black lower- and working-class residents suffered the most from this dysfunctional political arrangement. Many went to the worst schools, lived in substandard housing in the highest-crime areas, and worked in jobs that did not pay a living wage.

The problem in New Orleans was more than the narrowness of problem-solving activity. It was an inability to defer gratification. It is the collective-action problem in an acute form. There is little history of civic cooperation. The only major cooperative projects were loaded with selective material incentives and divisible benefits that had a short-term return.

While New Orleans is on the high side with regard to political-governmental dysfunction, it is not an isolated example either in the United States or throughout the world. New Orleans resembles Naples, where client-patron relations dominate. Clientelism, as Harold Savitch and Paul Kantor call it, "overrides broader values and touches everything, from business contracts to personal relationships. Whether Christian Democrat or Socialist, the culture is geared toward exchanging jobs and favors for social support or political votes." In Naples, government leaders choose favoritism and corruption over improving the lives of the citizens or promoting business prosperity. New Orleans has operated in much the same way. The dominant concerns for most local officials were patronage, power, and personal wealth. Other cities that have suffered from dysfunctional governance include East St. Louis, Illinois, and Camden, New Jersey.[10]

Machine-style patronage could be seen in New Orleans's dozens of boards and commissions that dealt with everything from the public belt railroad to law enforcement. According to one informant, those who sat on the various boards and commissions opposed change because they were cutting deals and enjoying mega-lunches at the taxpayers' expense. City government jobs and contracts were political in New Orleans. A person or business usually could not secure either without knowing someone in city government. As an example, a former member of the Orleans Parish School Board went to prison after she received $140,000 in kickbacks to help the brother of Congressman Jefferson secure an educational software contract.[11] Relatives of elected officials often worked in city government positions and held multiple municipal contracts.

From Reconstruction onward, the machine battled reformers for control over New Orleans politics. The machine, the strongest in the South, practiced patronage, doled out political favors, and resorted when necessary to election fraud and even violence. It tended to win. The machine went by different names over time—the Regular Democratic Organization, the Choctaw Club of Louisiana, the Ring, the Old Regulars, and later the Crescent City Democratic Association—but it dominated politics.[12]

Mayor deLesseps "Chep" Morrison (1946–1961) led the Crescent City Democratic Association and initiated several projects and reforms, such as the Mississippi River Bridge, the New Orleans Recreation Department, and a model city home rule charter. Referring to these changes as the illusion of reform, Edward F. Haas concluded that Morrison's machine was the last successful one to rule New Orleans. Black political organizations took off in the 1960s and 1970s and, like their white predecessors, practiced machine-style politics. Even though the golden era of the New Orleans machine may have ended with Morrison, machine-style politics, corruption, and exchange of patronage for political favors endured.[13]

The other political faction—the commercial-civic elite—had a conservative bent, opposed political corruption, and favored governmental reform as a way to weaken the machine. It ran candidates against the political machine but experienced limited success. Its accomplishments included the establishment of independent governing boards, which reformers thought would remove politics from government. The wealthy white Uptown elites and business interests who advocated reform in New Orleans created the Bureau of Governmental Research (BGR) in 1932,

known then as the Civic Affairs League, to combat the effects of the
Great Depression, Huey Long, and the Old Regulars. On its website BGR
states: "Good government requires constant vigilance on the part of the
governed. That's where BGR can help." BGR's successes over the years
include the drafting of a home rule charter (1950s), an action plan for
city finances, a report on the preservation of the Vieux Carré and the
rehabilitation of the Audubon Zoo (1970s), and, over the next several
decades, "high-profile work on Louis Armstrong New Orleans International Airport, government contracting, and property tax exemption and
assessment practices" and stoppage of the privatization of the Sewerage
& Water Board.[14]

The election of Ray Nagin as mayor in 2002 encouraged the
reform-oriented voters who put him into office. Nagin identified himself
as a reform candidate who would bring business acumen to city hall. Less
than four months into his first term, he authorized a raid on the city's
Taxicab Bureau and car inspection stations; police issued arrest warrants
for eighty-seven people, seventy-seven of whom were taxi drivers. Among
other charges, the authorities contended that city employees had accepted
bribes of $200 and even $1,000 to issue permits to drivers who did not
qualify for them.[15]

Nagin and his chief administrative officer said they wanted to show
the city and the nation that the old way of doing things in New Orleans
was over. The raid and these sentiments pushed Nagin's approval ratings
to more than 80 percent in public opinion polls. Seventy percent of black
respondents held favorable opinions of Nagin.[16]

The taxicab raid did not please everyone. Most of the people arrested
in the raid were blacks and Asians. Flyers distributed in black neighborhoods claimed that Nagin, himself black, employed too many whites, and
that blacks had lost contracts and jobs under the new mayor's administration. In July 2003 the *Atlanta Journal-Constitution*'s Drew Jubera
wrote: "There's also a suspicion among some residents in poorer African-
American neighborhoods that Nagin is beholden to business interests at
their expense. Elected with the overwhelming support of white voters,
Nagin is now the target of anonymous fliers that brand him, in a city
more than 60 percent black, 'the white man's mayor.'" The *New Orleans
Tribune*, which serves the city's black community, referred to the raid
as a "witch hunt" and claimed that Nagin was a tool for those with the
"specific intent of dismantling and disparaging 24 years of black political
control in New Orleans." Others claimed that the Nagin raids targeted
the poor.[17]

The raid produced only four guilty verdicts. District Attorney Harry Connick Sr. threw out fifty-three cases for lack of evidence. Some of the city workers who were arrested got their jobs back.[18]

The contest between entrenched interests and those who seek to displace them is a national and international phenomenon that has played out for more than a century. In the northeastern and midwestern parts of the United States, machines blocked change; in the West and Southwest, however, reformers championed and accomplished municipal reform. In his comparative study of northern and southern Italy, Robert Putnam concludes that reform of patronage and corruption improves democracy and the economy. In the case of New Orleans, opponents of reform claimed that governmental change violated democratic principles and local control.[19]

Reform had not taken hold in New Orleans in part because it lacked the kind of political arrangement that existed in so many other American cities. New Orleans's political arrangement—or any arrangement for that matter—is difficult to reform because those in positions of power and their supporters resist change. As the chapters that follow indicate, piecemeal reform took place before Katrina, but reformers had difficulty changing the arrangement as a whole. In the case of rebuilding New Orleans, businesses and the civic elite carried the reform banner into battle in the post-Katrina period. This active role was new for them. Business organizations and the civic elite concluded that reform was better for New Orleans than what had existed.

Racial, Social, and Governmental Divides

Multiple divides in public-sector relations characterized pre-Katrina New Orleans and made collaboration for the collective good next to impossible. People worked together when the project or policy satisfied their self-interested appetites. Fragmentation promoted the status quo. With so few looking out for the collective good, people focused on individual benefit, which led many to use government for personal gain. Patronage, corruption, and support for self-interested policies were the settled patterns of activity in pre-Katrina New Orleans. Racial, governmental, regional, societal, and class divisions also impaired reformers' ability to accomplish more.

Mayoral elections from 1969 to 2002 exemplify the racial split that characterized the New Orleans status quo. In a 1969 campaign debate, local media legend Alec Gifford asked candidates Maurice "Moon"

Landrieu and Jimmy Fitzmorris, both of them white, if either would appoint a black person to lead a city department. Fitzmorris claimed that he would use qualifications, not race, as the basis for his appointments. Landrieu declared that blacks would serve in several top positions in his administration. At the time of this election, blacks made up about 45 percent of the city's population. Landrieu won the election, becoming the first mayor to win the office without a majority of the white vote. Ninety percent of blacks and 37 percent of whites voted for Landrieu; black turnout was 75 percent.[20] That election established a trend: candidates could win office with a majority of the black vote and a sizable minority of the white electorate. Four years later Landrieu won reelection with the same coalition.

Then in 1977, Ernest "Dutch" Morial, a state appeals court judge, became the first black to win a mayoral election in New Orleans. In that election, 97 percent of blacks and 19 percent of whites voted for Morial, who won with 51.8 percent of the vote. At that time, blacks made up 43 percent of New Orleans's registered voters. Turnout for blacks was 76 percent in that election. Morial won a second term, although, according to historian Edward F. Haas, "the mayor's swash-buckling style, his own ambition and his quite vocal unwillingness to compromise on the question of African Americans' immediate right to political and economic power . . . alienated several influential white leaders." During Morial's administration the city's black middle class saw unprecedented access to municipal jobs and contracts, but poor blacks continued to suffer from unemployment and police brutality.[21]

In 1986 the white electorate played a new role, that of the swing vote. For the first time, blacks made up a majority, 51 percent, of the elector-ate. In one of his campaign commercials, white mayoral candidate Sam LeBlanc tells an audience, "This is our last chance."[22] With knowledge that a vote for the white candidate could ensure a win for then–State Representative William Jefferson, Dutch Morial's choice for his successor as mayor, white voters picked Sidney Barthelemy, a black member of the city council and one of Morial's greatest enemies. Poll after poll showed that white voters opposed what they viewed as Morial's confrontational style; they wanted to end Morial's influence over the mayor's office. Two black candidates advanced to the runoff for the first time, and Barthelemy garnered 86 percent of the white vote and 43 percent of the black vote to beat Jefferson, 58 percent to 42 percent. Four years later Barthelemy faced a white candidate in the runoff. This time, 86 percent of the black electorate voted for Barthelemy, compared to 23 percent of whites.[23]

Marc Morial, Dutch's son, became mayor through the support of black voters, who made up a majority of the electorate throughout his time in office (1994–2002). In 1994 Morial won the runoff with 54.5 percent of the total vote: 87.9 percent of the black vote and 7.3 percent of the white vote. Racial polarization of the New Orleans electorate intensified when white and black candidates were evenly matched, as they were in the 1994 runoff. In 1998, Morial ran without serious opposition and won the primary with 79% of the vote: 97% of the black vote and 37.5% of the white vote.[24]

In the 2002 runoff, Nagin, a general manager and vice president of Cox Cable, defeated Police Chief Richard Pennington with an electoral coalition made up of approximately 91 percent of whites and 49 percent of blacks. He carried white neighborhoods, prosperous black areas of the city, and precincts with few poor people and low numbers of registered Democrats.[25]

The election of Nagin showed that a substantial black middle class existed in New Orleans. According to Nagin's pollster: "If you look at the areas where Nagin did very well in the black community, it was in those middle-class areas. The black middle class has been developing for some time. This is probably the first time where they've been a principal force in the election of candidates."[26] John Maginnis, a longtime political analyst, agreed, noting that by contrast, "[Marc] Morial relied on the black lower class for votes and support. There never has been enough of a black middle class to make a difference in city politics. They're more conservative and business-friendly, and when you put them together with the whites who share their values, come pretty close to being the majority of the city."[27] From 1978 through the election of Ray Nagin, blacks served as mayor and, beginning in 1986, constituted a majority on the city council. Starting in 1994, five of the seven members of the city council were black.

Racial fragmentation occurs across and within groups in New Orleans. All four black mayors have been of Creole ancestry. In elections between two blacks, the Creole candidate beat a non-Creole. To further develop their power, many individuals created political organizations known by the acronyms BOLD, SOUL, LIFE, and COUP to win elections, gain access to patronage, and defeat one another, if necessary. These organizations lost steam over time because blacks came to control just about every elected position in New Orleans, their leaders grew old and no one replaced them, and patronage failed to benefit the entire black community.[28]

In 2011 post-Katrina recovery czar Edward Blakely described the racialized city this way: "New Orleans was and still is divided across 'subracial' lines embodied in the spoils of the city's political structure. Middle-class blacks escaped from the poorest neighborhoods by establishing Pontchartrain Park and then New Orleans East. That partly explains why the city encompasses so many internal political jurisdictions: each racial caste holds its perch in the political system by maintaining control of a local jurisdiction."[29]

Racial division can be traced as far back as the formation of New Orleans, when whites expelled blacks from higher ground into the lowest-lying areas of the city.[30] This meant that areas of New Orleans with high concentrations of blacks would face the worst of the floods if the levees broke.

Today, New Orleans is dominated by Mardi Gras. The *laissez les bon temps rouler* attitude permeates New Orleans throughout the year, but the influence of Mardi Gras extends beyond debauchery. A social aristocracy exists in New Orleans. A person's place of birth, grandmother's maiden name, and high school alma mater help determine where he or she ranks in New Orleans society. Outsiders are not welcome. The *Times-Picayune*'s Darran Simon once described New Orleans as "fiercely local."[31] One longtime minority leader believed that the difference between New Orleans and other southern cities was that other cities "had no inbred hierarchy, so the pie can get larger." The New Orleans business community has rejected outsiders because they fear that "our piece will get smaller."[32]

Mardi Gras reveals the social aristocracy in action. Different subgroups of the social elite belong to various local Mardi Gras parade organizations known as krewes. Lineage tends to determine whether a person can join a particular krewe and influences the kinds of krewes to which people can belong. Those at the top of the New Orleans social elite belong to old-line krewes—Rex, Mystic Krewe of Comus, Momus, or Proteus.

Each year on Mardi Gras day, "Rex," the designated king of carnival, receives a toast from the mayor and addresses his loyal subjects in front of Gallier Hall, which once served as city hall. Members of some of the elite Mardi Gras krewes belong to ultra-exclusive men's clubs with names like the Boston Club and the Pickwick Club.[33] Money cannot buy a person's way into these krewes and clubs. For much of New Orleans's history, members of these krewes and clubs dominated city politics and the New Orleans economy. But their influence waned as blacks became a majority of the population, and traditional industries, such as oil and gas and the Port of New Orleans, suffered.

Class, in the sense of economic status, divides New Orleans. In the week when Katrina hit, U.S. Census information revealed that 23.2 percent of New Orleanians lived below the poverty line. Orleans Parish, which is coterminous with New Orleans, had the seventh-highest poverty rate among counties in the United States. Blacks made up about two-thirds of the city's population but accounted for 84 percent of those living below the poverty line. The prevalence of poverty was most intense in parts of Mid-City, New Orleans East, and the Lower Ninth Ward. Concentrated neighborhood poverty increased by two-thirds in New Orleans from 1970 until August 2005, when Katrina struck. Residents of Uptown, the Garden District, and Lakeview were less likely to suffer from poverty.[34]

Of course, race, class, and social status are not mutually exclusive. Many wealthy whites make up the elite in New Orleans; poor blacks do not. Race, class, and social status are not determinative, either. Wealthy whites are not necessarily elites in New Orleans; the social aristocracy makes sure of that.

The move to desegregate Mardi Gras parades in the early 1990s illustrates the divisions within New Orleans and the cumulative effect of fragmentation on public policy. Dorothy Mae Taylor, who became the first African American female member of the city council in 1986, championed an ordinance to desegregate the city's exclusive luncheon clubs which maintained close associations with the old-line Mardi Gras krewes. In 1988 Taylor claimed that city business was conducted in these clubs and therefore they should be regulated by the city council.[35] Her focus then switched from the luncheon clubs to the krewes themselves. In 1991 Taylor introduced an ordinance to ban racial discrimination in Mardi Gras parades. She argued that the parades fell under the governance of the city council since they required city services such as police, sanitation, and the fire department. It was also the council that issued permits allowing the krewes to march.

Not all krewes are white-only, male-only, or limited to a specific religion, but Taylor's ordinance captured the attention of civil rights activists in the city as well as the leaders of the old-line krewes—the ones most likely to involve New Orleans's social elite. Taylor's original ordinance specified possible jail time and fines for violations, but the final

law—negotiated by a blue ribbon commission on carnival, Mayor Barthelemy, members of Mardi Gras krewes, and Taylor—simply required
"a krewe to swear that it has no 'written or unwritten' discriminatory
practices in order to receive a parade permit." Three old-line Mardi
Gras krewes refused to sign the ordinance and in 1992 withdrew from
the parade schedule. The Mystic Krewe of Comus, the oldest marching
krewe, stopped parading, as did Momus and Proteus. Proteus resumed
its parade in 2000, but at this writing, the other two had not held a
parade since 1991. A poll that year revealed that 79 percent of whites
had an unfavorable view of Taylor, whereas 67 percent of blacks held
either favorable or very favorable opinions of her.[36]

Catholics, Democrats, and blacks play prominent roles in New Orleans
politics, while Protestants, conservative Democrats and Republicans, and
whites dominate politics in other parts of Louisiana. The prominence of
conservatism and the Protestant religion in other parts of the state means
that people throughout Louisiana condemn New Orleans's *laissez les bon
temps rouler* attitude.

Over time, various governors, legislators, mayors, and other actors
played out the animosity—even hatred—that other Louisianans felt
toward New Orleans. Huey Long (governor 1928–1932) and Earl Long
(governor 1939–1940, 1948–1952, and 1956–1960 and lieutenant governor 1936–1939) typified north Louisiana's disdain for New Orleans,
especially its religion, racial composition, and culture. Debates over control of the city and race divided state and city after the Longs left office.
Governor Jimmie Davis (1944–1948, 1960–1964) opposed *Brown v.
Board of Education* and the integration of New Orleans's schools. In a
special session of the state legislature, Governor Davis and the legislators
passed a series of segregationist laws to circumvent that Supreme Court
decision. Davis took over New Orleans's schools to prevent desegregation and worked to pass rigorous anti-integration laws.[37]

In assessing Louisiana politics in the 1990s, Edward F. Renwick,
T. Wayne Parent, and Jack Wardlaw concluded, "Republicans have
enjoyed successes, though, largely owing to many of the same forces at
work throughout the region: racial polarization, the appeal of the GOP's
pro-business message to growing and prosperous suburban residents,
and the appeal of cultural conservatism in the more rural, less prosperous areas of the state."[38] David Duke, former Grand Wizard of the Grand
Knights of the Ku Klux Klan represented Metairie, a predominantly white
suburb of New Orleans, in the Louisiana House of Representatives. The

Republican ascendancy possessed an anti-New Orleans orientation: its racial polarization, cultural conservatism, and rural and suburban composition worked against New Orleans.

These differences between New Orleans and the rest of Louisiana play out in the state legislature, where many legislators oppose state subsidies for public amenities in New Orleans. From other parts of the state come arguments that New Orleans receives a greater share of Louisiana's resources than it contributes to the state's coffers.[39] Among other things, legislators from outside New Orleans have opposed state subsidies for the New Orleans Saints football team, the Superdome, a downtown arena, an amusement park, and the state's only land-based casino.

As New Orleans's population decreased from 627,525 in 1960 to 484,674 in 2000, the city's influence in the Louisiana legislature and state politics waned. In the past, candidates could win statewide office by carrying New Orleans by a large margin. In 1992, Bill Clinton won New Orleans by 81,242 votes and carried Louisiana by 82,525.[40] But the days when Democrats could count on New Orleans to help them win statewide were over by the late 1990s.

Parishes that surround New Orleans (in Louisiana, parishes function as counties do in other states) include some of the city's harshest critics. Many former residents of New Orleans moved to these outlying areas to avoid problems of education, crime, and race. When people in the surrounding parishes look at the city, it is to condemn its politics and policies. In 2003, Louisiana voters considered a constitutional amendment to allow a state takeover of failing schools, most of which were located in New Orleans. The highest vote percentages in favor of the takeover came from the parishes within the New Orleans metropolitan area, excluding the city itself.[41]

Leander Perez (1891–1969), the political boss of Plaquemines and St. Bernard parishes, both of which are located in the New Orleans metropolitan area, typified the racial disdain that surrounding areas felt toward New Orleans. Known as the Judge, Perez served only five years (1919–1924) in that position before becoming district attorney of Plaquemines and St. Bernard (1924–1960). In 1963 Perez threatened to imprison any civil rights worker who came to Plaquemines Parish. He opposed state and federal intervention in his local politics, masterminded state laws for his benefit, and punished anyone who got in his way. Perez led efforts at the state capitol to resist desegregation in schools even though he never served in the legislature. He supported Dixiecrat candidates and championed George

Wallace's run for president in 1968. Because of Perez's support, Wallace carried Louisiana in that presidential election.[42]

Fragmentation characterizes governmental activity inside New Orleans as well. New Orleans mayors need a majority on the city council to get their agendas passed. A lack of that majority on the council hampered Nagin's ability to accomplish much in his first term.

Before the storm, New Orleans had a board, commission, committee, or other governmental organization for just about every function in the city and metropolitan area. In 2004, James Brandt and Robert K. Whelan catalogued some of the independent boards, commissions, and special districts that were outside the direct authority of New Orleans's government: these included the Sewage and Water Board, Orleans Parish Law Enforcement District, Downtown Development District, Public Belt Railroad Commission, and Almonaster-Michoud Industrial District. They followed that list with another that featured independent state-created boards or agencies that were not under the control of city government: the Regional Transit Authority, Orleans Levee Board, New Orleans Exhibition Hall Authority, and Dock Board. Peirce Lewis described the levee boards as "worlds unto themselves" because they had no obligation to cooperate with municipal governments. State government granted authority to the levee boards "to levy taxes, expropriate land inside or outside their districts, run rights-of-way through lands belonging to other public bodies, and even maintain their own police forces." Lewis characterized levee boards as "intensely political" because their terms coincided with that of the governor who appointed them.[43]

The social oligarchy controlled these boards and commissions, appointing members of the elite and excluding blacks. Mayor Dutch Morial, who opposed the exclusive nature and independent power of these boards, sued the Board of Liquidation, City Debt, to end its "racially restrictive membership." Morial won in court, and a judge ordered the board to make a good-faith effort toward the consideration of nonwhites. By the end of Dutch's tenure as mayor, at least one black person was serving on most of the city's major boards and commissions.[44]

Nevertheless, these boards, commissions, agencies, and special districts sliced up authority and patronage in New Orleans. They fragmented government by making it necessary for people to deal with them in order to get something done within a particular policy area. For example, before Katrina, New Orleans had a board of seven elected tax assessors, who would endorse low assessments in order to secure reelection. The board of assessors divided governance, created another patronage entity, and constrained the city's ability to raise resources. In 1983, Michael Peter Smith and Marlene Keller concluded that the "[assessors] system is unlikely to change without a protracted political fight."[45]

New Orleans had not advanced far in the pre-Katrina period in part because this kind of fragmentation was an impediment to progress. Hurricane Katrina presented the possibility that instead of a pattern in which the various civic elites and business leaders continued along their separate ways, they might combine efforts around an expanded sense of common purpose. The question remained: To what extent, if any, would New Orleans's history of corruption and racial, societal, and governmental divides change or persist after Katrina?

What Hath Katrina Wrought?

Hurricane Katrina erased a city. Louisiana governor Kathleen Babineaux Blanco used these words to describe how Hurricane Katrina in general, and the flooding in particular, attacked every part of life in New Orleans. It is known as the "Crescent City" for its location on the Mississippi River, and the siting of the city has been questioned since its founding. Several years before Katrina, Christopher Morris called New Orleans's location a "Sisyphean struggle with nature that continues today." But there the city was built, persevering through centuries, until August 2005. At that point the "City That Care Forgot" appeared to have been forgotten by the federal government. As a result of breached levees at the 17th Street, London Avenue, and Industrial canals, water enveloped 80 percent of New Orleans. Of the 373,206 residents affected by the storm, 371,697 of them (99.6 percent) experienced some damage caused by flooding.[46]

Blacks accounted for 75 percent of New Orleans residents in damaged areas; the poor made up slightly less than 30 percent. The storm affected all of the city's Lower Ninth Ward, in which blacks and the poor made up the majority of residents, and the eastern part of the city known as the East or New Orleans East, where middle-, upper-middle-, and upper-class blacks constituted most of the residents. A number of Lower Ninth residents claimed that the levee breaches in the Industrial Canal were a result of detonations—an accusation criticized by many Americans unfamiliar with the Great Flood of 1927 and the resulting levee detonation intended to save the city.[47]

Even though blacks and the poor made up a majority of Katrina's victims, the storm also wreaked havoc on Lakeview, a section of New Orleans populated by many middle-, upper-middle-, and upper-class whites. No part of the city escaped the storm's effect, but residents in Uptown New Orleans and the French Quarter experienced the least amount of damage. They suffered from the loss of jobs, social networks, city infrastructure and services, and a variety of other problems that plagued the entire Gulf South. In testimony before a committee of the U.S. House of Representatives, the head of a New Orleans–area commercial real estate firm said, "Hurricane Katrina created the single largest need for housing in the history of our country."[48]

Katrina destroyed the city's infrastructure. Every part of New Orleans lacked basic services, including phone communication, electricity, potable water, and gas. One month after the storm, only 16 percent of the city's fifty-seven public transportation routes were operating, and nearly all bus service remained inoperative.[49] The streetcars that transport visitors and workers up and down St. Charles Avenue and into the edges of the French Quarter were out of service.

More than one month after the storm hit, only two of the city's twenty-two hospitals had reopened.[50] Because the New Orleans public school system closed every one of its 117 schools, the storm displaced 50,000 students in the public educational system alone. All of New Orleans's private schools closed as well, and the city's colleges and universities had to shut down just as they were preparing to start the fall semester. An estimated 100,000 students who attend colleges and universities in the New Orleans area were evacuated to other schools throughout the country.

Hurricane Katrina's devastation set the stage for major physical rebuilding. As a case study, New Orleans brings an extra dimension to the inquiry. The city's long history of patronage politics, corruption, lack of engagement by the civic elite and businesses, and multiple divides in public sector practices put New Orleans in line for possible political and governmental reconstruction along with the physical rebuilding. While it might have been unrealistic to expect a sudden and thorough transformation, it was reasonable to expect change to occur. How much change, what kinds of change, and who benefited and suffered as a result of these changes are the broad questions that this book addresses. Enough time has elapsed that we can look at durable change, not just immediate reactions and short-term rhetoric.

Disasters unfold in stages: mitigation, the emergency period, and short- and long-term recovery. Research focuses on the first three categories but pays less attention to the long-term consequences of disaster. We examine change in the first ten years after Katrina because the effects of disasters cannot be seen soon after their point of origin. It takes eight to eleven years to observe the outcomes of recovery and policy changes.[51]

Governance, politics, and policies were as damaged in pre-Katrina New Orleans as the infrastructure was afterwards. As the federal and state governments came to repair and rebuild New Orleans, would they use their resources and authority to change governance, politics, and policies? Would those who ruled in the past continue to do so after the disaster, or could newer actors set the agenda, enact policy, and produce a new set of winners and losers? Even though a sudden shock like Katrina upsets an entire city, how and why does it change governance, politics, and policies not directly associated with the disaster? In the chapters that follow, we explain how and why extra-local actors and reform-oriented local players used their resources and authority to change governance, politics, and policies throughout post-Katrina New Orleans.

2

Reform and Economic Development

With regard to economic development in pre-Katrina New Orleans, the city looked more like deindustrialized northeastern and midwestern cities than one in the Sunbelt. Like cities in the Northeast and Midwest, New Orleans lost jobs, population, and businesses in the thirty years before Katrina struck. During the same period, Miami, Atlanta, Houston, Dallas–Fort Worth, and Charlotte, among other Sunbelt cities, gained population, jobs, and major companies.[1]

Divisions of nearly all types prevented the creation of a cohesive economic development agenda in pre-Katrina New Orleans. In 1986, Michael Peter Smith and Marlene Keller concluded that two economies and two societies existed in New Orleans. Five years later, Robert K. Whelan wrote: "New Orleans continues to have a two-tiered economy and society. . . . One segment of the population is largely white and consists of affluent, well-educated people who hold professional positions within the community. Those who constitute the other segment, which is largely black but includes a sizeable white component, struggle with the problems of unemployment and marginal employment." When he analyzed economic development activity in New Orleans in the 1970s and 1980s, Whelan concluded that the neighborhoods had seen little activity or benefit from the projects the city pursued during this period.[2]

Public and private actors fought over development in the pre-Katrina period. One example of the divisions among civic elites, political leaders, and preservationists in New Orleans dates to 1946, when the New York "power broker" Robert Moses recommended to the city's elected leaders that they build a 40-by-108-foot six-lane highway along the Mississippi River in the Vieux Carré, or French Quarter, parallel to St. Louis Cathedral. Preservationists, members of affected neighborhoods, some civic elites, and Archbishop Philip Hannan stopped the expressway plan in 1969, finally defeating the city's business interests and their champions, including the Central Area Committee and the Chamber of Commerce, the leading civic elites, Congressman Hale Boggs, and city council member Moon Landrieu.[3]

During much of this period New Orleans did not receive any federal urban renewal funds because the Louisiana state legislature waited until 1968 to pass enabling legislation for accepting these dollars. Other cities used the funds to segregate themselves; New Orleans did not. Mayor Moon Landrieu eventually convinced other public officials in the city that it was all right to accept federal funding. Governors John McKeithen (1964–1972) and Edwin W. Edwards (1972–1980), in particular, warmed to the idea of federal aid because of their moderate politics and presidential aspirations.[4]

The building of the Superdome illustrates how economic development projects came to fruition in New Orleans in the late 1960s and early 1970s. Those directly involved benefited from the development. James Jones, a native of Dallas and president of the National Bank of Commerce in New Orleans, persuaded the Citizens and Southern Bank of Atlanta to purchase Superdome bonds.[5] Governor McKeithen championed the Superdome project in exchange for Jones's political support. Local land speculators and national developers joined the Superdome coalition because they saw profit in the projects and in the development of this land. As a trustee for construction accounts, Jones's bank received $100,000 and a $1 million return on the Superdome bonds. Developers realized profits from the construction of offices, retail stores, and a Hyatt hotel adjacent to the Superdome. In exchange for the support of local black leaders, Mayor Landrieu awarded a multimillion-dollar cleanup contract to Superdome Services, Inc., operated by Sherman Copelin, a black leader who ran the SOUL political organization.

Local banks, such as Whitney Bank, did not want non-local capital to play a role in and benefit from development in New Orleans. The social elites wanted the beneficiaries of this policy to be limited to their circle. They also opposed development that would raise taxes, increase traffic, or change the status quo. Good-government leaders opposed the Superdome as well because of the patronage it produced.

Soon, during the mayoral administrations of Moon Landrieu (1970–1978) and Dutch Morial (1978–1986), New Orleans's industrial economy began to fade. The city's third-largest industry, the port, lost its prominence internationally in the 1970s when its containerization technology failed to keep up with that at ports across the United States.[6]

Then, in the 1980s and 1990s, Amoco, Chevron, Mobil, Texaco, and Shell moved most, if not all, of their operations back to Houston. According to one executive: "We *had* to be in Houston. We did not have to be in New Orleans." The oil and gas bust of the 1980s exacerbated high unemployment, flight of the tax base, and a decline in the middle-class population. Between 1984 and 1988, the New Orleans metropolitan area lost more than 27,000 jobs. By 1990, one-quarter of Poydras Street's Class A office space—the best built, most modern, and best managed—was vacant.[7]

The federal government cut funding for cities and eliminated Urban Development Action Grant funding and revenue sharing under the Reagan administration. The decrease in federal funds made resources even scarcer in New Orleans. In 1975, federal aid accounted for more than 25 percent of the city's revenue and about 60 percent of its intergovernmental revenue; twenty-five years later, these figures had dropped to 7 percent and 29 percent, respectively. New Orleans's Community Development Block Grant (CDBG) money peaked at $20 million in 1980; when inflation is taken into account, CDBG funding to New Orleans dropped by 50 percent from 1980 to 2000. The city cut its operating budget by one-third from 1984 to 1988.[8]

In 1997 New Orleans was home to slightly fewer jobs than it had had twenty years before. The job losses came, as we have seen, in the port and manufacturing sectors, which experienced a 50 percent decline. In the late 1980s, hospitality services generated twice as many jobs in New Orleans as in the rest of the country. Reflecting on changes to the New Orleans economy throughout the 1980s, Robert K. Whelan and Alma Young wrote, "It is clear that tourism is now a dominant sector of the local economy."[9] In the years ahead, it would become *the* dominant sector of the local economy.

In the decades that followed the construction of the Superdome, New Orleans hosted NCAA Final Fours, Super Bowls, the 1988 Republican National Convention, an annual football game between Grambling and Southern universities, a papal visit, major rock concerts, and the annual Jazz and Heritage Festival and Essence Festival. In 1960 New Orleans had 4,500 hotel rooms; that number increased to close to 34,000 by 2000. The city had changed from a commercial-based economy to one centered on tourism.[10]

The 1884 World's Fair had helped develop the city's Uptown area around what is now known as Audubon Park. The 1984 version allowed the city to develop the riverfront and the Warehouse District. The state allocated $30 million to build the World's Fair's riverfront exhibition hall and a convention center and paid $14 million to the Dock Board for the relocation of two docks, while investors converted warehouses into restaurants and apartment lofts in the hopes of taking advantage of the event. The long-term effect of these investments was the revitalization of the Warehouse District, which became a place for young locals to live, eat, and play.[11]

Because state law prevented New Orleans from annexing its suburbs, the city and developers decided to build along the Mississippi River. Joseph Canizaro, a prominent developer of office space along Poydras Street, exchanged land he owned for a large city-owned parcel along the riverfront; his Canal Place project expanded development of the central business district (CBD) toward the river. Preservationists, small businesses, and French Quarter residents opposed the development, which they saw as a case of unrestrained growth. During Dutch Morial's second term, the city's Dock Board leased wharves for non-maritime purposes for the first time. These wharves were converted into space for James Rouse's Riverwalk Mall, which opened in 1986. Rouse had designed Quincy Market in Boston and the reclamation of the waterfront in Baltimore.[12]

The economic development centerpiece of Mayor Sidney Barthelemy's administration (1986–1994) was the $40 million ten-acre Aquarium of the Americas and Woldenberg Park, located on the riverfront in the French Quarter. The entire city council, as well as the Business Council, the Chamber of Commerce, the NAACP, and the Urban League, supported the project. The majority-black electorate helped pass the $25 million in bonds needed to build the aquarium. Throughout construction, Mayor Barthelemy and business leaders promised jobs and contracts to blacks and minority-owned businesses. Private entities, including the Friends of the Zoo and the Business Council, raised the additional $20 million needed to complete the project. Preservationists and merchants in the French Quarter opposed it, fearing that the aquarium would alter the historical integrity of the area and disrupt their businesses.[13]

Started by the president and chief executive officer of the Freeport-McMoRan corporation in late 1985, the Business Council included the heads of about fifty businesses in the New Orleans metropolitan area and leaders of national corporations with offices in the city. It aimed to improve the business climate in New Orleans and address corporate tax issues that businesses feared were likely to arise under Governor Buddy Roemer, who championed, but could not execute, tax reform in Louisiana. The Business Council included the chief executive officers of Coca-Cola, Consolidated Natural Gas, and the Louisiana Land and Exploration Company. These leaders, each of whom was relatively new to New Orleans, realized that a failing city would be bad for their businesses. In addition to promoting and funding the aquarium, the Business Council paid for a report on the city government's financial status and created a committee to evaluate gaming in New Orleans. It also funded the search for an Orleans Parish superintendent of schools after opposing all three of the candidates being considered in 1998. The organization nevertheless maintained a relatively low profile with an undisclosed membership list, and its accomplishments before Katrina were modest at best.[14]

Business leaders also formed MetroVision, Greater New Orleans, Inc. (GNO, Inc.), and the Committee for a Better New Orleans in an attempt to generate growth and jobs, but they exerted limited influence over economic development in the city. The consensus, even among people who belonged to these organizations, was that New Orleans's economic development profile lagged far behind that of the rest of the country. Economic development was haphazard and uncoordinated, and when it did occur, it proceeded in stops and starts.

As the 1990s arrived, New Orleans was not well positioned for economic development. The loss of the oil and gas industries, diminished federal funds, and the small size of the corporate community made resources scarce and deprived the city of potential leaders. Louisiana governors used their own resources and authority to complete several development initiatives in New Orleans.[15]

In his fourth term, Governor Edwin Edwards, a notorious gambler who later went to federal prison for racketeering, extortion, and fraud connected with casino licenses, signed into law a bill that authorized a land-based casino in New Orleans. In July 1994 Edwards and Mayor Marc Morial negotiated a deal that called for the state and the Harrah's corporation to pay $10 million to the city, for which Harrah's received a gambling license to operate the New Orleans casino.[16]

In 1995, Harrah's filed for Chapter 11 bankruptcy and halted the construction of its permanent casino at the end of Canal Street across from Canal Place and the French Quarter. Three years later, Governor Murphy J. "Mike" Foster (1996–2004) renegotiated Harrah's contract, which called for the company to provide a $100 million payment to the state each year the New Orleans casino was open. That deal and others negotiated by the governor, the mayor, and the city council saved the Harrah's casino, which opened in its permanent location at the foot of Canal Street in October 1999.

In 1993 Edwards championed and signed a bill to allocate $85 million for an arena adjacent to the Superdome in downtown New Orleans and $55 million for other sports facilities in the city's metropolitan area, including Zephyr Field, also known as the Shrine on Airline (Highway), and the Saints' training facility in Metairie, Louisiana. The first opportunity for New Orleans to secure an NBA team came in the spring of 2001, when the owner of the Vancouver Grizzlies was looking to move. New Orleans was the frontrunner at first, but in the end it was Memphis that attracted the Grizzlies when FedEx, Auto Zone, and other local companies guaranteed ticket sales and a revenue stream to the team's owners. New Orleans lacked the kind of private resources that drew this NBA team to Memphis.[17]

In the fall of 2001, the owners of the Charlotte Hornets planned to move their team. They wanted the same guarantees that the Grizzlies' owners had received from Memphis. Without the kind of private resources necessary to lure a team to New Orleans, city leaders asked the governor for help. As the result of a special session of the state legislature, Louisiana agreed to pay the Hornets' moving costs, spend $10 million to improve the arena, and give revenue from premium seats, advertising, the arena's naming rights, souvenirs, and parking to the Hornets. This time New Orleans was successful.

In the years before Katrina, New Orleans did not embrace development. Both historical preservationists and homeowners opposed growth. The city lacked a stable and long-lasting class of leaders interested in pursuing and executing development policy. The small number of pro-growth corporate leaders declined further over time, though it had never been large. Given the limited number of private actors with the resources and ability to spearhead a pro-growth regime, the governor took the lead on major development projects in New Orleans in the 1990s and early 2000s, and the state legislature financed these initiatives.

Economic Development in the Post-Katrina Era

Governmental reform topped the post-Katrina agenda in economic development. The civic elite and city business leaders placed reform at the top of the agenda. The governor, state legislature, and new members of the city council championed the changes and managed to enact some of them. Louisiana voters enacted other reforms. These forces linked change to economic growth. The process and implementation of reform proceeded more smoothly than planning for the rebuilding of the city, which was plagued by inter- and intragovernmental division and racial divides. Planning produced lots of outputs and activity in the post-Katrina period, but reform is where the outcomes and actions were. This is a critical point, because the reforms were the necessary foundation for business, which needed to regain trust in a reformed local governance structure.

In the weeks and months after the storm, some middle- and upper-class New Orleanians and business leaders claimed that levee protection was the most important issue the city faced. Without assurances that the levees had improved since Katrina, they argued, individuals and companies would not return to New Orleans. In an interview with CNBC two months after Katrina, Jay Lapeyre, chair of the Business Council, said that levee board reform was the number one issue that faced the city and the state at that time. Lapeyre and others framed governmental reform as an imperative that affected the economic health of New Orleans. According to one civic leader, the Business Council "became extremely engaged for the first time on a civic level" after Katrina.[18] When asked why civic engagement had increased among New Orleans's corporate community in general and the Business Council in particular, a business leader answered: "Everybody had enough with the Katrina thing. We were looking into the abyss. If we don't get busy, this city could end up being . . . no more."[19]

The ten boards that governed the levees throughout the New Orleans area exercised authority over parks, marinas, a police force, and an airport. Members of the board were not required to have expertise in engineering, geology, hydrology, or other areas relevant to levees and flood protection. All they needed were the political prerequisites for a gubernatorial appointment.

Governor Blanco called a special session of the state legislature in November 2005 to address the effects of Katrina on New Orleans and the state. Blanco proposed a new state agency to monitor the levee districts. Members of the city's corporate community, especially the Business Council, wanted the levee boards in southeast Louisiana consolidated from ten into one and a requirement that board members have expertise in engineering, geology, hydrology, or a related field. Blanco's plan did nothing to address the political patronage associated with the levee boards. The first special session of the legislature ended without levee reform.[20]

According to Ruth Frierson, a realtor in Uptown New Orleans, the public mood went from "mourning to outrage" after the first special session of the legislature.[21] Frierson gathered 120 New Orleanians at her Uptown home to discuss what they could do to bring about reform of the levee boards. They created an organization, "Citizens for 1 Greater New Orleans," and signed a petition to Blanco and the state legislature demanding the consolidation of the levee boards. Within two weeks, more than 45,000 people signed the petition.

The Business Council took out a full-page ad in the *Times-Picayune* to demand levee board reform. In a letter to Governor Blanco, the Business Council wrote: "The risk of economic collapse of New Orleans is real, and it will continue to increase if levee reform is delayed. . . . Politics-as-usual won't work." The letter continued, "A great city has been devastated, and yet the Orleans Parish Levee Board continues to protect the unqualified and the corrupt." Council for a Better Louisiana (CABL), Citizens for 1 Greater New Orleans, the Public Affairs Research Council of Louisiana, the Louisiana Association of Business and Industry, and the Louisiana Home Builders Association also wanted just one levee board.[22]

The pressure from Citizens for 1 Greater New Orleans and businesses in the city helped persuade the governor to change her position. In the second special session of the legislature, which began on February 2, 2006, Blanco endorsed the idea of a single levee board for New Orleans. She claimed that supporters of the current system were only trying to maintain the patronage positions and resources associated with the multiple levee boards.[23] Congress offered $12 million to Louisiana for flood control if the state consolidated the boards, thus exercising some authority over the creation of a single entity.

Blanco compromised with legislative leaders and proposed a constitutional amendment to create one levee board for the area west of the Mississippi River and another for the east. The bill passed the Louisiana House by a vote of 99–3 and the Senate by a 39–0 margin. On September 30, 2006, Louisiana voters ratified the constitutional amendment to create the two levee boards, with about 80 percent in favor of the change. After the vote Blanco said, "I think it shows that people really care about basic reform in Louisiana."[24]

Of all the post-Katrina reforms, levee board consolidation received the most widespread support. Ninety-seven percent of voters in the precincts with the highest percentages of whites favored the measure, while 90 percent of voters in the precincts with the highest percentages of blacks endorsed it. This 7 percent gap between white and black support was the narrowest margin for any reform in the post-Katrina period.

As a result of the levee board reforms, said one corporate leader, "the Business Council became a magnet for other civic organizations to make New Orleans a healthy place."[25] Citizens for 1 Greater New Orleans and the Urban League of Greater New Orleans, under the leadership of Nolan Rollins, who left to run the same organization in Los Angeles in early 2013, among others, remained partners with the Business Council throughout the post-Katrina period.

In the second special session of the legislature in February 2006, Speaker of the House Joe Salter introduced a bill to cut the number of tax assessors in New Orleans from seven to one. Blanco, the Business Council, the Bureau of Governmental Research (BGR), the Public Affairs Council, Citizens for 1 Greater New Orleans, the Council for a Better Louisiana, the World Trade Center, the Young Leadership Council, the Jefferson Business Council, the Northshore Business Council, and the New Orleans Chamber of Commerce, among other organizations, supported this proposal. They argued that the seven assessors undervalued property, produced variable judgments, were unfair and arbitrary, and had reduced assessments for non-damaged homes after the storm. The Legislative Auditors Office claimed that the consolidation would save about $574,000 in salaries alone.[26]

The sitting assessors opposed the consolidation. The Louisiana House Ways and Means Committee defeated the bill, 8–5. State representatives Jeffrey Arnold, the son of one assessor, and Alexander Heaton, the brother of another, cast the deciding votes. Lapeyre of the Business Council condemned the vote, saying that it "demonstrates the politically elite will fight to obstruct reform in order to protect their backroom property deals."[27]

Senator Ann Duplessis, a Democrat from New Orleans, reintroduced the assessor consolidation bill in the regular session of the legislature, which began in March 2006. Testifying before the Senate's Committee on

Local and Municipal Affairs, Governor Blanco said, "No city in our state is more in need of reform" than New Orleans. State Senator Cleo Fields, a Democrat from Baton Rouge, opposed the measure, arguing that the state should not interfere in city politics.[28]

The call for a constitutional amendment to consolidate the assessors passed the Senate, 35–2, and the House of Representatives, 98–2. State Senator Cedric Richmond tried to change the date of voter ratification of the amendment from the fall of 2006 to 2008, saying that he wanted to give New Orleanians time to return home before the vote.[29] That amendment failed.

The city's assessors campaigned against the consolidation. In a newspaper ad they argued, "A vote for Amendment 7 will take away each community's right to choose its own assessor who lives in that community."[30] On November 7, 2006, 78 percent of the voters statewide and 67 percent of the voters in New Orleans approved the constitutional amendment, and the change to a single assessor took effect in 2010. Voters in supermajority-white precincts in New Orleans were much more likely than those in supermajority-black districts to favor a single assessor: 85 percent of the electorate in supermajority-white precincts voted for a single assessor, but only 50.35% of voters in supermajority-black precincts supported this change. The gap of 35 percentage points between white and black districts represents the widest difference between these precincts for any post-Katrina reform vote.

In the February special session of the state legislature, Representative Peppi Bruneau, a Republican from New Orleans, introduced a bill to consolidate the city's three courts into one and eliminate half the sheriffs and city clerks in the city. Blanco, State Senator Walter Boasso, and State Representative Steve Scalise, a Republican who served Orleans and Jefferson parishes, argued that the consolidation of the court system would continue to send a signal that Louisiana and New Orleans were serious about reform. The Business Council's Lapeyre said: "What we're seeing is the recognition that if we don't get change now, you might as well leave town. And this is the time to change. Never in recent history have I seen the explosion of action I'm seeing now. It's the combination of disaster and its linkage to corruption and incompetence and business as usual."[31]

The measure drew immediate opposition from black legislators, especially those from New Orleans. State Representative Cedric Richmond, a Democrat from New Orleans and head of the Legislative Black Caucus, believed that race was driving this reform and the other measures designed to consolidate positions of power in New Orleans. He criticized these reform measures for taking place at a time when displaced New Orleans residents, many of whom were black, were living outside the city and state and were unable to have any input into these decisions. He referred to race as "the elephant that's been in this room the whole time," urging, "It may be uncomfortable, but let's address it."[32]

Black state legislators and legislators from New Orleans believed that the legislative session's priorities and agenda were misguided. State Representative Arthur Morrell, a Democrat from New Orleans, questioned why the governor and other legislative leaders were ignoring housing and other measures to ensure that people were able to return home. He argued: "The call is to dismantle New Orleans mainly. What does that tell New Orleans, that we don't want you anymore?"[33] Juan LaFonta, also a Democrat from New Orleans, declared: "I don't know what's more urgent than to get a roof over somebody's head. That is an urgent issue. The rest of it could wait."[34] Judges and sheriffs also opposed the consolidation.

In the middle of February, Blanco stopped her push for court consolidation. She said: "I know there's a resistance to change. It's very hard to get a focus on reform."[35] Bruneau introduced the court consolidation bill in the regular session, which began on March 27, 2006. He claimed that New Orleans's judicial and sheriff system was "at best, an ancient and arcane system created some time in the 19th century."[36]

The court consolidation bill passed the House, 96–1, but eight representatives were absent. Morrell, who had just been elected clerk of the criminal court for the city, did not vote. Neither did LaFonta. The governor could not get any New Orleans–area senator to introduce the court bill in that chamber, so a Democratic senator from Lake Charles sponsored the bill. The Senate approved the measure, 29–7, with three absences. Five African Americans senators cast "no" votes, three of whom represented New Orleans. The original law called for the consolidation to take place in 2009, but in 2008 the legislature approved a delay in implementation until 2014.[37]

In November 1995, 68 percent of New Orleans voters had approved revisions to the city's home rule charter, which included the creation of an Office of Inspector General and an ethics review board. Ten years later, the city had yet to implement these reforms, and no progress on these changes was in sight at the time Katrina struck.[38]

The Bring New Orleans Back Commission's governmental effectiveness committee now proposed the creation of an Office of Inspector General

(OIG), an independent agency to promote economic efficiency and prevent waste, fraud, and mismanagement. The city council approved the measure with a unanimous vote. In 2006, New Orleans voters elected four reform-minded city council members. Two of them—Arnie Fielkow and Shelly Midura—supported this position. Midura, a first-time officeholder who represented District A in Uptown, campaigned on reform and championed the creation of the OIG and an ethics review board when she took office. Fielkow, an attorney with a background in professional sports, was elected to an at-large council seat. A former executive vice president of the New Orleans Saints, he had been fired by team owner Tom Benson for his opposition to the Saints' remaining in San Antonio, their emergency home for the 2005 season, and his insistence that Benson keep the team in New Orleans.[39]

Ninety-one percent of the voters in predominantly white precincts and 64 percent in predominantly black districts supported the creation of the Office of Inspector General. Some black leaders in the city nevertheless regarded the creation of the OIG as a white power grab and an "instrument of whites to check black politicians."[40]

One early accomplishment of the OIG was an audit of the city's take-home vehicles. The city ordinance mandates the use of sixty city-owned vehicles that municipal employees could take home outside working hours—fifty for municipal workers and ten for the Fire Department—but the OIG found that the actual number of vehicles was close to 275. The inspector general also found a lack of controls on fuel for city cars, the assignment of take-home cars, and the number of cars in the fleet, among other things.[41]

In 2013, which the inspector general called the office's most productive year to date, the OIG discovered close to $10 million in avoidable costs. Its criminal investigations helped the city avert $4.4 million in potential losses. As of March 6, 2014, the OIG claimed to have saved the city more than $50 million in a three-year period that began in 2009.[42]

When Fielkow took his seat on the city council, he wanted to make many reforms, one of which was to the New Orleans Recreation Department (NORD). Fielkow had concluded that NORD suffered from underfunding, inconsistent leadership, and inequitable facilities. He pushed for the creation of a New Orleans Community Advisory Panel (CAP) to study the best practices of recreation departments around the country. Under Fielkow's leadership, the city council authorized the panel. An attorney, the CEO of Entergy New Orleans, and a local businessman who is the son of a famous New Orleans city council member served as the first tri-chairs of CAP.[43]

After studying other cities, including Baton Rouge, for three years and receiving public input from town hall meetings for a year, CAP recommended establishing a new model for governing the recreation department, creating a public-private partnership to raise additional funds for NORD, and increasing funding. BGR, Citizens for 1 Greater New Orleans, and *New Orleans CityBusiness* endorsed and promoted the change as well.[44]

On October 4, 2010, the charter changes to create a new NORD passed with support from 74 percent of the electorate, receiving 90 percent of the white vote and 61 percent of the black vote. The local NAACP opposed the changes, which it argued would allow the quasi-private NORD to ignore public input. In the first two years of the new NORD, Mayor Landrieu doubled city funding for recreation, and the NORD Foundation helped raise more than $200,000 from the local corporate community. Other accomplishments include more summer camps, increased community participation, and new programs.[45]

In 2003 BGR published "Runaway Discretion: Land Use Decision Making in New Orleans," which condemned the city's planning process and identified the city council as an obstacle to development in New Orleans. City council members deferred to their colleagues on land-use decisions because they wanted the same in return.[46] In 2006 BGR proposed amendments to the city charter to transform land policy and procedures in New Orleans. Under the law at the time, the city lacked a master plan, and the city council could change zoning ordinances with only four votes. Special exemptions created imbalanced land-use policy whereby commercial, residential, and mixed-use functions existed in the same area.

In 2008, at-large council member Jackie Clarkson recommended a charter change that would give an official master plan the force of law. Her original amendment mirrored the recommendations made in "Runaway Discretion." The proposed amendment passed without opposition from the city council.

The NAACP saw the master plan as a veiled attempt to shrink the city's footprint. Both the NAACP and the African American Leadership Council wanted the city's voters to approve a completed master plan. They did, by a vote of 52 percent to 48% percent. The wealthier areas of New Orleans supported the charter amendment, while 60 percent of the voters in the poorer areas of New Orleans East and the Lower Ninth Ward opposed the charter change. Of all the post-Katrina reforms, the master plan met with the greatest opposition from voters in white as well as black precincts. Sixty-two percent of voters in supermajority-white districts and 45 percent in supermajority-black districts voted to give the force of law to the master plan.[47]

Businesses, developers, elites, Citizens for 1 Greater New Orleans, BGR, and other white and wealthy residents supported the master plan change. Developers wanted a straightforward and consistent planning process. Under the system at the time, the rules changed often, and developers needed to go before several boards to get anything accomplished in the city. By contrast, some blacks feared that areas like New Orleans East and the Lower Ninth Ward would be left out of the recovery. An analysis of the city's recovery projects in 2008 revealed that District E, which includes New Orleans East, had 112 infrastructure projects, whereas in the other four council districts, between 129 and 171 such projects were planned or were under construction.[48]

Thousands of residents attended dozens of master plan meetings. The Goody Clancy planning firm scheduled meetings with council member Cynthia Willard-Lewis and other black leaders and moved a planning forum to New Orleans East to receive feedback from residents there. Citizens made 337 formal comments and suggestions to the city's planning commission, which incorporated 147 of those ideas into its final draft of the plan.[49]

Planning

A focus on reform lasted throughout the post-Katrina period. Actual development—and the plans that produced it—did not come with the same kind of cohesiveness or accomplishments. New Orleans experienced five citywide recovery planning schemes in the two years after Katrina.[50] FEMA, the mayor's Bring New Orleans Back Commission, the city council, the Louisiana Redevelopment Authority (LRA), and the city's Office of Recovery and Management, created by Mayor Nagin in late 2006, initiated separate recovery plans and processes. Each plan and process responded to the one before it.

By October 2005, Mayor Nagin had appointed a commission to help develop policies for rebuilding. The Bring New Orleans Back Commission

(BNOBC) had seventeen members, eight of whom were white, eight black, and one Latino. At least ten came from the business community, and two were religious leaders. A health care executive and a community organizer served as co-chairs. The BNOBC claimed that its mission was to "finalize a master plan to advise, assist, and plan the direct funding on the rebuilding of New Orleans culturally, socially, economically, and uniquely for every citizen."[51]

The BNOBC, which attempted to establish the kind of cross-sector cooperation that characterized pro-growth cities, linked public and private actors in an unprecedented way in New Orleans. Early in the recovery, Mayor Nagin told Congress that his "vision to rebuild New Orleans includes the citizens, the private sector and Government." The BNOBC created a way for government and business to talk to each other and plan economic development for the city's future. Its members wanted to move quickly, but that speed prevented the displaced from having a say in the rebuilding process.[52]

The BNOBC's attempt to create a long-lasting partnership among various sectors of New Orleans society and rebuild the city ended in January 2006, when local developer Joe Canizaro, co-chair of the commission's committee on city planning, suggested that the city impose a moratorium on building and living in areas prone to flooding. Black and/or the poor made up a majority of residents in these areas, which included New Orleans East, the Lower Ninth Ward, Gentilly, Mid-City, and Hollygrove. The Urban Land Institute recommended to Canizaro's committee that these sections of the city be returned to wetlands, which it referred to as investment zones. Canizaro agreed, but stipulated that residents should be allowed to build wherever they wanted for three years. "At the end of three years, we'll see who is there. And if a neighborhood is not developing adequately to support the services it needs to support it, we'll try to shrink it then."[53]

The *Times-Picayune* created a map based on the BNOBC's recommendations and put it on page one, above the fold. The newspaper used green dots to mark the areas that would not be redeveloped. This so-called green dot map provided clear proof that black neighborhoods were the least likely to be redeveloped. Lakeview, an upper-middle-class area with a majority of white residents, was also vulnerable to another storm, but the BNOBC did not recommend that it be turned into wetlands.

The plan and the process that produced it rekindled a fear among African Americans that the city's white elites wanted to use Katrina as a pretext to change the racial and economic composition of New Orleans and increase their authority and power. Former mayor Marc Morial, who was president of the National Urban League at the time, called the green dot map a "massive red-lining plan wrapped around a giant land grab."[54] He wanted levees built that could protect against Category 5 hurricanes, so that every part of the city could be safe.

At first, Mayor Nagin offered no opinion on the shrinking footprint issue. In January 2006 he appeared at city hall to commemorate Martin Luther King Day. In his speech Nagin recounted a conversation he said he had that morning with Dr. King on what King thought about what had happened to black people in New Orleans before, during, and after Katrina. Toward the end of his speech, Nagin said: "We ask black people: it's time. It's time for us to come together. It's time for us to rebuild a New Orleans, the one that should be a chocolate New Orleans. And I don't care what people are saying Uptown or wherever they are. This city will be chocolate at the end of the day. This city will be a majority African-American city. It's the way God wants it to be. You can't have New Orleans no other way; it wouldn't be New Orleans."[55]

This address, which became known as the Chocolate City speech, kicked off Nagin's reelection campaign, one in which he stressed racial differences between him and the rest of the largely white field. In 2002 Nagin had won the mayoral runoff, 59 percent to 41 percent, over Police Chief Richard Pennington, who was also black, with 85 percent of the white vote and somewhere between 35 and 40 percent of the black vote. Four years later, Nagin beat Mitch Landrieu with 80 percent of the black vote and 20 percent of the white vote. Racial identity was the most prominent factor affecting voter choice in 2006. Voters did consider Nagin's performance after Katrina but emphasized that it was the federal government, not the mayor, that deserved most of the blame.[56]

The Chocolate City speech ended the BNOBC's attempt to create a cross-sector and biracial partnership dedicated to development. The shrunken footprint issue and an impending mayoral election eliminated the discussion of neighborhood viability from subsequent redevelopment plans. The reaction to the BNOBC caused just about every elected official and candidate for office to promise that displaced residents had a right to return to every neighborhood in the city. The government would not guarantee services to every part of the city, but if residents wanted to return, it was not going to stop them. The city would not promise that levees could protect certain parts of New Orleans, but after the green dot map controversy, safety took a backseat to the right to return.

According to some civic leaders, the green dot map ended rational discourse about the rebuilding of New Orleans. BGR leaders wanted a fair, criteria-driven approach for dealing with the spatial mismatch and mitigation issues. In its December 22, 2005, report, titled "Wanted: A Realistic Development Strategy," BGR stated: "The City of New Orleans owes its residents a plan laying out exactly which parts of the city can be rebuilt and when. The plan must be based, not on political considerations, but on careful analysis of the physical and demographic realities facing the city."[57] That kind of plan would not exist after the green dot map.

Entities outside New Orleans ensured that the city had a rebuilding plan. The LRA contributed $3 million. The Rockefeller Foundation in New York and the Bush-Clinton Katrina Fund provided $3.5 million and $1 million, respectively, to create the Unified New Orleans Plan (UNOP) in April 2006. The Rockefeller Foundation insisted that all sectors of society provide input, the best planners create the strategy, and the plan be completed quickly, and then provided the money to amalgamate the early plans and create a uniform strategy.[58]

Locally, the Greater New Orleans Foundation created the New Orleans Community Support Foundation, a nonprofit that would allocate $7.5 million for a process and a plan. UNOP provided the kind of cross-sector participation and comprehensive planning that the LRA and the Rockefeller Foundation demanded. At the end of June 2007, the LRA approved UNOP and released $117 million so that the city could work on some of the ninety-five capital and infrastructure projects contained in the plan. Who exactly would control those dollars was already an issue.[59]

Nagin had created the Office of Recovery Management (ORM) at the end of 2006 to develop a recovery strategy. At the beginning of 2007, Ed Blakely, an internationally recognized expert on planning and recovery who'd led Oakland's comeback after the 1989 earthquake, agreed to serve as director of ORM. The city council and the LRA approved Blakely's plan in June 2007.[60]

Blakely's citywide strategy, which he labeled the target area plan, divided the city into three kinds of areas according to need: rebuild, redevelop, and renew. The rebuild areas, the Lower Ninth Ward and New Orleans East, had experienced the most severe damage and had the longest way to go toward recovery. Some recovery had already taken place and some resources existed in the six redevelop areas. Renew areas were those that needed "relatively modest public resources to complement the investments of the private and non-profit sectors that were already underway." Forty percent ($289.6 million) of the citywide plan focused on projects recommended by community and neighborhood groups and residents. Fifty-five percent ($398.2 million) went toward citywide projects.[61]

In February 2007, Blakely said he envisioned cranes in the sky by September. Nagin expressed reservations about the prediction in light of the difficulty the city had had in completing large-scale projects in the past. A year later, still without many cranes in the sky, critics argued that economic development in the city was proceeding too slowly.[62]

It took twenty-two months to devise a rebuilding plan that included voices at all levels and covered each part of the city. According to the former director of city planning in New Orleans, the problem with planning in general, and the post-Katrina process in particular, is that planners and elected officials do not collaborate and the city tends not to use plans. Two outside entities—the LRA and the Rockefeller Foundation— forced the mayor, city council, residents, and civic organizations to work together to create a citywide plan. The Rockefeller Foundation worked with the mayor, city council, and planning commission for at least a month to define these entities' roles in the recovery and to ensure that UNOP became the city's official recovery plan.[63]

Eventually the city would see significant numbers of large-scale construction projects. By May 10, 2013, eighty capital projects were under way. The previous year the city had finished twenty-five capital projects at a cost of $60 million. Nagin's successor, Mayor Mitch Landrieu, announced that libraries, parks, playgrounds, and public safety facilities were his top priorities with regard to capital projects. During his 2013 State of the City speech, the mayor promised that new hospitals in Mid-City and New Orleans East, an $826 million renovation of Louis Armstrong Airport, more streetcars, completed upgrades to City Park, and public space at the foot of Canal Street would be completed by the city's three hundredth birthday in 2018.[64]

But before this building boom began, rebuilding occurred in a piecemeal fashion. Some civic leaders condemned this planning process, which one called "a bunch of fluff" and "junk food." Citizens were suffering from "planning fatigue" because they "participated in one silly process after another." Out of what this leader called "complete chaos" came some substance, namely neighborhood rebuilding plans constructed by qualified firms. Nevertheless, the reaction was largely negative. One civic leader complained that Nagin had "no agenda" after the storm. Another charged that the mayor had turned the keys over to Blakely, "who was like a bull in a china closet," adding, "There was that failure at the federal level to really provide any guidance and leadership, and there was a failure at the state and local levels as well to provide guidance and leadership to the people." As a result, the people had to take it upon themselves to decide, in his words, "Are we coming back, and if so, how, and what do we want?"[65]

Civic Engagement

The BNOBC on the one hand and a perceived lack of city leadership on the other spurred civic engagement in the rebuilding process. The BNOBC's early 2006 report insinuated that low-lying neighborhoods should no longer exist if they could not prove their viability. More than six hundred Broadmoor residents, some returning from as far away as Houston, joined together to rally against the green dot map. Prior to the storm, the Broadmoor section of the city was about two-thirds black, comprising mostly lower- to middle-income residents, and half the homes were owner occupied. LaToya Cantrell, leader of the Broadmoor Improvement Association (BIA), took the report's insinuation as a challenge. She and her neighbors created seventy-two committees with tasks that ranged from grass-cutting to pool-covering, and held more than 125 meetings from January to August 2006. The BIA's major objective was to track down the neighborhood's displaced residents, determine if they wanted to return, and encourage them to come back. Two years after Katrina, two-thirds of Broadmoor's 2,900 homes were livable or under renovation. That number rose to 85 percent by the sixth anniversary of Katrina.[66]

The BIA enlisted Harvard University to develop a 319-page recovery plan. Harvard helped the BIA draft the plan and ran neighborhood forums to develop leaders and address recovery issues. Shell Oil sponsored the costs for Harvard interns to come to New Orleans and provided funds for leadership forums. Bard College in New York mapped the neighborhood to assess and catalogue damage. The BIA worked with PlanReady, a California-based company, to design the neighborhood's emergency preparedness plan and recovery system.[67]

At the conclusion of a six-month planning process, the BIA began work on three development priorities for Broadmoor: a school, a library and community center, and a health and wellness facility. In large part because of the BIA, the Andrew Wilson Elementary School was one of five schools to receive the fast-track distinction from the Recovery School District. The BIA partnered with Edison Learning to operate the charter school.[68]

The Clinton Global Initiative helped raise $5 million for a library and community center, with the Carnegie Foundation donating $2 million of that total. In March 2012, Cantrell, the BIA, and others celebrated the opening of the $6.8 million Rosa Keller Library and Community Center. Walter Isaacson, a native of Broadmoor, was instrumental in securing funding for the redevelopment. A coffee shop within the new building was named the Green Dot Café; it features a framed picture of the green dot map along with the *Times-Picayune* article in which it first appeared.[69]

The Gentilly Civic Improvement Association (GCIA) got its start after the storm when leaders of that area's twenty-one neighborhood groups formed a single organization. Like the BIA, the GCIA proved its neighborhood's viability. Its education committee brought Holy Cross High School, a Lower Ninth Ward facility destroyed by the storm, to Gentilly. GCIA worked with its constituents to make sure that homeowners knew how to navigate the city's Lot Next Door ordinance, which allowed residents to buy abandoned property or lots adjacent to their homes maintained by the Road Home program. It held a Rebuild Gentilly Fair, which featured every type of business that homeowners would need to repair or rebuild their houses.[70]

Like the BIA in Broadmoor, the GCIA organization helped its neighborhood secure one of the city's five Quick Start schools. Also like the BIA, the GCIA partnered with private organizations. In early June 2008, Entergy announced that the GCIA would become the first Entergy Joint Venture Neighborhood Partner. Through this partnership, Entergy worked with the group to assess the needs of the neighborhoods and assist in strategies to improve the rebuilding of the Gentilly area. When asked how the GCIA received this distinction, Entergy's economic development director replied, "This joint venture partnership designation signals that Gentilly is organized and prepared for growth." According to one former GCIA leader: "The neighborhoods rebuilt the neighborhoods. We brought the resources." This kind of partnership between communities and major companies not only characterizes post-Katrina New Orleans but also represents a new form of urban governance in the twenty-first century.[71]

Not only did neighborhood and community groups explode in number in post-Katrina New Orleans, but also these entities differed from
their pre-Katrina predecessors. According to Frederick D. Weil, they
displayed increased organizational capacity and autonomy, a new strategic sophistication, more citizen participation, and a new cooperative
orientation. Neighborhood groups, such as the Lakeview Civic Association, organized by block and appointed captains for each block. This
structure, replicated to a degree by other groups like the BIA, resembled
the manner in which old-style political machines had operated. The BIA
illustrated its strategic sophistication when it plastered signs all over the
area insisting that "Broadmoor Lives," even though many residents had
yet to return. Weil concluded that the signage "helped create a critical
mass, or tipping point, to forge solidarity in the service of recovery."[72]

The Neighborhood Empowerment Network Association (NENA) is
one of the best examples of the spirit of collaboration in the new umbrella
groups. NENA, a collaboration of residents, homeowners, and survivors
of Katrina in the Lower Ninth Ward, "pioneered a community land trust
to leverage subsidies and ensure affordability and sustainability of the
land, homes, and businesses that they rebuild."[73] It organized property
swaps, coordinated volunteers to help build houses, and provided information, counseling, and case management to residents who looked to
return or receive benefits and aid from other institutions. It received government and private grants to assist homeowners. It also championed the
construction of a high school in the Lower Ninth Ward.[74]

Another such organization is Beacon of Hope, a nonprofit in Lakeview created by Denise Thornton, wife of Doug Thornton, who runs the
Superdome and New Orleans Arena. Beacon of Hope provides information about building permits, utility reconnections, contractors, and other
topics to residents looking to return to Lakeview or elsewhere in New
Orleans. Like NENA, Beacon of Hope coordinated volunteers to improve
its neighborhood. Former New Orleans Hornets owner Ray Wooldridge
gave seed money, which Thornton leveraged for a full-time office, staff,
a tractor, an all-terrain vehicle, and other equipment that residents could
borrow. Saints quarterback Drew Brees's foundation, Brees Dream Foundation, allocated $60,000 so that Beacon of Hope could expand to other
parts of New Orleans, including Gentilly and the Lower Ninth Ward.[75]

Other groups, such as the Irish Channel Neighborhood Association,
canvassed each block of their neighborhood to assess damage, repair
and rebuild homes, and encourage displaced residents to return. In the

Vietnamese community of New Orleans East, the Mary Queen of Vietnam Catholic Church helped its members evacuate then relocate and recover, and it blocked the location of a landfill in its area. The high levels of organization in the Mary Queen of Vietnam community and Gentilly that had existed before Katrina proved instrumental in helping people return home after the storm, share information, and rebuild. Harry Connick Jr. and Branford Marsalis led and helped fund Musicians' Village, seventy-two affordable single-family homes for musicians and five duplexes for senior citizen musicians, in the Upper Ninth Ward. The Musicians' Village includes a performance space and theater for its residents and other musicians. The village was built by eighteen thousand volunteers from Habitat for Humanity.[76]

Five years after Katrina, Senator Mary Landrieu told the committee she chaired on the progress of New Orleans after Katrina, "Civic participation and nonprofit activism are at an all time high, providing the region with a new framework and engine for self-determination and renewal."[77] Just about every stakeholder interviewed regarded civic engagement by people in the neighborhoods as the most positive outcome of Hurricane Katrina. Some credited the "resiliency and tenacity of the people"; another observer said that New Orleanians created a "civic structure" after the storm, "a sense of civic engagement that wasn't there before Katrina. That's one of the most important legacies of Katrina."[78]

Civic engagement was nevertheless uneven, and therefore contributed to the unevenness of the recovery. Areas of New Orleans with greater resources, which were less likely to have experienced damage in the first place, were more likely to have residents who participated in the recovery, and more likely to have a stronger community revival. At least one study found that the most heavily organized areas of the city were the ones least likely to have FEMA trailers located in them. Community groups and faith-based institutions that helped with disaster recovery in New Orleans were motivated, flexible, and creative, but they were not powerful enough to achieve an equitable recovery, overcome limited resources, and ensure accountability and coordination.[79]

Although civic engagement affected the rebuilding of neighborhoods, it did not determine the public agenda, which was set by business, civic elites, reform-oriented members of the city council, and the governor and state legislature, among other resource providers and authority holders. Rebuilding neighborhoods was a bottom-up enterprise. The public agenda and its implementation were driven from the top down.

The Lower Ninth Ward, which was wiped out by Hurricane Katrina, recovered slowly. Before the storm, this area lacked a grocery store; residents shopped at Walgreen's and small convenience stores in their neighborhoods. Six years after the storm, most of the commercial buildings, churches, and schools were still vacant in the Lower Ninth Ward, which also lacked a fire station. At the time, only one-third of the area's 5,500 residents had returned.[80]

The Lower Ninth Ward experienced few victories in the post-Katrina era. With a fight, the Dr. Martin Luther King Charter School was the first school of this kind to open in the district. Brad Pitt's Make It Right Foundation built 100 modern and eco-friendly homes close to the levee, with the goal of building 150. Civic engagement and protest also led to promises of a new high school building, which had not yet opened nearly ten years after Katrina hit.[81]

New Orleans East also rebuilt slowly. A Walmart in that area did not open until more than eight years after Katrina. This area still did not have a hospital more than nine years after the disaster.

In the post-Katrina period, Weil observed increased citizen participation and more cooperation among civic groups in New Orleans as "a virtuous circle of growing mutual trust and civic engagement began to displace the old vicious circle of distrust and disengagement." But he also found that "blight was most reduced, since Katrina, in areas with (a) higher individual resources (esp. income), (b) stronger social capital and civic engagement, and (c) organizations that focused on blight reduction and, importantly, cooperated with each other."[82]

Organizational capacity does not tell the complete story of rebuilding after Katrina. By all accounts, Gentilly is one of the better-organized sections of the city, but seven years after the storm, parts of that area looked and remained depressed. Even though Walmart was scheduled to replace Gentilly Woods Mall, that facility was vacant and boarded up with grass growing in the parking lot. Ground was not broken on the Walmart project until more than eight years after Katrina. Lake Terrace Shopping Center, a prominent commercial facility before the hurricane, also remained shuttered for more than eight years after Katrina. Backed by heavy neighborhood involvement, the city fined the owners of the property and went to court—and won—in order to get the shopping center returned to commercial use. The owners had received $162,500 in public funds but had not rehabilitated the property.[83]

Neighborhood organizations and churches were not the only nongovernmental entities to contribute to the rebuilding of New Orleans. In the post-Katrina period, the community organizing group ACORN assisted residents with mortgage and credit issues, organized survivors, developed a rebuilding plan, and campaigned for everyone's right to return to the city. But maintaining its combative style, the NGO went from a strong and powerful organization to total collapse after three incidents: embezzlement of $1 million by Dale Rathke (brother of founder Wade Rathke); allegations of fake registration for nonexistent voters, including Mickey Mouse, in eight states; and a controversial videotape which suggested that ACORN staff had advised two anti-ACORN activists disguised as a prostitute and her pimp about how to cheat on taxes and establish brothels using underage girls. Significantly, U.S. attorneys never found an illegal vote cast or recorded because of ACORN, and forty-five federal, state, and local investigations "exonerated ACORN from all wrongdoing" in regard to the prostitution allegations. The videotapes were determined to be "doctored, edited, and misleading."[84]

Although Wade Rathke blamed "Neo-McCarthyism," Congress took action to prohibit ACORN from receiving federal aid. Private donors too canceled funding after the videotape incident. ACORN filed for Chapter 7 bankruptcy on November 2, 2010, effectively shutting down the organization. Wade Rathke, who was ousted by ACORN, became chief organizer for ACORN International, a separate entity that works overseas. He purchased Fair Grinds Coffee House, near the racetrack in New Orleans, as a way to continue his activism in the city.[85]

The second generation of social movement organizations in the city included the New Orleans Women's Health Clinic, the New Orleans Women's Health and Justice Initiative, Safe Streets/Strong Communities, and the New Orleans Workers' Center for Racial Justice. They provided services and organized communities in order to address Katrina-related issues and ongoing social problems while building their membership.[86]

A Public-Private Partnership Emerges

More than a year after the storm, academics and business and government leaders in New Orleans agreed that the pace of economic development had not improved since the disaster. In 2006 Whelan concluded that "economic development does not seem to be a high priority at this point" and "there is a lack of vision in the political and business leadership."[87] City council member Stacy Head gave an "F-minus" to the city for its incapacity to deal with business issues.[88] According to the former chair of MetroVision and Greater New Orleans, Inc., "the ineptitude of the economic development in this parish [New Orleans] over the past 20 to 30 years is just sad."[89]

In November 2007 the city council—with Arnie Fielkow as its president—approved a plan to create a formal public-private partnership to recruit and retain businesses, a project Fielkow had been attempting to initiate since he was first elected to the council. Although the Chamber of Commerce and GNO, Inc., supported this partnership, Mayor Nagin remained uncommitted until his State of the City address in June 2008, when he promised $2 million from the city's economic development fund to start the partnership and $1 million each year thereafter; he reserved a cabinet position for the executive director of the partnership.[90]

On the day the city council forwarded the names of board nominees to the mayor, however, Nagin suspended the creation of the organization. He objected that the list of nominees, which was put together by the presidents of the universities in New Orleans, lacked racial and gender diversity; he also criticized the private sector for its minimal financial contributions to the partnership. Fielkow countered that Nagin's rejection was revenge for the city council's 4–3 vote against the mayor's proposal to move city hall to the Chevron Building, a vote that split along racial lines. The formal business partnership would have to await new mayoral leadership.[91]

On July 8, 2009, Lieutenant Governor Mitch Landrieu, who was widely expected to enter the mayoral election scheduled for February 6, 2010, announced that he would not run. In his official statement Landrieu said, "There are many capable people who will make themselves available and who will serve well, if elected."[92] But after he watched one inexperienced candidate after another join the race and no frontrunner emerge, Landrieu changed his mind. Five months to the day after announcing he would not run, Landrieu, the son of former mayor Moon Landrieu and brother of Senator Mary Landrieu, declared his candidacy for mayor.[93]

In 1969, when Moon Landrieu was first running for that office, one of his political ads asked, "Can an honest man become mayor of New Orleans?" In 2009 the question was "Can a white man become mayor of New Orleans?" Despite the lack of qualified high-profile candidates of any race other than Mitch Landrieu, most people were unsure that a city that was still about 60 percent black would elect a white mayor; but changes had already taken place. In 2007 the New Orleans city council became a majority-white body for the first time in twenty-two years. By the time of the 2010 mayoral election, every major elected office since Katrina had been won by a white candidate, except the mayor's office. While the city focused its attention on the Saints' upcoming appearance in the Super Bowl on February 7, 2010, the day before the game, one-third of its voters went to the polls and gave 66 percent of its vote to Landrieu, who won 365 of the city's 366 precincts. He captured 62 percent of the vote in predominantly black precincts.[94]

Some might argue that the political and policy changes—and in fact all changes—resulted because the city's demographics had changed: whites were winning because blacks no longer made up the electoral majority. Census data, however, do not support that argument. In post-Katrina New Orleans, blacks remained the majority. In 2012, blacks made up 59.45 percent of the city's population, down from 66.7 percent in 2000. The U.S. Census estimated that New Orleans lost 103,881 black residents and 14,984 white residents from 2000 to 2012. The number of blacks dropped from 323,392 to 219,511, and the number of whites decreased from 128,871 to 113,887.[95]

Voter registration data also demonstrate that while the percentage of white voters eventually increased after Katrina, by 2014 whites still made up only a third of registered voters, while blacks remained a majority (see table 2). Public opinion data presented throughout this book indicate that although black voters were not as enthusiastic as whites about proposed reform measures, a majority of them supported change and helped elect a white mayor.

Others might argue that policy changes occurred because the demographics of the city's black community changed. Census data reject this assertion as well. According to the Greater New Orleans Community Data Center, the share of middle- and upper-class black households in the city dropped from 35 percent of the city's total black households in 1999 to 31 percent in 2011. The proportion of New Orleans's black households in the nation's lowest income quartile (less than $20,432) rose from 42 percent of the black households in 1999 to 44 percent in 2011. White candidates clearly had to appeal to black voters if they hoped to win citywide office.

After his election, Landrieu committed his administration's support to the public-private partnership. Nearly five years after Katrina, New

TABLE 2

No. (%) of white and black registered voters in New Orleans, 2004–2014

Year	White	Black	Total voters
2004	91,987 (30.42)	191,163 (63.21)	302,409
2006	89,542 (30.32)	186,341 (63.09)	295,361
2007	83,926 (30.16)	175,768 (63.16)	278,307
2008	86,304 (30.43)	177,018 (62.41)	283,638
2009	84,048 (30.85)	168,710 (61.93)	272,399
2010	86,052 (31.33)	168,409 (61.31)	274,672
2011	77,239 (33.26)	137,787 (59.33)	232,221
2012	83,647 (33.27)	148,698 (59.14)	251,439
2013	82,063 (33.74)	142,750 (58.70)	243,204
2014	81,515 (33.87)	140,972 (58.58)	240,656

Source: Louisiana Secretary of State.

Orleans created a formal partnership, the Business Alliance. that would be responsible for business recruitment and expansion, marketing, and planning, among other priorities. The board of directors included partners in law firms and the CEOs or owners of the New Orleans Saints, Royal Engineers, Whitney Bank, Bayou Equity Mortgage, and Entergy New Orleans. The city allocated $1.5 million from its special tax-generated economic development fund, and the private sector pledged $500,000 annually. The money would pay for a CEO and five staff members.[96]

Mayor Landrieu charged the Business Alliance with business retention and expansion. It would negotiate with businesses that expressed an interest in coming to New Orleans. The alliance's duties also included "marketing, small business services, entrepreneurship initiatives, international business development, and strategic planning." The mayor and city departments maintained responsibility for "business licenses and permits, neighborhood economic development and programs, workforce development, federal grants, housing, [and] historic preservation," among other things. The Business Alliance worked with other organizations to form the Hornets Business Council, which helped sell enough tickets to games in order to keep the NBA franchise in the city.[97]

Landrieu also placed business leaders on his transition committees. He signed executive orders to create the position of chief procurement officer, outline a competitive selection procedure, and make public all documents related to contracting. The new mayor received widespread public praise for these decisions.[98]

The presence and power of businesses organized after Katrina can be seen in the actions of Mayor Landrieu and post-Katrina city councils. In anticipation of the 2010 mayoral election, the Business Council partnered with more than thirty other civic, neighborhood, and business organizations to create Forward New Orleans, a coalition that would create an agenda it expected local elected officials, especially the mayor and the city council, to follow. Principled reform, accountability, transparency, fiduciary responsibility, and best practices were at the heart of this agenda. The priorities covered crime, blight, city finance, economic development, city services and infrastructure, city contracting, and public education.[99]

In its 2013 progress report on the city's commitments to its initiatives, Forward New Orleans noted that the mayor and city council had made "good progress" on its economic development priorities. It applauded the mayor's establishment of the NOLA Business Alliance, the launching of a One Stop Shop for permits and licenses, and the creation and full funding of an Office of Supplier Diversity, among other things. The report also concluded that the "Mayor and the City Council have been appropriately supportive of key economic engines, including tourism, the hospitality industry, and the biomedical corridor, though we urge work toward policies that drive economic development in destination health-care and research commercialization."[100]

Economic Development Projects

The two largest economic development projects in the post-Katrina period were reminiscent of the sporadic character of development in the pre-Katrina era. One, the renovation of the Superdome, followed the pre-Katrina playbook in its commitment to a tourism-based economy in New Orleans. In the other case, Louisiana State University, a state entity, and the Veterans Administration, a federal one, led and financed the construction of a massive medical complex in Mid-City. This signaled a shift toward a "meds and eds" focus for New Orleans in the post-Katrina period. Resources from extra-local and nongovernmental actors funded these projects; locally based public and private actors played almost no role in either one. The coalitions that led and financed the Dome and the medical complex did not collaborate on other economic development projects.

After the first week of September 2005, when the sports facility became a chaotic refuge for city residents displaced by the storm, the Superdome commission chairman, the legal counsel for the Superdome, and the operator of the New Orleans Arena and the Dome estimated that they would need at least $400 million to restore these two facilities. Among other problems, 70 percent of the Dome's roof had failed; much of the electrical, heating, air-conditioning, and plumbing infrastructure needed repairs; and elevators, the football field, carpeting, suites, scoreboards, and 35 percent of the seats had to be replaced. The next month, Governor Blanco fast-tracked repairs to the Superdome.[101]

State Representative Cedric Richmond objected, saying, "It sends a bad message when it's an emergency to repair the Superdome for events uncertain when we have people still living in shelters."[102] A state senator from Shreveport said that the Superdome should be at the bottom of the list of things to do in terms of the recovery. Other legislators thought that the governor should focus on reopening Charity and University hospitals, two state-owned medical facilities located in New Orleans.[103]

At the time Blanco agreed to make these repairs to the Dome, the city of San Antonio, Texas, had already hosted three Saints home games during the Katrina emergency, and that city's mayor was attempting to keep the NFL team there permanently. The Dome by now symbolized pain, suffering, and public incompetence. Blanco wanted those images to fade. The governor reasoned that a restored Superdome would show that the city had recovered and was open for business.[104]

The rehabilitation of the Superdome cost about $185 million. FEMA paid $116 million, the Louisiana Stadium and Exposition District refinanced Superdome bonds and paid $41 million, the NFL contributed $15 million and another $5 million subject to a match by the state, and Louisiana allocated $13 million. The coalition of the governor, the Louisiana Stadium and Exposition District, and the NFL came together, renovated the facility, and disbanded.[105]

Charity Hospital, a much more historic local landmark, opened in New Orleans in 1736 as L'Hôpital des Pauvres de la Charité, an institution funded by a French sailor and shipbuilder. During the Great Depression, Huey Long promoted Louisiana's charity hospitals as a way to serve the poor and uninsured. He commissioned the architects of Louisiana's state capitol building, the largest of its kind in the country, to design a new Charity Hospital in New Orleans. Funded by the Works Progress Administration, Charity opened in its present location in 1939. Thirteen years later the federal government opened a VA hospital behind Charity, which took up 1 million square feet of space in Downtown.[106]

In addition to serving the city's needy, Charity Hospital was a level-1 trauma center and operated as a teaching hospital, where medical students from LSU and Tulane learned their trade. Because of funding cuts, however, Charity had closed nine operating rooms even before Hurricane Katrina. In late May 2005, the American College of Surgeons, Charity's accrediting agency, warned LSU that it would have to reopen some of the operating rooms or it would lose its distinction as a level 1 trauma center.[107]

According to a statewide poll conducted in 2004, 85 percent of Louisiana residents wanted to maintain Louisiana's ten charity hospitals, a result hardly changed from seven years earlier, when 87 percent of the state's residents had endorsed these hospitals. Although the support cut across race and region, the greatest support came from the New Orleans metropolitan area, where 91 percent of residents preferred to keep the state's charity hospitals. Doctors, patients, and historical preservationists all wanted Charity rebuilt and restored. That discussion resumed after Katrina.[108]

The storm caused $340 million worth of damage to Charity Hospital. In late September, LSU, which had exercised authority over the charity hospitals since 1997, shuttered the building, declaring that the facility was unsalvageable. But in late October 2008, post-Katrina recovery chief Blakely told students at Loyola University that the city's economy needed to be repositioned. He cited the biomedical field as a potential area of expansion.[109] A few weeks later, LSU and the Veterans Administration announced that they would build a medical complex on sixty-seven acres of land in the Mid-City section of New Orleans.[110]

According to Darwin BondGraham:

In New Orleans, the ensemble of organizations working alongside BRAF [the Baton Rouge Area Foundation] to privatize Charity Hospital health care system has assisted in the state university's bid to permanently shutter the Avery C. Alexander Charity Hospital (the third largest in the nation), and build a new LSU medical center. . . . [T]his redevelopment project in its sheer physical scope is the largest in post-Katrina New Orleans. It has required eviction of hundreds of homeowners and businesses from the lower–Mid City neighborhood, and was purposefully excluded from the city's highly controversial Master Plan by the City Council for fear that opponents to the new "Taj-Mahospital" as it has been pejoratively named, would stall the multi-billion dollar project. Closure and replacement of Charity is intended to both eliminate the public health care system with a medical services economy paid for by private insurance, and to serve as the anchor for an entire medical and biotechnology industrial district in Downtown and Mid City New Orleans.[111]

The plan, initiated by Governor Blanco, state legislators, LSU and Tulane University, and members of the VA, was to create a medical complex consisting of a University Medical Center (UMC), which would serve as a teaching hospital, and a VA hospital in the Mid-City section of New Orleans. The cost would be $1.2 billion, of which the federal government allocated $475 million, $300 million came from the state, and the rest from state bonds. Congress appropriated $800 million for the VA hospital.[112]

The National Trust for Historic Preservation opposed the project in order to protect 165 homes in a National Register–listed historic district. The National Trust filed a lawsuit contending that FEMA and the VA had violated the National Environmental Policy Act because they had not assessed the environmental effects of the medical complex's construction and operation on the area around the site. When the lawsuit failed, preservationists worked with city council member Kristin Gisleson Palmer and Mayor Landrieu on a compromise. The city would pay $3.2 million to a nonprofit organization that would move homes on the construction site to land owned by the city. As of late 2012, many of the houses were so badly damaged that they needed to be destroyed. At that point, twenty-eight had been restored.[113]

The idea of replacing Charity Hospital with the VA-LSU medical center included a strong racial and class component. Charity served the poor, and many of the city's black population had been born there. The new medical facility did not guarantee the kind of care for the poor that the old Charity had provided. In contrast to the success of the Vieux Carré Commission in its battle over the expressway forty years earlier, this time the preservationists lost.[114]

Tulane University, which would continue to teach its medical students at the UMC, constituted the main local actor involved in the creation of these hospitals. The rest of the leadership behind these facilities came largely from outside the city of New Orleans. The funds emanated from outside the city as well. While these are government facilities, it is important to note that state and federal actors—not private ones in the city—maintain the greatest responsibility for large-scale economic development in New Orleans.

Political Arrangement for Economic Development

There were winners and losers in the transition to a post-Katrina New Orleans. The beneficiaries of political patronage were among the losers. Sitting members of the levee boards, all but one assessor, employees of the Orleans Parish courts, and city clerks and sheriffs lost their positions of influence. The Office of Inspector General was created to limit governmental corruption and mismanagement in the future. The poor also lost in post-Katrina New Orleans because public and private resource providers did not prioritize their return, shelter, or health care.

Black males lost in the post-Katrina economy. They continue to earn lower median wages than white males, participate in the labor force at lower rates than white males, and suffer from higher levels of poverty than white males in New Orleans. In 2011, 27 percent of black men in New Orleans were living in poverty, compared to 15 percent of white men. In the same year, the median earnings of the city's black men working full-time was $31,018; the median earnings for non-Latino whites was $60,075. In 2011 dollars, the median earnings of black men in New Orleans working full-time, year-round had decreased from $35,036 in 1999, while the figure for white males had increased from $55,144.[115]

Post-Katrina New Orleans is divided along racial lines, but the electoral chasm between whites and blacks is not as wide or divisive as most people might think. Voters in predominantly white districts endorsed reform to a much greater extent than voters in predominantly black districts, but the holding power of the past did not stop reform. Voters in supermajority-white and supermajority-black precincts approved a new

TABLE 3
Reform votes in majority-white and majority-black precincts in New Orleans

	Percent vote for in majority-white precincts	Percent vote for in majority-black precincts	Percent difference between vote in majority-white and majority-black precincts
Consolidation of levee boards	97	90	−7
Reduction in the number of assessors	85	50	−35
Creation of the Office of Inspector General	91	64	−27
Changes to the New Orleans Recreation Department	90	60	−30
Authorization of a binding master plan	62	45	−17

Note: These numbers include the 123 precincts in New Orleans in which African Americans made up at least 90 percent of the voting population and the 35 precincts in New Orleans where whites made up 90 percent or more of the voters in 2003.

Source: Louisiana Secretary of State.

levee board, the reduction in the number of assessors, the creation of an Office of Inspector General, and changes to the New Orleans Recreation Department (see table 3).

Land-use issues sustained black-white divisions in New Orleans. Black leaders and their constituents opposed the green dot map. As a result of this opposition, the BNOBC lost its legitimacy, people could live anywhere in the city they chose, and every candidate for office guaranteed the right of displaced residents to return. Voters in supermajority-black precincts did not support the idea of a binding master plan, which many viewed as just another attempt to exclude blacks.

Both white and black voters supported Mayor Landrieu. In 2010, 75 percent of New Orleans voters approved or strongly approved of his performance, including 71 percent of black voters and 79 percent of white voters. More than half of the white voters strongly approved Landrieu's job performance, and 39 percent of black voters felt the same way. In 2013, 65 percent of the city's voters approved or strongly approved Landrieu's performance; 78 percent of white voters and 60 percent of black voters expressed this opinion.[116]

Greater racial division appeared in perceptions of the city council's performance. In 2008, 68 percent of the voters approved or strongly approved of the council. That percentage dropped to 47 percent in 2013.

In 2013, 62 percent of white voters but only 38 percent of black voters approved the performance of the council. The makeup of the council went from 57.1 percent white and 42.9 percent black in 2013 to 28.5 percent white and 71.4 percent black after the 2014 municipal elections.[117]

Some claim that the internal division among blacks continued and intensified after Katrina. According to BondGraham:

> The post-Katrina neoliberal redevelopment of the Gulf Coast has employed numerous black political elites, and even a handful of black capitalists, who have served alongside white business leaders and elected representatives to support and execute various privatizations of the public sector, all of which has been made possible by the chronic displacement of New Orleans' black poor. Thus even before losing its black majority in late 2007, the City Council's black representatives voted in favor of many of the neoliberal economic and planning policies promoted by the region's economic elite. . . . While the vast majority of dispossessed citizens in post-Katrina New Orleans have been black—a clear proof of the racist effects of these policies—the beneficiaries have included a handful of African Americans who embraced their identities as neoliberal politicians or members of the bourgeoisie over that of their blackness.[118]

The divide between public and private resource providers shrank after Katrina. Even after the first attempt at cross-sector collaboration failed under Mayor Nagin, reform-oriented members of the city council, a new mayor, and business organizations kept the issue alive and established a formal and permanent public-private partnership in New Orleans. Just the attempt to build a partnership constitutes a difference from the pre-Katrina era, when collaboration occurred sporadically at best. On the fifth anniversary of Katrina, Mayor Landrieu told a congressional committee, "As we move forward, I do want to reiterate how much better everybody is working together."[119]

New Orleans voters' economic outlook improved over time as well. From 1986 through 2008, an average of 17 percent of survey respondents expressed optimism about new jobs and industry entering the city. From 2011 to 2013, that average increased to 32 percent. In 2013, 42 percent of New Orleans's registered voters believed that the "likelihood of new jobs and industry coming into the parish" was good (33 percent) or very good (9 percent).

The political arrangement that governed economic development changed after Hurricane Katrina. Business organizations assumed a prominent role in agenda setting and enactment of reform policy. Organized elites also set the agenda. Actors at the federal and state levels authorized structural reform and paid for economic development projects. Foundations from outside the city used their fiscal resources to dictate the terms of post-disaster planning. A new, reform-oriented city council and a new mayor also initiated and executed governmental reform.

The poor had lost before Katrina and continued to struggle afterwards. Their concerns and even their return to the city did not make the policy agenda. Some blacks lost political power. Elected officials no longer descriptively represent the majority-black population. Some black elected officials complained that policy change and the agenda violated democratic principles, but the black population as a whole supported reform and joined in electing a white mayor. While the black electorate's power has diminished a bit and descriptive representation has lessened, black people in New Orleans maintained a voice in the new arrangement that governed economic development.

Business organizations, white elites from the Uptown section of the city, and new members of the city council assumed prominent positions in the new political arrangement. They completed their mission to change official structures and attack patronage. The governor and state legislature used their authority to propose and enact change, but without this new arrangement, it is unlikely that large-scale reforms would have taken place.

A clear economic development agenda emerged after Katrina. It came from the newly constituted inner core of leaders and focused on government reform. Unlike in the pre-Katrina period, civic elites and business collaborated on a vision, one that sought to remove from authority those who practiced machine politics. Their strategy worked. They set the public agenda, and the governor, state legislature, city council, and state- and citywide voters enacted these changes.

Not everything was new in the post-Katrina period. The governor and state legislature continued to lead and finance major economic development projects in the city. Local actors played little to no role in these projects, which were concentrated in the central business district. The federal government also financed and led some of these projects, which provided benefits to businesses and developers but not to the city's poor. This federal stance serves as a contrast to earlier policies that attempted to ensure social equity. The new federal tack has been to pursue policies that emphasize the free market. The financial community reciprocated in March of 2015, increasing the city's bond rating to a higher grade than it held before the storm.[120]

The reform agenda of the new political arrangement eliminated patronage positions. It uprooted embedded interests. The leaders of the new arrangement discredited local authority in the wake of Katrina. They argued that levee boards, assessors, sheriffs, and other patronage positions weighed down the city's economic development profile. Business leaders and civic elite won this battle. They set the recovery agenda.

Civic engagement expanded in the post-Katrina period. It did not set the recovery agenda, but it helped determine which neighborhoods came back and the speed with which they returned. If we compare the preferences of businesses and the civic elite to those of neighborhood leaders and groups, we see that the public agenda focused on the concerns of the former, not the latter.

Resources and authority ruled in the post-Katrina era. One common theme throughout the period is that local entities lost their authority. As far as economic development is concerned, the patronage-producing institutions saw their authority usurped. Katrina provided an opportunity for reformers to discredit institutions afflicted by preexisting problems such as corruption, mismanagement, and poor services. After Katrina, reformers linked cleaning up the actions of these institutions to New Orleans's survival. Resource providers such as the federal and state governments as well as businesses and the civic elite set this agenda, and the voters and others supported it. The governor, the state legislature, the federal government, and the mayor and city council used their authority to discredit these institutions. They were the winners in economic development and other policy areas, including the field of education.

3

Democracy versus Reform in Pre-Katrina Education

The division present in pre-Katrina economic development was even more pronounced in the public education policy arena prior to the storm. Different types of actors dominate urban school districts. In the past, in Newark, Detroit, Gary, Baltimore, and many other cities, the school board, superintendent, and school administrators ran the educational system, and teachers' unions and school employees supported them. This type of arrangement, also known as the education cartel, the employment regime, or the status quo regime, serves the financial and material interests of school employees and is characterized by corruption, patronage, nepotism, and bloated and mismanaged budgets. The education cartel excludes other stakeholders such as the local corporate community; it often neglects the needs of children in the school system; it aims above all to maintain the status quo; and it buffers the existing arrangement from political interference. This kind of regime opposes reform because its members know that change equals a redistribution of resources in a system that benefits them.[1]

In an educational system dominated by corporate involvement, school reforms concentrate on management, fiscal responsibility, and improved scores on standardized tests. It rejects members of the education cartel, empowers non-local actors, and promulgates policies that attempt to nullify the effects of the employment regime. As Dorothy Shipps notes, this type of political arrangement, which she calls a market regime, restructures "schooling in the image of the marketplace . . . to facilitate choice or increase system efficiency." This arrangement focuses on reform. Before Katrina, the Orleans Parish System District (OPSD) typified an education cartel.[2]

Amid poor performance, low high school graduation rates, substandard facilities, violence in schools, a lack of basic supplies, financial mismanagement, and micromanagement by the school board, Mayor Marc Morial considered a mayoral takeover of city schools in March 1998. New Orleans mayors had steered clear of education politics; the Orleans Parish School Board (OPSB) handled the schools and excluded outsiders from influence, but Morial had had enough. At the mayor's request, a group of business executives formed the Greater New Orleans Education Foundation in March 1998. As its first task, the foundation reviewed every aspect of the school system. The month after its creation, the foundation announced it would hire faculty from local universities to visit and assess New Orleans schools. It raised $1.2 million to conduct the evaluation and perform other activities in its first year.[3]

Robert Reilly, co-chair of the foundation and vice president of William B. Reilly & Company, which manufactures Luzianne coffee, wanted to integrate the community and the school system in a way that had not existed before. The report concluded that teachers spent the equivalent of one day per week on nonacademic issues, such as student socializing, discipline, and classroom management. The increased participation of business made school board president Bill Bowers uneasy. He wanted the board to "reserve its options to say that we must maintain our independence."[4] In October 1998 the foundation and the OPSB announced that they would develop a strategic plan for the school district. Paul Pastorek, a member of both the state Board of Elementary and Secondary Education (BESE) and the foundation, called the agreement "the day this district began to march toward reform."[5]

In November 1998 all but one of the members of the OPSB signed a Declaration of Intent to Reform (DOI), an outline of eleven principles that guided the foundation's views on the transformation of education in the city. Extended summer school, afterschool programs for at-risk children, a lower student-teacher ratio, and the end of social promotion made up the core of the strategic plan. The foundation wanted the school board to make policy and the superintendent and other administrators to execute those policies.[6]

Cheryl Mills, the one school board member who opposed the DOI, referred to the plan as a "one-sided view of how the school system should

operate," adding, "There are ways to do things that would be more col-
laborative and that will not be the board responding to directives and dictates from organizations over which many of us have had little involvement."[7] Nat LaCour, president of the teachers' union in New Orleans,
regarded the move to fire teachers whose students performed poorly as a
way to sidestep tenure.

The school board opposed the continuation of Al Davis Jr. as chief
executive officer of the Orleans Parish school system; the foundation
supported Davis and took out a full-page ad in the *Times-Picayune* to
announce its support of the CEO. Two new board members, Jimmy Fahrenholtz and Ellenese Brooks-Simms, joined Mills in questioning the role
of the foundation in education policy making. They too refused to sign
the DOI. Fahrenholtz said, "I don't think I can sign a document that a
private group wants me to do. How would my constituents feel?"[8] Business interests spent $8,500 in an unsuccessful attempt to defeat Brooks-
Simms, a former principal and school administrator.

In a March 1999 column in the *Times-Picayune*, Lolis Eric Elie wrote
that the education foundation was fatally flawed because a majority of
its members (seven out of ten members of the executive committee) were
white, while a majority of the students in the school system were black.
Elie wrote: "Has there ever been an example in the history of the repub-
lic when a majority black committee has been entrusted with the power
to make policy materially affecting a population that is more than 80%
white? I think not."[9] At the time, the battle between reform and democracy came down on the side of the school board, the voters, and local
control.

Corruption

In 2000 Al Davis Sr. made $70,691 working as a janitor at George Wash-
ington Carver High School, more than the principal of the school and
most other principals in the system. The previous year he'd made less
than half of what he earned in 2000. In 2002 his salary totaled about
$66,000. Davis claimed that his salary had been inflated by overtime
because the school at which he worked underwent an $8 million ren-
ovation project in 1999 and 2000 and required constant attention. In
2000 Davis collected $38,754 in overtime pay on top of a base salary
of $27,738. According to one estimate, Davis worked 1,850 hours of

overtime to reach this pay level. Records indicated that at one point, Davis worked sixty-three consecutive days. In 2001 he supposedly worked more than eighteen hours in one day. When confronted with the evidence, the OPSD's CEO Al Davis Jr., son of Al Davis Sr., said it was "entirely probable that he worked all these hours."[10]

The district attorney and the state auditor launched investigations into the matter. District Attorney Harry Connick Sr. concluded that construction projects at Carver High School had indeed increased Davis Senior's pay. The *Times-Picayune* wanted to know how Davis's overtime hours continued in 2001, a year after the Carver construction project had ended. State Auditor Dan Kyle contended that Davis had done nothing wrong but that overtime pay and hours were loosely monitored and organized.[11]

The school board hired a private auditor, Compensation and Benefits Consulting Services (CBCS) of Pennsylvania, to examine insurance practices in the educational system. Stuart Piltch acted as CBCS's lead investigator. Kyle's and Piltch's investigations led them to Carl Coleman, the school system's insurance department manager. Coleman wore expensive suits and had built a half-million-dollar home. As a result of his investigation, Kyle believed that Coleman had deposited public money into his checking account and used government workers and funds in constructing his house.[12]

The federal government discovered that Coleman had accepted close to $400,000 in kickbacks from Jeff Pollitt, an unlicensed contractor, in exchange for nearly $4 million in fire damage contracts. Pollitt did not complete most of the work for which he had been contracted. A lawsuit filed by the school system further alleged that Coleman and Pollitt had negotiated a $2.4 million contract to clean up after a fire at the Lusher Charter School, a fire that would not occur for another month. Coleman and Pollitt pleaded guilty in U.S. District Court to charges of conspiracy, extortion, and tax evasion. In exchange for a reduced sentence, Coleman told federal authorities about several insurance brokers, including the aunt of former mayor Marc Morial, who had kicked back thousands of dollars to him so they could secure and maintain health insurance contracts. Those involved in these schemes received various penalties including prison time, probation, and tens of thousands of dollars in fines.[13]

In the process of his investigation, Piltch discovered that the school system had allocated checks to nearly four thousand people who did not deserve them and paid insurance premiums for two thousand people who no longer worked for the schools; some of those who collected checks were retired, fired, or dead. The school district had allocated more than fifteen thousand erroneous checks in all, at a cost of $11 million. Among other things, Piltch found that the school system had issued five hundred handwritten checks. Once the school system required signatures for all paychecks, at least three hundred checks went uncollected.

In light of Piltch's findings, federal prosecutors—along with the FBI and IRS—launched a new investigation into the payroll irregularities on June 25, 2003. U.S. Attorney Jim Letten had already started investigations into Coleman and the insurance fraud. On April 19, 2004, an intergovernmental taskforce that included representatives of the FBI, the U.S. attorney's office, the New Orleans District Attorney, the New Orleans Police Department, the state legislative auditor's office, and the U.S. Department of Education's inspector general launched an investigation of the Orleans Parish School District. As of October 12, 2007, the task force won convictions on twenty-six of the twenty-nine indictments it secured.[14]

Reform?

After three years as superintendent Davis resigned, but he was unlikely to have had his contract renewed in light of the problems with the system and his father's overtime. In late January 2003 the Orleans Parish School Board selected Anthony Amato to replace Davis as superintendent of schools. The vote for superintendent divided along racial lines. A black-white coalition picked Amato, who is Puerto Rican and had served most recently as superintendent of the Hartford, Connecticut, school district. A group of three African American school board members preferred Andre Hornsby, an African American who served as superintendent of the Yonkers, New York, school system. Some of the school board members who favored Hornsby argued that black students, who made up more than 90 percent of the school district, needed an African American role model.[15]

The tension over the selection of a Puerto Rican superintendent over an African American candidate is not surprising, given that the modern Orleans Parish School District was built on a foundation of racial discord. On November 14, 1960, four six-year-old black girls integrated the New Orleans public schools. According to Alan Wieder: "School desegregation in New Orleans was neither peaceful nor successful. Black children and their families were harassed by the crowds at both schools, and there was violence throughout the city. The boycott by whites of McDonogh 19 [one of the integrated schools] was total, and by the end of the school year only two white families remained at Frantz [the other integrated school]."[16] Protests and violence inside and outside New Orleans schools characterized the early 1970s.[17]

The integration of New Orleans's public schools precipitated white flight from the system. At the time of the *Brown v. Board of Education* decision, whites and blacks each made up about 50 percent of the New Orleans public schools. Each group attended schools with only members of their own race. In 1970, whites constituted nearly one-third of the school system, a figure that dropped to 20 percent in 1975. By 1985, blacks made up nearly 90 percent of the student body, and in that year the city appointed its first black superintendent of schools. In 2003, blacks constituted 93 percent of the students in New Orleans public schools, an increase of more than 40 percentage points since the 1950s.[18]

In 2003 the school board claimed that it wanted a reformer, and Amato seemed to fit that description. He invited the intergovernmental task force to investigate the school system and provided office space to this team. Upon taking the job, Amato admitted, "I can't tell where we are fiscally."[19] He relied on the federal task force to identify, mitigate, and eliminate corruption. Amato also worked with Piltch to get a better sense of the financial status of the school district.[20]

At the end of June 2003, Piltch estimated that the school system had misspent $7 million on payroll and benefits, misused federal grant money, overspent on equipment because it did not use a central purchasing office, rented an unnecessary warehouse, failed to pay taxes on time, and overspent on banking, investment, and health care contracts, among other things. In February 2003 Piltch received a death threat in which someone had drawn a hangman and written, "Stay out of New Orleans." Piltch understood the reason for the threat: "There's a lot of money here." He joked to Brooks-Simms, then the chair of the school board, that they would end up in a swamp with an anchor tied to their necks.[21]

Unbeknownst to Piltch at the time, Brooks-Simms was working with Mose Jefferson, the brother of U.S. Representative William Jefferson, to ensure that the school system purchased educational software sold by Mose, who made more than $900,000 in commissions. In exchange for this assistance, Jefferson kicked back approximately $140,000 to

Brooks-Simms. For her part in this corruption, Brooks-Simms was sentenced to eighteen months in federal prison.[22]

Gail Glapion, a member of the school board, attacked Piltch's work and findings, claiming, "[Piltch's] allegations need to be supported by factual evidence, and I haven't seen the evidence." Glapion disliked Piltch's use of the words "mismanagement," "theft," and "fraud" to describe the school board's performance. She also complained about the $450,000 fee for Piltch's services, his increasing estimates of the cost of mismanagement and fraud, and his evolving job description. Amato, however, judged that Piltch and another auditing firm had saved the district at least $12 million through tighter financial controls and reasoned that Piltch should stay as long as he continued to find ways for the school district to save money. The school board disagreed.[23]

The board unanimously rejected CBCS's contract extension with the auditing firm and ended Piltch's involvement with the school district. Members claimed that the board could not afford to continue paying Piltch's company, which had already earned $1.9 million for twenty-two months' work. When Amato's new deputy superintendent of administration told him that the school district would be ready to assume control over the system's finances in three months, Piltch responded, "You're smoking dope."[24]

The Groundwork for Post-Katrina Reforms

The state legislature took actions in 2003 and 2004 to gain greater control over the OPSD and mitigate the acts of the school board. More than five years before No Child Left Behind mandated it to do so, Louisiana monitored public school achievement through standardized tests, student attendance, and dropout rates. In response to chronic underachievement, Leslie Jacobs, one of the governor's three representatives on the state Board of Elementary and Secondary Education, developed a constitutional amendment that empowered BESE to supervise, manage, or operate any failing public school or appoint others to carry out these functions. BESE would thus control the financial affairs of any school characterized as failing. Forty-seven percent of Orleans Parish schools were rated academically unacceptable, and 70 percent of Louisiana's seventy-nine academically unacceptable schools were located in New Orleans. Republican governor Mike Foster made the state takeover amendment a major piece of his legislative agenda in 2003.[25]

The takeover measure passed overwhelmingly in the state legislature and went to the voters for ratification. In October 2003, three-fifths of the Louisiana electorate ratified the amendment. It received a high level of support, 60–70 percent, among parishes in the New Orleans Metropolitan Statistical Area, not including Orleans Parish. New Orleans supported the takeover measure with 56 percent of the vote. In the 123 precincts in New Orleans in which blacks made up at least 90 percent of the voting population, voters rejected the takeover amendment by a total of 59 percent to 41 percent (see table 4). In the thirty-five New Orleans precincts in which whites made up 90 percent or more of the voters, the electorate supported the takeover amendment by a margin of 82 percent to 18 percent.

In a unanimous vote, the New Orleans School Board endorsed a resolution against the takeover amendment. The Louisiana Federation of Teachers, the Louisiana School Board Association, the Louisiana Association of School Superintendents, and the United Teachers of New Orleans, among others, also opposed the takeover. The teachers' federation called the takeover "little more than a scheme to allow big business interests or universities with little experience running a K–12 school to tap into public funds."[26]

Daniel Kiel explains the situation: "Attached to the constitutional amendment was a legislative package, known as Act 9, which defined the process by which BESE could exercise its ability to intervene in local schools. . . . Enacted in 2003 upon ratification of the constitutional amendment, Act 9 created the Recovery School District to serve as the state's authority for operating any local school taken over pursuant to the constitutional amendment's power." He notes, "The framework created

TABLE 4

Percent for and against the school takeover amendment in the New Orleans voting precincts in which African Americans or whites make up more than 90 percent of the electorate, 2003

	Percent (total) in favor of the takeover amendment	Percent (total) against the takeover amendment
Predominantly African American voting districts (N = 123)	41 (11,004)	59 (15,592)
Predominantly white voting districts (N = 35)	82 (7,764)	18 (1,700)

Source: Office of Louisiana's Secretary of State.

by Act 9 would help enable the actions of the state to further intervene following Hurricane Katrina in 2005."[27]

After the passage of the takeover amendment, the state legislature observed that the actions of the Orleans Parish School Board interfered with the superintendent's ability to run the system on a day-to-day basis. Representative Karen Carter from New Orleans proposed a bill to expand the authority of superintendents of districts that were academically in crisis. The law defined "schools in crisis" as those in which more than thirty schools are rated academically unacceptable according to state accountability standards or more than half of the students attend academically unacceptable schools. At the time, the Orleans Parish school system was the only one in the state that fit these criteria.[28]

The law enabled the superintendents of systems in academic crisis to promulgate policy and operate the district without the approval of the school board. The board retained its authority to meet financial obligations incurred prior to the activation of the superintendent's expanded powers. The law mandated that school boards would need a three-fifths vote, instead of the traditional majority, to fire the superintendent of a system in academic crisis. In the case of New Orleans, it allowed the superintendent to enter into contracts on behalf of the OPSB for no longer than five years.[29]

Digging in against the measure to strip them of their power, four school board members called a meeting. The purpose was clearly to fire Amato, though the four denied it, two divorcing themselves from the incident, and the other two, including Brooks-Simms, contending that dismissal represented only one option. The federal judge who extended a restraining order preventing the school board from firing Amato referred to these denials as "disingenuous at best."[30] The board's actions hastened the legislature's movement on Act 9, which passed overwhelmingly in the House and Senate and was signed into law by Governor Blanco.

In the 2004 elections for school board, three of the four board members (Cheryl Mills, Ellenese Brooks-Simms, and Elliot Willard) who had called the meeting to reevaluate Amato lost their reelection bids. The fourth did not seek reelection. The voters rewarded Amato when they reelected Fahrenholtz and Una Anderson, the superintendent's biggest supporters. In one of her first board meetings, new member Phyllis Landrieu, sister-in-law of former mayor Moon Landrieu, called for everyone to work together to fix the city's educational problems. To that end, the new board called itself "the team of eight," a number that included Superintendent Amato.[31]

When asked for her views on whether collaboration among various stakeholders was possible, Brenda Mitchell, the president of the teachers' union, UTNO (United Teachers of New Orleans), said that she distrusted the business community and had a problem with "other people outside of education trying to lead this parade," adding, "There's a conscious effort by 'people who have' to keep 'people who don't have' from getting an education, so they can keep them working for $5.50 an hour in hotels and motels."[32]

By 2005, Amato's support on the school board was slipping. In January the U.S. Department of Education's inspector general reported that the Orleans Parish School District had failed to document its use of $71 million in Title I grant dollars from July 2001 to December 2003. Amato was running the school district for two of the three years in question. At a meeting in the middle of February, the inspector general told Cecil Picard, the state's superintendent of education, that New Orleans schools could lose federal funding if the operations of the district were not rectified immediately.[33]

Picard proposed an oversight committee, which he and legislative auditor Steve Theriot would lead. Under the guidance of this committee, a financial project manager would control OPSB finances, institute standard fiscal procedures, and alleviate accounting abnormalities. In response to Picard's plan, Fahrenholtz said, "When you get that kind of culture of dishonesty, it's almost impossible to break it from within."[34] Jimmy Reiss, chairman of the New Orleans Business Council, said, "I think the business community wants to see something draconian happen."[35]

Amato came under increased scrutiny after the accumulation of a series of incidents that included the use of district employees to board up his house before Hurricane Ivan in 2004, a request to the mayor for between $15 million and $18 million to meet payroll, reports of a secret plan to create an elite white public high school in Uptown New Orleans, and escalating gun violence in city schools. At an emergency session on April 11, 2005, the school board passed resolutions to address each of these problems. In a unanimous vote, the board agreed to pay $1.5 million to outside consultants to run the fiscal side of the district for three months. The board agreed to take out a $50 million loan to pay district employees. It agreed to measures that limited Amato's ability to enter into contracts without its approval and ordered the superintendent to cut $10 million in contracts. Amato resigned the day after this meeting.[36]

In the wake of Amato's resignation, State Senator John Hainkel said that the Orleans Parish schools needed to start from scratch, something that seemed highly unlikely at the time. The president and CEO of the New Orleans Chamber of Commerce advocated "some radical steps." The president and CEO of Greater New Orleans, Inc., called for a super-intendent who would possess dictator-like powers and remain on the job for two to three years.[37]

Secretary Picard continued to push for a special project manager and a team of outsiders to operate district finances for as long it took to rectify the situation. He would pick the person to be in charge of the district's finances, and the project manager would report to him and an oversight team. Picard insisted that this reform did not constitute a state takeover of the school district, but he warned the school board that a takeover was imminent if his plan failed to gain the board's approval.[38]

The president of the Orleans Parish School Board framed the creation of a fiscal czar as tantamount to privatization. He and at least two other school board members complained that Picard's plan circumvented local control. But neither Picard nor the federal government would accept a plan that called for the fiscal czar to report to the school board. Picard wanted to maintain control himself. At this point, school politics centered on a debate about democracy: Should local leaders, elected by city voters, continue to make decisions about education, or should actors at the state level, who maintain the ultimate authority over police powers, dictate policy?[39]

Even before this latest controversy arose, Mayor Nagin had remarked, "Our school system scares the bejesus out of me."[40] The mayor proposed that his office take over all or some of the functions of the OPSB's central office. School board member Anderson advised the mayor to take care of his own problems, including job loss and crime. Leaders of the local teachers' and principals' union opposed the move as well. Even advocates of reform did not support Nagin's attempt to gain some authority over the school district.

By the time Amato resigned, Nagin did not think the OPSB would survive. In his State of the City address in the spring of 2005, he proposed Project FOCUS (For Our Children's Ultimate Success), a program in which the mayor would lead a school district composed of the twenty lowest-performing schools. BESE's Leslie Jacobs did not believe that

Nagin could accomplish this feat. School board vice president Lourdes Moran agreed. "The city can't handle its own problems," she said. "How in the world do they see themselves taking on the responsibility of 20 failing schools?"[41] Brenda Mitchell, president of UTNO, dismissed the plan as well; she felt that Nagin had launched it simply as a ploy to gain votes in his reelection bid.[42]

The Fiscal Takeover

In early May 2005, the state takeover was under way. Superintendent Picard selected Alvarez & Marsal, a New York–based company, to reform the New Orleans school system's fiscal practices and control district finances. The $16.8 million deal needed the approval of the Orleans Parish School Board. Picard warned that he would withhold federal and state education funds totaling $300 million annually if the board refused to confirm the agreement.[43]

The vote to approve the financial takeover split along racial lines: the three white members and one Latina supported the takeover; the African American members opposed it. Board president Torin Sanders charged that Alvarez & Marsal's contract disenfranchised him and the people who had elected him. Even Phyllis Landrieu, the only board member to speak in support of the measure, was hesitant to vote for the financial takeover until she realized that the OPSB's anticipated debt was $25 to $30 million by the end of the fiscal year.[44]

Picard and the school board empowered Alvarez & Marsal to manage the school system's business operations. The school board retained approval over the firm's recommended spending cuts, school closures, and layoffs. Alvarez & Marsal now did the hiring and firing in the district's central office and assumed authority over any contracts that pertained to central office activities.[45]

Mitchell, president of the teachers' union, opposed state intervention. In response to the move to grant Alvarez & Marsal control over OPSB finances, Mitchell said: "Let me tell you, people across the state are making plans for us whether it passes or fails. I go to the Legislature, and they don't like Orleans Parish. They talk about us as the 'people below the interstate' and, yes, racism has something to do with it."[46]

The *Times-Picayune* labeled Alvarez & Marsal "hatchet men," suggesting a business-style approach to school reform. In 2003–4 Alvarez

& Marsal had operated the schools in St. Louis, Missouri, where they closed twenty-one schools, cut $79 million from the budget, privatized certain services, laid off more than a thousand employees, none of whom were teachers, and hired 130 new teachers. In St. Louis, teachers and school employee unions opposed Alvarez & Marsal's practice of cutting jobs while increasing executive salaries.[47]

The Alvarez & Marsal intervention in St. Louis came with a racial dimension. School closings and job losses within the system predominantly affected African Americans. A black talk show host protested the intervention in St. Louis, saying, "There's a willingness of people to believe that 'We've just tried everything' in black school districts, and so we have to do something drastic."[48] African Americans boycotted the first day of school and carried coffins to protest Alvarez & Marsal's presence in St. Louis.[49]

In the 2002–3 school year, African Americans made up 93 percent of the students in the New Orleans school system, compared to 47.8 percent of the students statewide. Nearly 75 percent of the students in New Orleans attended public schools, whereas nearly 84 percent of students went to public schools statewide. Twelve of sixteen schools closed by Alvarez & Marsal in the summer of 2003 were located in the city's poorest neighborhoods.[50]

Bill Roberti headed the firm's turnaround efforts in New Orleans. When he first began to wade through the school system's fiscal swamp, he realized that the "situation was as bad as any [he] had ever seen."[51] Putting it bluntly, "This is a mess," he said.[52] Roberti's colleague Sajan George told him that the Orleans Parish School Board's financial management "makes St. Louis look like a Fortune 100 company."[53] In late July 2005, Roberti characterized the school system's financial data as unreliable and requested that two more certified public accountants be added to his team to help solve the district's fiscal mysteries. The addition of the accountants increased the number of Alvarez & Marsal consultants in New Orleans to thirty. A so-called clean audit, one that reliably gauges finances, had not been conducted in the district in four years, and according to the *Times-Picayune*, "even that one is questionable."[54]

The district lacked a clear idea of what it owned. Alvarez & Marsal could not even determine how many people the school system employed or what the employees were hired to do. It estimated that Orleans Parish schools employed more than six thousand, but according to the Associated Press, "how many more would be a guess."[55] In an attempt to count the number of people working for the school district, George required each employee to bring identification and sign up for health benefits in person.[56]

Roberti referred to the school district as "a candy jar," used by certain people to enrich themselves at the expense of the children.[57] Alvarez & Marsal cut the number of people with access to payroll and other financial accounts from fifty-three to one; an employee of the firm was now the only person with access. In the course of its audits and investigations, Alvarez & Marsal determined that the school board had overestimated its revenue stream and underestimated its costs when it passed its most recent budget in late July. The budget, which the school board claimed was balanced, had a $48 million hole.[58]

Less than a week after the schools opened for the year, Alvarez & Marsal announced that the district would lay off 150 school employees, starting immediately. Sticking to its St. Louis model, the firm wanted to make all the cuts outside the classroom. Fahrenholtz speculated that between 1,000 and 1,200 employees would be laid off "before this is all over."[59]

Prior to the 2005–6 school year, the state had opened four charter schools in New Orleans, which were operated by nonprofit organizations. Seventy of the seventy-five teachers at Lusher Alternative Elementary School, which was also petitioning to expand to high school level, approved the conversion to a charter school as well. Parents were about to vote on the measure, but Katrina got in the way.[60]

The Pre-Katrina Political Arrangement for Education

In pre-Katrina New Orleans, a coalition of entrenched local actors battled local business leaders, reform-oriented members of the school board, the mayor, and state-level actors over how to educate students and govern the school system. A policy agenda tennis match occurred between the school board and the teachers' union on one side versus the city's business community, the state board of education, the head of the state's department of education, some state legislators, and newer members of the school board on the other. Business organizations served policy reform, which the school board initially supported but eventually batted back. The old OPSB maintained the status quo while attempting to limit the influence of the city's corporate community and superintendents of schools. Amid the attempts at reform, the public education policy arena remained stubbornly concentrated among the inner core of the governing arrangement, which was inadequately educating children but continued to demonstrate strong policy fidelity.

Mayor Marc Morial and a business-led organization placed school reform on the public agenda. They favored community and private involvement in schools and a variety of policy reforms that included summer school, expanded afterschool programs, the end of social promotion, and disciplining underperforming teachers. A state auditor, the FBI, and the OPSB made a public issue of school corruption and mismanagement. BESE board member Leslie Jacobs joined the mayor and newer members of the school board in seeking changes to the governance, curriculum, and operations of New Orleans's schools. They received support from the Business Council, the Chamber of Commerce, GNO, Inc., and an influential state senator from New Orleans.

To change or not to change: those were the primary pre-Katrina policy option choices in education. Some members of the OPSB framed increased involvement by business as tantamount to the privatization of schools. They felt that the democratic process could be ensured only if the school board continued to rule New Orleans's schools. They feared that any attempt to include outside actors as decision makers diminished local control and representative democracy. Members of the OPSB and the teachers' union emphasized that the board needed independence from outside forces, namely business and state government, which sought control over the school system.

Extra-local actors began to chip away at the power of the school board. The U.S. attorney's office, the FBI, and the IRS investigated, prosecuted, and convicted the beneficiaries of the employment regime. BESE, the governor, state legislators, and voters throughout Louisiana worked to amend the constitution to allow the state to take over poorly performing schools. This constitutional change introduced charter schools to New Orleans. The secretary of Louisiana's department of education stripped the OPSB of its control over finances and dictated which private company would manage the finances of New Orleans's schools.

After the election of reformers to the school board in 2004, the OPSB gave up its control over finances to private actors. The election of this reform board not only indicated that New Orleans voters endorsed change but also provided local support for the transformation of city schools. For a long time, actors outside of elected office had few allies in positions of authority within the school system.

The pre-Katrina education cartel empowered those who plundered the school system. The OPSB did little to stop corruption and mismanagement.

On a number of occasions it prevented reformers from investigating and stopping the corrupt behavior. In at least one case, a member of the OPSB participated in the corruption.

Extra-local players, private actors, and reform-oriented New Orleanians won some policy battles before Katrina. They initiated charter schools and state takeover and secured control over the district's finances. Those who wanted to see the purveyors of the education cartel punished also experienced some victories before Katrina.

Pre-Katrina education politics was characterized by division and fragmentation. Entrenched local actors tried to prevent private actors, the state and federal governments, and new members of school board from altering education politics and policies. Race played a prominent role in this divide. White reformers from the local business community, the state legislature, the federal government, BESE, and the governor's office worked to take authority and power away from local black political actors, many of whom had been elected to make decisions about the city's schools. Voters in predominantly black districts of New Orleans opposed the constitutional amendment to allow state takeover of underperforming schools. Voters in predominantly white districts in New Orleans supported the amendment.

OPSB votes on a new superintendent of schools and the financial takeover also split along racial lines. The president of the teachers' union claimed that racism played a role in state-level decisions on education reform in New Orleans. The president of the OPSB argued that the fiscal takeover of Orleans Parish schools by a private company disenfranchised voters, two-thirds of whom were black. The expansion of Lusher School to include high school grades, as well as its conversion to a charter school also carried racial overtones, as black leaders saw it as a move to create a divided school system in which white students, but not black, could attend elite and selective public schools.

Battles over authority affected the governance of schools in the pre-Katrina period. Business leaders wanted education policy and school governance to change, but they were not elected officials. Elected members of the OPSB used their authority to maintain control and the status quo. While members of the local school board attempted to protect the employment regime, the governor, BESE, and state legislators enacted market-based reforms, opening charter schools and taking over failing schools. Alongside these actions at the state level, the election of reform-minded members of the OPSB pointed toward decreased local control as the future of New Orleans's schools. The question became: Which authority would ultimately rule city schools and allocate the city's educational resources?

Piecemeal reform was already under way when disaster hit. After Katrina, the question became whether the disaster would expand the scale of reform that people were already thinking about and acting upon. In the case of education, the answer was yes.

4

The Most Reform-Friendly City in the Country

Hurricane Andrew, which hit Florida in August 1992, set a new American standard for destruction. It produced 43 million cubic yards of debris in the Dade County metropolitan area. Hurricane Katrina shattered that record, creating 100 million cubic yards of debris in the New Orleans metro area. Andrew damaged each of Dade County's 287 public schools, but facilities in the southern part of the county bore the brunt of the storm. Schools didn't reopen until three weeks after Andrew struck. On the day of the reopening, 250,100 students—79 percent of the 318,000 pre-storm enrollment—returned. By January 1, 1993, the district claimed to have lost 10 percent of its pre-Andrew student population. As a result, the county faced a surplus of three hundred teachers. The school district allowed the extra teachers to tutor students in its fifty-seven elementary, middle, and high schools.[1]

The federal government used its resources to get Dade County to expand school reforms. According to Eugene F. Provenzo and Sandra H. Fradd, Lamar Alexander, U.S. secretary of education, told the superintendent of Dade County schools four days after the storm that federal money would be available if "the school system created an innovative program for rebuilding the schools that would meet the educational needs of the Twenty-first Century."[2] In response, local education leaders expanded initiatives such as school choice, a competency-based curriculum, implementation of research-based models, outreach and alternative programs for at-risk students, and parental participation. Because of these efforts, the U.S. Department of Education gave the county $82 million to help rebuild the schools. Although the community supported the proliferation of these policies, teachers balked at the pace and timing of these innovations. Like their counterparts throughout the county, Dade County teachers voted against new school programs. As a representative of the teachers' union put it, "Teachers are tired, they've had a difficult year and they need time to recover."[3] Another said, "We want to slow the train down."[4]

In New Orleans in the wake of Hurricane Katrina, schools remained closed for a year, and some never reopened; surplus teachers were let go; the federal government financed the rebuilding of schools and, as in Florida after Hurricane Andrew, used its resources to initiate policy reforms. The governor of Louisiana, the state legislature, and policy entrepreneurs within New Orleans also used their resources and/or authority to initiate and expand reform post-Katrina. Teachers again wanted to slow down or prevent these changes.

Post-Katrina Reforms with Pre-Katrina Antecedents

The Louisiana state legislature had used its authority to promote and enact school reforms before the storm, and it expanded these reforms after Katrina. A 1995 state law had created a pilot program authorizing charter schools in Louisiana on a voluntary basis; in 1997 an amendment to that law enabled the state Board of Elementary and Secondary Education (BESE) and local school boards to authorize charters. In 2003, as we saw in the preceding chapter, Act 9 allowed the Recovery School District (RSD) to open and operate charter schools. As a result of these laws, five types of charters existed in Louisiana. Type 1 charters are created and authorized by local school boards. Type 2 charters are transferred to or authorized by BESE. Local school boards may convert existing schools into Type 3 charters. Type 4 charters are startups or conversions "operated as a result of [a] charter between a local school board and BESE." Type 5 charters are those transferred to the RSD and authorized by BESE. Before Katrina, nine charter schools were operating in New Orleans.[5]

On September 30, 2005, the U.S. Department of Education committed $20.9 million to New Orleans to reopen, expand, and create charter schools in the city.[6] This money provided the impetus for New Orleans to pursue a charter school system in the wake of Hurricane Katrina. As they

had in Dade County, Florida, the federal government and some local education leaders used the natural disaster as a springboard for authorizing
and funding existing reforms.

Extra-local actors played a larger role in reform in New Orleans than
they had in Dade County because local resistance to reform was greater
in New Orleans. Louisiana's secretary of education, Cecil Picard, mandated that charters were the only kinds of schools to be opened, since neither the state nor the city of New Orleans possessed the money to open a
traditional school. Sajan George of Alvarez & Marsal agreed, noting that
the Orleans Parish School Board had only $74.9 million at hand, which
was about $134.1 million less than it needed to open schools on the
West Bank area alone. Nor could the district depend on state per-pupil
funds because by now, displaced New Orleans students were enrolled in
schools in other places. One education leader pointed out that charters
could also be opened more quickly than traditional schools.[7]

On October 7, 2005, the same day the Orleans Parish School Board
approved twenty charters, Governor Blanco used her authority to waive
aspects of the charter school law.[8] Executive Order 05–58 suspended eligibility requirements establishing which children could attend charters;
it ended the provision that required professional faculty and staff of the
preexisting school and parents and guardians of its students to approve
the conversion of a traditional school into a Type 4 charter; and it eliminated timelines for applications and approvals for charter schools and
suspended the minimum number of instructional days required for a
school year. Blanco's executive order allowed for a massive expansion of
charters in the city of New Orleans. The first two public schools opened
on November 28, 2005, a day short of three months after the hurricane
hit New Orleans. Both were charters.

The new system allowed schools to bypass the seniority system and
select teachers they wanted regardless of how many years they had
taught.[9] Under the old system, tenure and the collective bargaining agreement protected teachers. Under the new system, teachers worked under
one-year contracts with incentives for high performance.

Like his predecessor Brenda Mitchell, Larry Carter, the new president
of the teachers' union, wanted to know why schools could reopen only
as charters. In an August 24, 2009, opinion piece in USA Today, titled
"Be Wary of Charter Schools," Carter complained that charter schools
advanced privatization and limited the benefits and professional rights of
teachers. Furthermore, he argued, it was traditional schools, not charters,

that maintained responsibility for special education students. And some charter schools received major private donations whereas others did not, leading to an inequitable education even among charters.[10]

Yet a Tulane University survey conducted in November 2007 indicated that 70 percent of voters and 69 percent of parents thought that charter schools had improved public education in New Orleans.[11] Whites and other non–black voters (70 percent) were more likely than black voters (64 percent) to believe that public charters had improved public education in New Orleans. Regardless of race, however, the majority of voters had a positive view of the effect of public charter schools (see tables 5 and 6).

In its first full year, New Orleans's new decentralized school system included seventeen schools under control of the Orleans Parish School Board, two operated by BESE, and thirty-nine RSD schools. Of those numbers, twelve OPSB schools were charters, both BESE schools operated under a charter, and the RSD had seventeen charter schools. Fifty-six percent of New Orleans students attended charter schools. The next year those figures remained about the same, but the number of students attending charter schools had risen to eighteen thousand from fewer than

TABLE 5
Attitudes (%) toward charter schools, 2009

Public charter schools have improved public education in New Orleans.

	Total voters	White and other voters	African American voters
Somewhat/strongly disagree	13	6	18
Uncertain	6	10	3
Somewhat/strongly agree	70	77	64

Source: "Public Education through the Public Eye: A Survey of New Orleans Voters and Parents," Cowen Institute for Public Education Initiatives, Tulane University.

TABLE 6
Support (%) for charter schools, 2009

As you may know, a majority of public school students in New Orleans now attend public charter schools. Charter schools are independent public schools that operate with freedom from many of the regulations that apply to traditional public schools. Given this information, do you support or opposed charter schools?

Oppose	10
Support	74

Source: CABL New Orleans Voter Survey, 500 registered voters, field dates: August 6–11, 2009.

fifteen thousand. At that time, New Orleans had the highest percentage of charter schools in the country. Washington, D.C., ranked second, with 31 percent of its students attending a charter school.

At the start of the 2009–10 academic year, 60 percent of students in New Orleans attended one of the city's fifty-two charter schools. At the start of the next school year, the Thomas B. Fordham Institute named New Orleans the most reform-friendly city in the country because sixty-one of the city's eighty-eight public schools were charters. By the 2013–14 school year, the RSD ran five traditional schools and authorized the operation of fifty-six charter schools; BESE provided charters to four schools, and the OPSB operated six traditional schools and issued fourteen charters.[12]

Governance of Schools

At the first post-Katrina meeting of the Orleans Parish School Board, which took place on September 15, 2005, in Baton Rouge, school board member Phyllis Landrieu offered a motion to fire interim superintendent Ora Watson, hire former U.S. secretary of education Rod Paige as acting chief academic officer, and name Bill Roberti of Alvarez & Marsal superintendent of schools. Teachers, principals, and school employees made up most of the audience at that meeting, and they roared with disapproval when Landrieu announced her motion. The vote split along racial lines: the three white members and one Latino on the board supported the measure; the three African American members opposed the motion. Since a supermajority was required to hire or fire a superintendent, the initiative failed.[13]

School board president Torin Sanders charged that race factored into the decision to try to remove Watson, who, like Sanders, is black. He cited Watson's doctorate, and his ability to represent the students and parents of the district, as evidence of the interim superintendent's qualifications to run the district. Board member Jimmy Fahrenholtz, who is white, called it "shameful that the race card got played immediately."[14]

In a special legislative session on Hurricane Katrina, Governor Blanco asked the legislature to change the scope and authority of the Recovery School District to allow this entity to operate the lowest-performing schools in post-Katrina New Orleans. Under Blanco's measure, known as Act 35, the RSD would run schools in which students finished below the state average on the school performance score (SPS). Before Katrina, the state considered schools to be academically unacceptable if they scored below 60 on the SPS. Under the old takeover law, the state would have operated thirteen schools in New Orleans. Act 35 would enable the state to assume authority over entire school districts with more than thirty failing schools, those with a minimum of half their student population in academically unacceptable schools, or those declared to be in academic crisis.[15]

Although the legislature's black caucus and members of the New Orleans delegation complained that displaced residents lacked input into the decision, and the teachers' union agreed, the state legislature passed the takeover law by a vote of 33–4 in the Senate and 89–16 in the House. All four senators who voted against Act 35 were black; three of them represented New Orleans.[16] According to one education leader, "there was a desire to use the hurricane to wipe the slate clean."[17] In fact, less than a week after Katrina, the Heritage Foundation was already encouraging Congress to expand opportunities to develop more charter, private, and religious schools in New Orleans. The teachers' union felt that groups pushing the reforms—conservative and national leaders, the state board of education, a well-financed national network of charter school advocates, the governor, and the local actors who made up the new education arrangement—were excluding parents, students, and other stakeholders from participating in the process of making changes to the school district.[18]

Nevertheless, in November 2009, a survey by the Cowen Institute at Tulane found that two-thirds of the city's voters agreed with the state's decision to take over most of New Orleans's public schools after the storm, but opinions varied by race.[19] Fifty-seven percent of black voters endorsed the state takeover, whereas 80 percent of non-black voters favored the intervention (see table 7). These results resemble those for other policy areas. Both white and black voters support reform, but the former are much more enthusiastic than the latter.

TABLE 7
Attitudes (%) toward state takeover of public education, 2009

The state of Louisiana made the right decision to take over most schools in New Orleans after Hurricane Katrina.

	Total voters	White and other voters	Black voters
Somewhat/strongly disagree	21	10	28
Uncertain	13	10	15
Somewhat/strongly agree	66	80	57

Source: "Public Education through the Public Eye: A Survey of New Orleans Voters and Parents," Cowen Institute for Public Education Initiatives, Tulane University.

Less than a year after Hurricane Katrina, the head of BESE declared that New Orleans had a new model and framework for urban education. Before a congressional hearing, Linda Johnson testified:

> In New Orleans, the state's takeover is the reverse of other efforts nationally. The local school board and its superintendent were left intact, and the board retained the right to run 16 schools and remains the taxing and bonding authority for all public schools in Orleans Parish. The state, in essence, took over empty school buildings, the right to operate the schools, and the money (local, state and federal) to educate the students attending state controlled schools. The state did not take over the central office; it did not retain existing employees, it did not inherit existing policies and procedures.

She concluded by calling New Orleans "the most free market public education system in the country."[20]

Old Actors Out, New Ones In

The RSD allowed individual charter schools to negotiate with teachers' unions if they desired, but the state senate's education committee rejected a proposal to permit the collective bargaining agreement to apply to RSD schools. UTNO represented 6,300 school employees before the storm but only 300 at the end of the school year. In the middle of April 2007, the OPSB denied the union's request to discuss a new collective bargaining agreement. That vote, like others on education, split along racial lines. The three white members and one Latino on the school board voted against the resolution to start talks about a new contract; the two African American school board members supported the motion, while the third was absent. The NAACP, Southern Christian Leadership Conference, and ACORN favored the initiation of talks on a new collective bargaining agreement.[21]

With two weeks left before its contract with the OPSB expired, UTNO wanted the board to extend the collective bargaining agreement. The OPSB refused and the collective bargaining agreement which had stood for thirty-two years ended on July 1, 2006. Following a settlement agreement to restart contract talks, and after close to a year's worth of negotiations, the school board rejected a new deal. Three whites and one Latino opposed the contract, and three African American school board members voted for the contract.[22]

Teachers recruited by outside organizations, including New Schools for New Orleans, the New Teacher Project, New Leaders for New Schools, TeachNOLA, Teach for America (TFA), and the Knowledge Is Power Program (KIPP), promoted, sustained, and expanded New Orleans's charter schools movement. New Schools for New Orleans, which was founded in 2006, incubated five charter schools in New Orleans after Katrina. New Leaders for New Schools, a New York–based nonprofit that started in 2000, came to New Orleans in early February 2007 to recruit, train, and support forty principals for charter schools over four years. The New Teacher Project, a national nonprofit formed in 1997, offers an alternative way to recruit, train, and hire teachers in urban districts. TeachNOLA is the New Teacher Project's training academy in the New Orleans area. From 2006 until the summer of 2012, TeachNOLA trained more than 230 non-teacher professionals in the New Orleans metropolitan area to become teachers. The teachers' union opposed the influx and dominance of these organizations.[23]

Fifty-four percent of voters believed that new teachers improved public education in the city, 29 percent were uncertain, and 17 percent somewhat or strongly disagreed (see table 8). Fifty-seven percent of white voters and 54 percent of black voters believed that the new teachers had improved education in the city.

TFA, New Schools for New Orleans, New Leaders for New Schools, and other similar organizations provided the human capital and technical

TABLE 8
Attitudes (%) toward new teachers, 2009

The many new teachers coming into public schools in New Orleans have improved public education in the city.

	Total voters	White and other voters	Black voters
Somewhat/strongly disagree	17	9	21
Uncertain	29	34	26
Somewhat/strongly agree	54	57	54

Source: "Public Education through the Public Eye: A Survey of New Orleans Voters and Parents," Cowen Institute for Public Education Initiatives, Tulane University.

expertise to sustain charter schools, accountability, choice, and most of the post-Katrina education reforms in New Orleans, while outside foundations and the federal government provided the financial resources to realize the reforms. Paul Pastorek, who at the time was a New Orleans attorney and former chair of the state board of education, provided the legal work to create the Louisiana Disaster Recovery Foundation, a private nonprofit that collected more than $6 million in deposits in the month after Katrina and facilitated the privatization of schools in New Orleans.[24]

In mid-December 2007, Pastorek, by now the state superintendent of schools, told an audience: "Change is coming. Yes it is. . . . Ladies and gentlemen, today marks recognition by national foundations that the planets have aligned in New Orleans."[25] Pastorek made this pronouncement because on this day, three major national nonprofits—the Doris and Donald Fisher Fund, the Eli and Edythe Broad Foundation, and the Bill and Melinda Gates Foundation—committed $17.5 million to New Schools for New Orleans, Teach for America, and New Leaders for New Schools. The Fisher Fund gave $2.5 million each to TFA and New Schools for New Orleans; the Broad Foundation allocated $3 million to TFA, $2 million to New Schools for New Orleans, and $1 million to New Leaders for New Schools; and the Gates Foundation provided $5.5 million to New Schools for New Orleans and $1 million to TFA. One year after Katrina, Broad committed $2.45 million to KIPP so that organization could operate two schools and plan three more. The U.S. Fund for UNICEF also promised $450,000 to two KIPP charter schools for renovations, extra learning time, and social workers.[26]

Capital One Bank allocated $1 million to create its own charter school in May 2006. It provided $50,000 to New Schools for New Orleans and distributed another $1.5 million to local and national nonprofits that operated in the New Orleans area. The Walton Family Foundation, which is connected to Sam Walton and Walmart, gave $6.37 million to the RSD to redesign school plans. Entergy, the local energy company, donated $1.5 million so that New Orleans public schools could get solar power equipment.[27]

In late April 2006, the Greater New Orleans Foundation allocated $500,000 to New Schools for New Orleans to fund business services, recruit quality teachers, and train and develop staff. By September 2006, the Bush-Clinton Katrina Fund (BCKF) had raised $130 million for the Gulf Coast region. TFA received money from the BCKF to recruit and retain teachers. Personnel development and educational assessment, as well as creating school investment and serving as a resource for area public schools, were among the ways in which New Schools New Orleans used its BCKF money. The Foundation for the Mid-South provided $20,000 to New Schools for New Orleans to facilitate its goal of expanding charter schools in New Orleans and nationally.[28]

Lawrence Vale and Thomas Campanella write, "Even the most horrific acts of destruction have been interpreted as opportunities for progressive reform, and the process whereby the narrative is assembled often happens very quickly."[29] One of the dominant post-Katrina narratives focused on how the storm presented a chance for a new beginning to New Orleans. The president of Tulane University said that the $20 million from the U.S. Department of Education and other resources provided New Orleans with "an unprecedented opportunity to transform its public education system."[30] Paul Pastorek told his fellow New Orleanians: "We have the most extraordinary opportunity ever in the modern history of dealing with public education. We have a clean slate."[31]

About two months after the storm, Leslie Jacobs of the BESE said, "I think this is a once-in-a-many-a-lifetime opportunity to restart public education in New Orleans in a system that's been broken many times over."[32] Most of the experts in education in New Orleans consider Jacobs one of the most powerful players in this policy arena. She wields power because she allocated large sums of money to candidates who ran for offices that maintain authority over education.

The U.S. Department of Education mandated the opening of charter schools in post-Katrina New Orleans as a condition for $21 million in aid it allocated to the educational system after the storm. In August 2010 the department awarded $30 million as part of its Investing in Innovation (i3) grant to New Schools for New Orleans for that organization to expand charter schools in the lowest-performing areas of New Orleans, Memphis, and Nashville. The American Recovery and Reinvestment Act, also known as the stimulus bill, provided the money. TFA and KIPP received $50 million in grants from the i3 fund to improve schools in New Orleans. In September 2010 the Department of Education provided an additional $13.7 million Teacher Incentive Fund (TIF) grant to New Schools for New Orleans.[33]

On February 15, 2007, state superintendent Cecil Picard died after a long battle with amyotrophic lateral sclerosis. Pastorek, the New Orleans attorney who had chaired the recovery school district's advisory committee, replaced him. Pastorek had helped develop the state's accountability and testing program during his eight years (1996–2004) on the BESE board and regarded accountability, capacity building, and partnership as three pillars of education policy. He wanted to communicate a clear vision for the RSD and provide more resources to RSD superintendent Robin Jarvis; he believed that the districts affected by Hurricane Katrina, and by Hurricane Rita less than a month later, needed more attention. Reformers like Pastorek drove home the accountability narrative in post-Katrina New Orleans. Before Katrina, the schools had lacked accountability for poor performance and corruption, but not the post-Katrina schools, reform advocates argued. Pastorek saw Katrina as an opportunity for New Orleans "to recreate education as we know it."[34]

In early April 2007, Paul Vallas, then the chief executive officer for the School District of Philadelphia, provided advice to the RSD on teacher recruitment, facilities, academics, and finances. Robin Jarvis announced her resignation as head of the RSD a month later, citing a lack of community and media support as well as difficulties associated with hiring teachers, opening schools, providing hot lunches, and separation from her family as reasons for the decision. Other problems facing the RSD during Jarvis's tenure in the post-Katrina period included shortages of books and teachers, as well as student violence.[35]

For years, U.S. Senator Mary Landrieu had been recruiting Vallas to lead New Orleans's schools. When asked why he'd come to New Orleans, Vallas answered, "I am here because Mary Landrieu asked me to be here." Leslie Jacobs believed that Vallas would not have come to New Orleans if New Leaders for New Schools and New Schools for New Orleans had not preceded him.[36]

Vallas had experience running troubled and uniquely governed school districts in Chicago as well as Philadelphia. In Chicago, Vallas's district built and renovated schools, reconstituted failing schools, and expanded pre- and after-school programs. The percentage of Chicago students who scored at or above average on assessment tests rose from 30 to 45 percent in math and from 28 to 35 percent in reading during Vallas's first four years as CEO of the school system, although test scores leveled off and then dropped at the end of his tenure.[37]

After a failed run for governor of Illinois, Vallas took over as CEO of Philadelphia's state-operated school system in 2002. He embraced the diverse provider model, school choice, and charter schools, which had been initiated before he arrived in Philadelphia. Student test scores jumped under Vallas's leadership there. The percentages of fifth and eighth grade students who earned scores of "proficient" or "advanced" rose by 26 points in math and 36 in reading. The percentage of students in the lowest-scoring group in math decreased by 26 points and by 12 in reading.[38]

According to *Education Next*, "Vallas lasted longer in both Chicago and Philadelphia than most urban school leaders . . . but he wore out his welcome in both places."[39] Vallas explained the reaction to him this way: "What happens with turnaround superintendents is that the first two years you're a demolitions expert. By the third year, if you get improvements, do school construction, and test scores go up, people start to think this isn't so hard. By year four, people start to think you're getting way too much credit. By year five, you're chopped liver."[40]

Pastorek called Vallas one of "the top tier superintendents in the country" and cited Vallas's ability to raise test scores in Philadelphia in addition to his reputation and contacts as reasons for the hire.[41] Calling "the opportunity to build a school district from the ground up . . . too good an opportunity to turn down,"[42] Vallas said, "This will be the greatest experiment in choice, charters and in creating not a single school system, but a system of schools."[43] The managing director of the Broad Foundation referred to Pastorek and Vallas—"the Pauls"—as the "New Hope."[44] One education informant said that "the Pauls" were each other's champions and noted that they had relatively free rein over the New Orleans schools because BESE supported their actions.

The environment provided what Vallas regarded as the perfect conditions for reform. He had no school board to deal with, no collective bargaining agreement, and a teachers' union without leverage. Vallas ran with the narrative that "the hurricane wiped out the district" and provided "a clean slate." In 2009 he said that Hurricane Katrina "took politics out of the school system." He wanted to hire and fire on the basis of merit and promote on the basis of ability, and he believed that he now had the ability to do so. "You can do what you want to do," he said of his role in the new school district.[45]

Vallas sought to convert as many of the RSD's traditional schools into charters as possible. Charters made up sixty-one of the eighty-eight schools in New Orleans at the start of the 2010–11 school year; 70 percent of the city's forty thousand students attended a charter. Vallas referred to the charter school movement as a "rebellion against the institutional obstacles to designing schools to benefit kids."[46]

As for Pastorek, he espoused the principles expressed by Professor Paul T. Hill in *It Takes a City;* the main concept behind the new system was Hill's diverse providers model. At the outset of the post-Katrina period, Hill preached that the New Orleans school district should not rebuild the old district structure. "In the case of post-hurricane New Orleans," he said, "American school planners will be as close as they have ever come to a 'greenfield' opportunity." Hill advocated choice, charters, new teachers, and autonomy for New Orleans. The school district adopted his recommendations.[47]

In response to arguments that an elected school board provides checks and balances and local control, Pastorek said: "Democracy is a good thing. But having a pure democracy and running an education system creates challenges, and you've got to balance those challenges. Right now it's out of balance. Superintendents and principals are not able to maintain high academic standards in their environment."[48] As the state's superintendent of education, Pastorek attempted to change the arrangements that governed local education throughout Louisiana. He sought to enhance the authority of superintendent and diminish the role of school boards in order to take patronage out of the hands of school board members. Local boards opposed these reforms, which the state legislature rejected.

Vallas complained that "democracy moved slowly" as far as the Orleans Parish schools were concerned. To him, the kind of reform required in the New Orleans schools would not come quickly enough if the system relied on an elected board and officials to change it. Katrina accelerated things.

Opponents of the reforms, including African American leaders and some residents who rejected change, disliked the fact that education policy in city schools post-Katrina was being made and executed by non-elected officials from outside the city, who did not descriptively represent the population of New Orleans. They disapproved of the lack of public input into the educational changes that were occurring in the aftermath of the storm. Some scholars described privatization and charter schools as emanating from the business ideology of education, which dictates that "all children should be educated to develop work skills and compete in this knowledge based economy."[49] They argued that the political right was using the disaster to advance its own interests.[50] According to Kristen Buras, writing in the *Harvard Educational Review,* "New Orleans charter schools are less about responding to the needs of racially oppressed communities and more about the *Reconstruction* of a newly governed

South—one in which white entrepreneurs (and black allies) capitalize on black schools and neighborhoods by obtaining public monies to build and manage charter schools."[51]

As Pastorek and Vallas saw it, the democracy argument was being advanced by those who wanted to regain access to patronage positions and money. Vallas believed that charter boards allowed New Orleans to exert local control to a greater extent than in any other place in the country. Opponents of this view, including at least one member of the post-Katrina OPSB, referred to the charter movement in New Orleans as the privatization of public schools.

The takeover law required underachieving schools to remain in the RSD for five years. BESE had to decide how RSD schools would be operated at least six months before the five-year period ended. It had until December 9, 2010, to determine the fate of sixty-eight RSD schools. The takeover law did not mandate a return to the locality even if the school excelled.[52]

A survey conducted August 6–11, 2009, by the Council for a Better Louisiana (CABL) indicated that the plurality of respondents (45 percent) did not want BESE ever to return schools to local control; 38 percent advocated a return to local control within five years; and close to 20% were uncertain (see table 9). CABL also asked whether people wanted to keep the changes to the school system or revert to the way education had operated prior to Katrina. A little under 75 percent wanted to continue with the changes, and 12 percent wanted a return to the old ways; 14 percent were undecided (see table 10).[53]

In another poll conducted November 3–14, 2009 (see table 11), Tulane's Cowen Institute found that 40 percent of voters favored a plan to allow RSD to control all of the schools and 39 percent opposed this

TABLE 9
Attitudes (%) toward local control of public schools, 2009

In 2010, the state Board of Elementary and Secondary Education will consider whether state officials should return schools to the Orleans Parish School Board or continue to operate them within the Recovery School District in New Orleans. Which of the following do you prefer?

Return schools in the next year or two	21
Return schools in the next three to five years	17
Not return schools at all	45
Uncertain	18

Source: Council for a Better Louisiana (CABL), 2009.

TABLE 10

Attitudes (%) toward change in public education, 2009

A number of changes in public education have taken place in New Orleans since Katrina. If given a choice, would you prefer to continue with the changes in public education since Katrina or go back to the way it was before Katrina?

Continue with the changes in public education since Katrina	74
Go back to the way it was before Katrina	12
Uncertain	14

Source: Council for a Better Louisiana (CABL), 2009.

TABLE 11

Attitudes (%) toward public school oversight, 2009

Now I have a few options to read to you about what groups should have oversight and control over public schools in New Orleans. Please tell me if you favor or oppose each of the following options.

	Total voters somewhat or strongly favor	Total voters somewhat or strongly oppose	White and other voters somewhat or strongly favor	African-American voters somewhat or strongly favor	White and other voters somewhat or strongly oppose	African American voters somewhat or strongly oppose
Create a new citywide elected board	74	17	69	78	22	13
Change almost all schools into public charters	46	37	54	41	29	43
Give control of all schools to the RSD	40	39	42	40	34	42
Give control of all schools to OPSB	34	55	25	40	63	49
Create a new mayor-appointed board	13	80	6	18	85	77
Give control of all schools to the next mayor	7	83	6	9	82	83

Source: "Public Education through the Public Eye: A Survey of New Orleans Voters and Parents," Cowen Institute for Public Initiatives, Tulane University.

idea. About the same percentage of white and African American voters supported this plan, but blacks (40 percent) were more likely than
whites (34 percent) to oppose this change. White voters (54 percent)
endorsed a conversion of all schools to public charters to a greater extent
than African American voters (41 percent).

Fifty-five percent of the voters surveyed rejected the idea that the old
OPSB should be reestablished. A little less than half (49 percent) of African American voters opposed the return of a fully empowered OPSB,
whereas 63 percent of whites and other voters rejected this change. Furthermore, 40 percent of black voters favored giving complete control of
schools to the OPSB. In a March 2, 2009, interview with NPR, when
asked about the return of a single school district, Jacobs said, "New
Orleans is never going back to that."[54]

In the end, Pastorek's plan provided that successful RSD schools
should be allowed to decide whether to remain under state control or
return to their previous governing authority (PGA). Local charter boards
would make those decisions, though chances were slim that any charter
school would choose to return to local rule. Pastorek called the plan
a victory for local control because communities with successful schools
would have the right to determine whether they wanted to remain under
the RSD or return to the PGA. In places where RSD schools had not
done well, communities could operate a school through either a charter
or the local education authority. Senator Landrieu commended Pastorek
for the superintendent's engagement of the local community; the education
chair of Citizens for 1 Greater New Orleans endorsed the revised plan.[55]

In December 2010 the entire BESE body approved the Pastorek plan
for deciding whether or not to return to local control. Eligible schools
could not leave the RSD until the 2012–13 school year, and at that point
in 2010, according to Pastorek, only five schools met the criteria for considering leaving the RSD.[56] Some members of the OPSB still opposed
Pastorek's plan because they felt that the new and improved school board
had shown that it could be trusted.

Perceptions of School Reforms

A little more than a year after Katrina, UTNO issued a statement charging
that the state had created a separate and unequal school system in New
Orleans. RSD schools—both traditional and charters—served the poorest

students, the teachers' union claimed; indeed, RSD students were nearly twice as likely as their OPSB counterparts to have been eligible for free or reduced-cost lunches before Katrina. The union complained that most of the reopened schools were in affluent white neighborhoods, far from areas where people of color lived. Union members understood that most of the schools in African American neighborhoods had been destroyed, but they argued that the RSD was not using facilities that had incurred only minor damage in these minority areas.[57]

Furthermore, UTNO argued that by using size limits, selective admissions criteria, and early registration to restrict their enrollments to higher-achieving students, the charter schools were turning traditional RSD schools into places of last resort. The union offered statistics to back up its claims. One-third of all students attended state-run RSD schools, but only 5 percent of gifted and talented students went to these schools. More than two-thirds of the gifted and talented students attended OPSB charters, while 20 percent of all students attended these schools. Thirty percent of the New Orleans public school student body were attending highly selective schools in 2006–7. UTNO felt that these and other factors—such as admitting low numbers of special education students—explained why OPSB charter schools were outperforming their traditional counterparts. Nor were the non-RSD schools as accessible as state and city education leaders claimed. Limited or nonexistent transportation options made many schools inaccessible to poor and black students[58]

The reuse of Fortier High School in the Uptown neighborhood of New Orleans exemplified these issues. Prior to the storm, Fortier had served a predominantly black student body. After the storm, the school district gave the building to the Lusher School, a selective-admissions charter school that serves predominantly white, middle-class to upper-middle-class students.[59]

A 2010 report by the University of Minnesota Law School's Institute on Race and Poverty likewise claimed that the OPSB and charter schools—regardless of authorizing institution—used various policies and practices to create a multi-tiered and inequitable system. White students attended the highest-performing schools. Eighty-seven percent of white students attended an OPSB or BESE school, but only 18 percent of African American students went to one of these schools. Three-quarters of the African American students in New Orleans went to an RSD school; by contrast, 11% of white students went to a school operated by the RSD. The report concluded that black students were twelve times more likely than white students to attend a school in a high-poverty area. To enter a charter school, students had to sign a contract, and the school expelled students who violated their contracts; RSD schools had to take any student who wanted to enroll and they dealt with discipline problems to a much greater extent than charters.[60]

BESE and OPSB charter schools tended to be situated in low-need areas; high-need students lived closest to the RSD schools. In 2009, six of the charter schools did not provide transportation, so the poor, who have limited access to cars, could not take advantage of these schools; two OPSB schools offered limited public transportation.[61]

One education leader observed that "tiering" occurred not only within the public school system but also among private and parochial schools, which "in addition to selective admissions schools like Ben Franklin and Lusher provide a safety net for middle and upper-middle class parents and students. These parents won't send their children to RSD schools."[62]

At the start of the 2014–15 school year, a report conducted by the website Trulia found that the New Orleans metropolitan area had the highest percentage of students attending private schools in the nation: more than one-quarter of students in the metropolitan area attended private schools. Other sources support this finding. In 2002, 26.5 percent of the 96,245 students in Orleans Parish attended private schools; in 2013, 30 percent of the 65,725 Orleans Parish students attended private schools. The superintendent of Catholic schools believed that the strength of the Catholic faith in New Orleans explained these statistics. The authors of the report noted, however, that enrollment in private schools across the country rises as public school performance drops and the level of income inequality increases.[63]

In 2008 a publicly funded voucher program was instituted in New Orleans and was expanded statewide by Governor Bobby Jindal in the fall of 2012. In the 2011–12 school year, about 2,500 New Orleans public school students used vouchers to attend private schools. By January 2014, approximately 6,750 low-income students were attending private schools on these vouchers. Eligibility depended on either attending a substandard school or entering kindergarten.[64]

Tulane's Cowen Institute for Public Education Initiatives agreed that schools in New Orleans were segregated by race and class but argued that the segregation predated the reorganization of the schools. It concluded that charter schools were not free to locate wherever they wished. Unlike charters in other parts of the country, those in New Orleans received their buildings from the city's educational system. The uneven development in New Orleans necessitated the location of school buildings in more heavily populated areas.[65]

Led by James Carville, Tulane University and Democracy Corps surveyed likely voters from April 5 to 14, 2009. This poll found that a majority of whites (63 percent) and a plurality of blacks (42 percent) believed that New Orleans public schools had improved after the storm. Blacks (21 percent) were twice as likely as whites (10 percent) to believe that the public schools had worsened after Katrina. They were more likely than whites (30 percent to 18 percent) to contend that schools were about the same pre- and post-Katrina (see table 12).

In an opinion piece in the *Wall Street Journal* on the fifth anniversary of Katrina, Leslie Jacobs wrote: "From the flood waters, the most market-driven public school system in the country has emerged. Education reformers across America should take notice: The model is working."[66] Jacobs cited test scores and the CABL and Cowen Institute poll results as evidence of the model's effectiveness. She believed that cooperative competition, which she labeled "co-opetition," school choice, and decentralization were the reasons for this success. Jacobs concluded with the following words: "Hurricane Katrina devastated New Orleans. But the disaster gave state officials the opportunity to accelerate education reform. Other cities shouldn't wait for their own cataclysm to do the same."[67] She supported many of the positive narratives about post-Katrina schools in New Orleans, including the importance of choice, decentralization, autonomy, and competition.

TABLE 12
Attitudes (%) toward Public Schools, 2009

Do you feel New Orleans public schools are getting better, getting worse, or about the same since Hurricane Katrina?

	Total voters	White voters	African American voters
Getting better	50	63	42
About the same	25	18	30
Getting worse	17	10	21
Don't know/refused to answer	8	9	7

Source: Tulane University/Democracy Corps, New Orleans, April 5–14, 2009.

Achievement and Assessment

RSD schools in New Orleans sustained increases in every measure of academic success, including LEAP (Louisiana Educational Assessment Program) tests, SPS (School Performance Scores) and DPS (District Performance Scores), at-grade-level proficiency, and a reduction in the percentage of academically unacceptable schools. Students in all kinds of New Orleans schools witnessed improved performance over time after Hurricane Katrina. New Orleans students' scores rose regardless of the type of school they attended. The RSD-run schools had the lowest levels of achievement, while students in OPSB charter schools turned in the best performance in the city. In the years after Hurricane Katrina, New Orleans students cut the achievement gap between themselves and the rest of the state, but the city's students continued to rank well behind the Louisiana average for percentage of fourth- and eighth-grade students scoring "basic" or above on the English and math portions of the LEAP tests (see tables 13 and 14).

U.S. Secretary of Education Arne Duncan held the view that raw scores do not matter nearly as much as positive change. Speaking before the annual BGR (Bureau of Governmental Research) luncheon in December 2014, Duncan commended the changes in New Orleans education, saying that the scores indicated that the city's schools were "getting better faster" than most other schools in the nation. He told his audience that New Orleans's schools were headed in the right direction and that those changes were "helping lead the nation."[68]

In his analysis of RSD student performance from 2005 to 2011, consultant Charles J. Hatfield, co-founder of Research on Reforms, expressed a different view:

> Whether assessing the 2010–2011 status of the RSD schools using the current achievement performance labels or applying the new letter grade system that will be implemented in the fall, it is clear that the SPS achievement status for the vast majority of the RSD schools is at best pathetic. The public continues to be fed the propaganda by the LDOE, RSD, and various support advocacy groups as the tremendous progress made by schools in the RSD. . . . [I]t is extremely difficult to understand how anyone could propose that the transformation of New Orleans Public schools serve as a national model for educational reform.[69]

TABLE 13

Louisiana Educational Assessment Program (LEAP) and Graduate Exit Examination (GEE) performance (%) by school type in New Orleans, 2007–2011

Grade Level	School type	2007 English, language, arts (ELA): basic & above	2009 ELA: basic & above	2011 ELA: basic & above	Growth over time, 2007–2011	2007 math: basic & above	2009 math: basic & above	2011 math: basic & above	Growth over time, 2007–2011
4th Grade	OPSB Charter	79.9	88.9	95	15.1	74	82.1	91	17
	OPSB-Run	80.2	94.3	92	11.8	76	89.5	91	15
	RSD-Charter	48.6	59.7	62	13.4	41.8	55	60	18.2
	RSD-Run	18.6	43.7	54	35.4	14	30.3	44	30
	New Orleans	48.9	61	67	18.1	43.4	52.9	63	19.6
	Louisiana	70	73.9	76	6	65	67.2	73	8
8th Grade	OPSB Charter	74	84.1	95	21	74	86.3	92	18
	OPSB-Run	58	71.5	78	20	44	66.2	57	13
	RSD-Charter	34	49.4	59	25	34	48.9	60	26
	RSD-Run	14	24.3	36	22	17	19.8	34	17
	New Orleans	38.6	46.6	62	23.4	36.6	44.4	60	23.4
GEE	OPSB Charter	68	70.6	75	7	72.3	77.2	81	8.7
	OPSB-Run	47.3	61.1	64	16.7	52.7	65.4	68	15.3
	RSD-Charter	25.4	45.8	54	28.6	45.6	67.9	69	23.4
	RSD-Run	8.9	18.4	24	15.1	13.	26.9	33	19.4
	All New Orleans	37.3	48.6	54	16.7	43.4	57.8	63	19.6

Sources: "2008 OPSB & RSD LEAP/GEE Scores in Context," May 2008, Cowen Institute for Public Education Initiatives, Tulane University; "Public School Performance in New Orleans: Supplement to the 2008 State of Public Education in New Orleans Report," January 2009, Cowen Institute for Public Education Initiatives, Tulane University; "A Close Look at the 2010 LEAP Scores and Their Gains and Declines over Time," June 2010, Cowen Institute for Public Education Initiatives, Tulane University; "NOLA by the Numbers: School Performance Scores," October 2010, Cowen Institute for Public Education Initiatives, Tulane University; "NOLA by the Numbers: High-Stakes Testing," May 2011, Cowen Institute for Public Education Initiatives, Tulane University.

TABLE 14

School performance labels for public schools in New Orleans, 2005, 2009, 2010

School performance score (SPS)	Percent of 2005 schools by performance levels	Percent of 2009 schools by performance levels	Percent of 2010 schools by performance levels
Academically unacceptable (below 60.0)	64	41.9	26.5
One star	20.2	29.7	5.9
Two stars (80.0–99.9)	6.1	16.2	22.1
Three stars (100.0–119.9)	6.1	8.1	8.8
Four stars (120.0–139.9)	1.8	2.7	2.9
Five stars (140 and above)	1.8	1.4	4.4

Sources: "2008 OPSB & RSD LEAP/GEE Scores in Context," May 2008, Cowen Institute for Public Education Initiatives, Tulane University; "Public School Performance in New Orleans: Supplement to the 2008 State of Public Education in New Orleans Report," January 2009, Cowen Institute for Public Education Initiatives, Tulane University; "A Close Look at the 2010 LEAP Scores and Their Gains and Declines over Time," June 2010, Cowen Institute for Public Education Initiatives, Tulane University; "NOLA by the Numbers: School Performance Scores," October 2010, Cowen Institute for Public Education Initiatives, Tulane University; "NOLA by the Numbers: High-Stakes Testing," May 2011, Cowen Institute for Public Education Initiatives, Tulane University.

According to one black leader, the educational system was "very successful in achieving its goals, which were to create an uneducated docile labor force to supply cheap labor to the service industry."[70]

In a 2013 piece in the *New York Times*, the *Times-Picayune*'s former education reporter brought up another shortcoming of the massive reforms: "Consider the cost to many veteran educators, who formed the core of the city's black middle class. After the flood, officials fired 7,500 school employees. . . . Test scores might have risen, but fewer educators are considered part of the community fabric and understand the social and cultural context in which their students live."[71] Furthermore, as Luis Mirón concludes: "Not so good is the number of high schools and the quality of high school instruction available to communities left behind by Hurricane Katrina, in particular in majority black neighborhoods in the mostly poor and overwhelmingly black Lower Ninth Ward and the middle-class black neighborhood of Pontchartrain Park. As of the 2014–2015 school year, there is one high school in the Lower 9 and no high schools at all in Pontchartrain Park."[72]

The question of education illustrates the difficulty in assessing change in post-Katrina New Orleans. Those at the top of the political arrangement for education could—and do—tout the structural changes, improved test scores, increased harmony, and appearance of less corruption and patronage and say: "Look how far we have come. The system is better." They would be right. Those who sit lower in the new arrangement could—and do—oppose the two-tiered system, the poor test scores, and the still precarious position of most New Orleans students. They would be right too. Positive change has occurred. And the system continues to struggle.

The Post-Katrina Political Arrangement for Education

In the aftermath of Hurricane Katrina, Louisiana's governor, legislature, and department of education dismantled New Orleans's school employment regime and replaced it with one focused on reform and performance. These extra-local actors used the state's constitution and laws to limit the authority of the Orleans Parish School Board and the city's teachers' union. They expanded the scope of the RSD and charter schools to reduce the power of those who ran and benefited from the employment regime. Within New Orleans, reform-minded members of the OPSB blocked a return to the status quo. The new agenda received financial support from foundations and the federal government and was implemented by the RSD, KIPP and other charter providers, TFA, New Schools for New Orleans, and New Leaders for New Schools, among others. Although the education policy arena remained concentrated (governing arrangements) and strong (policy fidelity), the actual policies and the governing arrangements radically changed after the storm.

Those who opposed the pre-Katrina education cartel won in post-Katrina New Orleans. The state government and the federal government promulgated rules and financed reform that diminished the strength of the employment regime. Foundations assumed a role in the governance of schools in New Orleans; they financed policies favored by national and local business leaders, particularly charter schools. The state and federal governments along with big business and foundations won. They ruled.

Charter schools won; traditional schools lost.

New, younger teachers won; the teachers' union lost.

Charter boards gained authority; the OPSB lost authority.

Poor and black students continued to attend the lowest-performing schools. Students who attended elite public schools won.

Reform and status quo continued to battle each other in post-Katrina New Orleans education politics and policies. State secretaries of education, the governor, some state legislators, and reform-oriented members of the OPSB wanted to expand pre-disaster changes to school governance and the delivery of education. Some long-standing members of the OPSB and the teachers' union either opposed change or resisted the speed and scope of reform.

As was the case in economic development, racial divides over post-Katrina education policies were not as wide as many might expect. Like any group, African Americans are not monolithic. In this case, some support the changes, others oppose them, and some see both strengths and weaknesses in the transformation. For the most part, blacks support changes to public education in New Orleans. A majority of black voters approved the state takeover and school choice and believed that charters and new teachers improved public education. A core of blacks—about 20 to 25 percent—opposed changes to public education. Racial divisions persisted at the elite and elected levels in post-Katrina New Orleans. Blacks were less likely than whites to endorse the changes to public education. According to one civic leader, in 2011 polls indicated that "75 percent-plus of the citizen body as a whole supported the mayor and the changes under way." This leader concluded that the most vocal opponents of change were members of the "old power structure, who screamed an alternate reality."[73]

The agenda of the new performance arrangement—charter schools, choice, enhanced accountability, and autonomy—was set by the U.S. Department of Education, the state department of education, the governor, mostly white legislators from outside New Orleans, a core group of reformers on the Orleans Parish School Board, and national foundations. State secretaries of education and heads of the RSD also promoted a reform agenda. Conservatives, foundations, and a national network of charter schools encouraged the state to adopt charter schools and hire new teachers after Katrina.

The black caucus of the state legislature and the teachers' union believed that displaced residents should be able to provide input on the governance and policies of post-Katrina schools. The state secretary of education and the head of the RSD claimed that too much democracy had created these problems in the first place. They sought to limit elected officials' control over education decisions and expand educators' influence over school policy.

The school reforms in New Orleans were a series of choices on the part of those who had resources and/or authority. The U.S. Department of Education funded only charter schools. Federal grants financed the new teacher organizations that ran charter schools. The governor, mostly white legislators from outside New Orleans, and the state department of education accepted the money and promoted a charter system. The governor relaxed the rules for a local jurisdiction to convert a traditional school into a charter. Governor Blanco and state legislators, except many from New Orleans and some African American lawmakers, expanded the definition of schools in need so that the RSD could take over almost the entire district in New Orleans. These decisions allowed New Schools for New Orleans, Teach for America, and New Leaders for New Schools to expand their presence. Outside foundations furthered the mission of these organizations through their financial resources.

Education in New Orleans did not so much take a new direction after Katrina as Katrina accelerated a change already in motion. The RSD, charter schools, extra-local actors, and private entities had piece-meal control over aspects of New Orleans's educational system before August 29, 2005. The governor, state legislators, and the state depart-ment of education expanded these reforms after Katrina. This new education arrangement put system-wide reform on the public agenda. It enacted choice, accountability, new governance, and new education policies. The educational cartel wanted to open schools as quickly as possible, reestablish the OPSB as the chief operator of city schools, and renew the collective bargaining agreement. The new arrangement rebuffed these choices.

New Orleans's post-Katrina system of schools differed from the pre-Katrina arrangement, but education did not start anew after the storm. An intergovernmental public-private partnership ruled educa-tion in New Orleans post-Katrina. State government and charter schools ran the new arrangement. Foundations held power in the arrangement because they used their resources to help implement their policy goals, particularly the expansion of charters in New Orleans. The old education cartel lost power as a result of the post-Katrina reforms. The OPSB oper-ated few schools, and the teachers' union lost its collective bargaining agreement in the post-storm period. As it had in economic development, the post-Katrina political arrangement favored education reform and attacked sources of patronage.

The OPSB lost its authority in the post-Katrina era. Even before Katrina, the state stripped authority from OPSB in the form of charter schools, the RSD, and the financial takeover. In this instance, corrup-tion, mismanagement, substandard services, and sheer chaos led to the discrediting of this institution. After Katrina, the state government made certain that the OPSB could exercise its authority in only small doses. This action mirrored those taken by reformers to limit the influence of levee boards, assessors, and sheriffs in economic development.

5

From Mismanagement to Reform in Housing

As with economic development and public education, division and tension characterized the political arrangement governing public housing policy in pre-Katrina New Orleans. In December 1995 the Office of the Inspector General of the U.S. Department of Housing and Urban Development (HUD) recommended a federal takeover of the Housing Authority of New Orleans (HANO), the local entity responsible for administering public housing projects. At a congressional field hearing in New Orleans, Mayor Marc Morial testified against the takeover. Under a Cooperative Endeavor Agreement (CEA), an executive monitor from Tulane University would oversee HANO operations for HUD. This CEA transferred HANO's functions to the HUD secretary or his designee. HUD Secretary Henry Cisneros opted to placate Morial, a strong supporter of Cisneros's boss, President Clinton. The CEA was supposed to last for two years, but HUD extended it until 2002.[1]

In 1997 Congressman Richard Baker, a Republican from Baton Rouge, proposed the creation of a committee of housing managers, city officials, and private representatives to monitor HANO's activities. Fearing that HANO's fiscal mismanagement and decrepit properties were continuing to worsen, Baker expressed concern about delays in more than $400 million worth of construction to some of the city's public housing complexes.[2]

In 1998 Congress passed the Quality Housing and Work Responsibility Act, which created an advisory council for the Housing Authority of New Orleans. A combination of local and federal housing officials and federally appointed experts from outside New Orleans served on the committee. They had eighteen months to gather evidence and write a report to Congress. That report—and subsequent congressional testimony by the HUD inspector general—confirmed Baker's suspicions.[3] HANO had spent $832 million but without revitalizing any of the city's public housing units. It had failed to administer more than $65 million in HOPE (Housing Opportunities for People Everywhere) VI federal grants and to follow procurement procedures. The report recommended that HUD break HANO into several housing authorities and end the CEA, which it claimed did not work.[4]

Baker wanted to shut down HANO and impose a federal takeover as soon as possible. Mayor Morial saw no need to change HANO's leadership, but if that was inevitable, he preferred judicial receivership over HUD control of the housing agency, since he believed that a federal judge would be able to cut through red tape. A federal court judge denied the mayor's request to stop the federal takeover of HANO, and in March 2002, HUD named a Washington, D.C., consultant to run HANO's day-to-day operations. HUD inspectors general and Congressman Baker had put HANO's performance on the public agenda and influenced the way HANO's governance changed.[5]

After the federal government assumed direct control over HANO, it focused on the redevelopment of the Guste public housing project in Central City, the Desire and Florida projects in the Ninth Ward, Fischer on the West Bank, and St. Thomas in the Lower Garden District.[6] HUD was pushing homeownership for public housing residents. Some tenants of traditional public housing would return to the site of their old homes and live in mixed-income communities at reduced rents. Others would receive Section 8 housing vouchers to live in apartments throughout the area.

In 1969, *Gautreaux v. Chicago Housing Authority* concluded that segregated public housing violated Title VI of the Civil Rights Act of 1964. It ordered an end to high-rise public housing construction and required HUD and the city to build scattered-site public housing projects in white neighborhoods. The *Gautreaux* case extended beyond Chicago, and by the mid-1980s to the early 1990s, mixed-income scattered-site housing and the use of Section 8 vouchers became the dominant housing policy in the United States, as well as in Canada, Australia, and western Europe. Started in 1992, HUD's $5 billion HOPE VI grants became the vehicle through which the federal government created mixed-income housing.[7]

Researchers continue to debate the efficacy of mixed-income housing. Their results are as varied as the attitudes toward this approach. Some conclude that the intent of mixed-income housing is to build community for public housing residents, reverse racial segregation in urban America, deconcentrate poverty, move residents out of poverty, revitalize neighborhoods, improve services, and create a cross-racial, cross-class network. Scholars have found that mixed-income housing lasted longer and was better managed and less socially troubled than traditional public housing. Mixed-income housing revitalized neighborhoods, improved residents' surroundings, decreased their stress, and built community.[8]

Others claim that mixed-income housing neither integrates public housing residents nor builds community or social networks; nor does it deconcentrate poverty, reduce inequality, or improve services. Edward G. Goetz concluded that efforts to create mixed-income housing in Minneapolis–St. Paul resembled the political battles of the urban renewal era, when minority residents fought to save their homes from slum clearance.[9]

The conversion of the St. Thomas housing project in the Lower Garden District into mixed-income housing and a retail center drew the most attention in the pre-Katrina period. HUD hired local developer Pres Kabacoff's Historic Restoration, Inc. (HRI), to construct privately owned condominiums, moderate- and low-income housing, and public housing units. The St. Thomas housing complex included 1,500 apartments; at the time of this deal, 700 were occupied. The new complex, named River Garden, would include 296 units of multifamily rental units, of which 174 would be market-rate apartments and 122 would be low income. HANO also sold six acres near the St. Thomas site to HRI so that the developer could build seventy-three single-family homes, fifteen of which would be affordable housing. HANO and HRI shared the revenue from the sale of the homes.[10]

A $25 million HOPE VI grant to HANO and HRI helped pay for some of the construction, but Kabacoff needed more revenue to build the market-rate units. In June 2001 Walmart announced it would build a 203,000-square-foot superstore on the former St. Thomas housing site. In October 2002 the New Orleans city council agreed to transfer $20 million in sales tax revenue from Walmart to HRI. State capital outlay funds, the city of New Orleans, and private funding also paid for the River Garden redevelopment.[11]

The desirable location of the St. Thomas property explained the attention it received from HANO and private developers. As Alexander

J. Reichl wrote in the planning stages of its redevelopment: "The St. Thomas development is, in effect, a crucial missing link needed to complete an unbroken chain of economically valuable city neighborhoods. . . . St. Thomas, therefore, has been of increasing concern to the business and real estate interests who see the future of economic growth in the city around that pivotal location."[12]

Mayor Nagin, the influential University of New Orleans economist Tim Ryan, and Edgar Chase III, the dean of Dillard University's business school, among others, supported the St. Thomas transformation. Nagin hoped to capture millions of lost sales tax dollars from New Orleanians who shopped at the Walmart stores in the city's suburbs. A black mayor's support for the reconstruction of New Orleans's public housing represented a shift from earlier administrations. Nagin could endorse the Walmart project and the St. Thomas renovation without fear of backlash from the black electorate, which Christine C. Cook and Mickey Lauria described as the intractable barrier to earlier regeneration strategies.[13]

Preservation groups worried that the supercenter would destroy the historic feel of the Lower Garden District, which is on the National Register of Historic Places. The chair of the Neighborhood Council of the Preservation Resource Center declared, "This is a sweetheart deal for developers in town that is being crammed down the city's throat."[14]

A public-private partnership implemented the St. Thomas transformation. HANO and the city council provided legal authority and some financing, and HRI redeveloped the area, recruited a large retailer to provide additional resources, and profited from the sales of apartments and homes. The city council collected $5 million from Walmart for the general fund. In response to the city's limited local control over the St. Thomas demolition, Morial proposed an ordinance requiring a permit to demolish any building in New Orleans that had at any time been used for public housing. The city council passed the ordinance in January 2002; each subsequent demolition of a New Orleans public housing unit needed its approval.[15]

HANO's plans to demolish and renovate public housing extended beyond St. Thomas. HUD and HANO used their authority and fiscal resources to turn the Desire housing projects in the Upper Ninth Ward into a mixed-income community, tear down the Fischer high-rise, demolish 465 low-rise units at Guste, knock down the entire Florida project, and demolish 240 units at B. W. Cooper.[16]

The agenda before Katrina focused on changes to public housing that would result in less dense living environments, mixed-income communities, and a dispersed poor population. HUD, HANO, and the New Orleans city council and mayor chose demolition, decreased density, and mixed-income complexes over rehabilitation, garden-style homes, and traditional public housing. HANO and HUD exercised authority over public housing in New Orleans, but the mayor and city council played roles as well. When HUD announced it would spend $180 million to complete the demolition and renovation of the Fischer, Florida, and Guste projects, it asked the city of New Orleans to contribute $39 million toward building infrastructure in these areas. Nagin supported the idea, and the city council agreed to allocate $14 million for infrastructure. It requested a detailed plan by HUD before it would release the rest of the city's $39 million contribution.[17]

In 1995 Cook and Lauria asked whether downtown public housing and urban regeneration could coexist in New Orleans. They found downtown public housing to be a "more intractable barrier to regeneration strategies than . . . skid rows or other privately owned slum neighborhoods."[18] In 1986, an earlier report commissioned by the mayor's office had described the city's public housing as "unmanageable and beyond repair."[19] It called for reduced density in each of the city's public housing projects. Downtown business interests had demanded that Mayor Barthelemy do something about public housing, particularly the Iberville complex, which sat in Mid-City "in the shadow of Canal Street, the major commercial corridor for New Orleans."[20] The Downtown Development District and merchants on Canal Street believed that Iberville was hurting their businesses.

Business interests funded three of six new police officers who patrolled the area; they also established a police substation in the Iberville neighborhood. Iberville's residents complained that the police unit cared most about the perimeter of the Iberville complex and the protection of merchants' interests. Despite recommendations that Iberville be demolished, the city's elected officials refused to follow through, fearing that the political fallout would be too great for them to withstand. According to Cook and Lauria: "The growth coalition underestimated the political value of public-housing tenants in an African-American majority city. The inherent instability of the electoral coalition of the political members of New Orleans' governing coalition forced them to be sensitive to organized African-American political pressure and, at least temporarily, retreat to their previously faltering spatial-containment strategy."[21] This tension between the electorate, which possessed public resources, and business leaders, who controlled financial capital, paralyzed growth in the city of New Orleans.

In 2001 HANO's executive monitor cited Iberville's 92 percent occupation rate as one of the reasons to maintain the complex as public housing. He felt compelled to make these statements because news reports had surfaced that Saints owner Tom Benson wanted to convert the Iberville project into the site of a $450 million open-air stadium for his football team. The stadium would be the centerpiece of a $1 billion revitalization of the Iberville section, following up on the Urban Land Institute's recommendation three years earlier that Iberville be demolished as a way to revitalize upper Canal Street. Although Mayor Morial referred to the redevelopment plan as "completely insensitive" and said it would never happen, public housing advocates and Iberville residents predicted that the renovation trend that was sweeping the nation and the city would find its way to Iberville.[22]

The reconstruction of New Orleans's public housing put the plight of the city's poor on the public agenda. Residents of public housing and their advocates wanted to know where they would live while the reconstruction took place and whether they could return once their old homes were rebuilt. HANO announced that Section 8 vouchers would allow former residents to maintain a roof over their heads. In theory, at least, very low income families, the elderly, and the disabled provide these vouchers to landlords to secure housing in the private market. Section 8 vouchers cover 70 percent of rent for low-income tenants. Both HANO and HRI also claimed that many former residents would be able to return to St. Thomas.[23]

In 2005, residents of Eastern New Orleans, a middle-class black area of the city, persuaded their city council member, Cynthia Willard-Lewis, to sponsor restrictions on the kinds of apartments available to Section 8 recipients. According to State Representative Austin Badon Jr., New Orleans East "was designed as a place for the traditional nuclear family. People who bought homes out there invested in their homes. They want a return on their investments." Willard-Lewis, Badon, and their constituents did not want Section 8 tenants, many of whom were black, in their neighborhoods because they felt that these residents brought with them low-income support services such as shelters for battered women and check-cashing businesses, thus bringing down property values.[24]

Renovation of public housing had taken precedence over concerns about both the short- and long-term living arrangements for the displaced tenants of these homes.[25] When asked about these tenants, the federal receiver of HANO replied: "I have to publicly say that they weren't handled as well as they could have been. We won't repeat the mistakes of the past."[26] She made this claim about two months before Katrina hit.

Federal law had required that each unit of public housing that was demolished be replaced by a new unit of public housing. In 1995 Congress repealed that law, and HUD and HANO chose not to replace the public housing they demolished on a one-for-one basis. Residents of public housing viewed HOPE VI and the overall redevelopment of New Orleans's public housing as a way to displace the city's poor.[27]

Before Hurricane Katrina, about 54 percent of the city's population rented their homes, a figure 20 points higher than the average in the United States at that time. The New Orleans homeownership rate was about 47 percent, compared with 67 percent nationally. Fifty-nine percent of the residents in the Lower Ninth Ward owned their homes. In a ten-year period beginning in 1995, HUD and HANO demolished about half of New Orleans's fourteen thousand public housing units. Governmental reform, demolition, and mixed-income living were the trajectories for public housing in the city prior to Katrina.[28]

The Pre-Katrina Political Arrangement for Public Housing

As we have just seen, HUD used its resources and authority to dictate much of New Orleans's housing policies before the storm, while state government played little to no visible role. HUD's inspectors general, a member of the U.S. House of Representatives from Baton Rouge, and the U.S. Congress put the governance of HANO on the public agenda, and HOPE VI grants ensured that the redevelopment of housing projects followed federal priorities. Business in general favored mixed-income housing, while businesses in the central business district pressed for the demolition of public housing. Developers wanted to build homes and commercial businesses on the sites of former public housing complexes, and the Iberville housing project on the edge of the central business district was their number one target.

Obviously, the federal government controls federal housing policies. In the case of New Orleans, however, the federal government, namely HUD, removed from local control a housing authority that should have been governed by people living in New Orleans.

The HUD-led HANO enacted most of the changes that businesses wanted. HANO used HOPE VI grants to reconstruct and demolish additional public housing complexes. The housing authority hired a local developer to convert the St. Thomas housing projects into a Walmart and private homes. City council–approved tax increment financing allowed the developer to realize his plans. The city council also allocated $39 million for infrastructure improvements.

HUD and HANO opposed traditional public housing and one-for-one replacement of demolished units. They instead enacted scattered-site housing and mixed-income housing. Mayor Morial supported the conversion of public housing into retail centers because he wanted the revenue for the city. The city council and planning commission backed these policies. Despite the preferences of businesses and developers, Iberville remained intact and untouched. Morial ensured increased local control over the fate of public housing when he shepherded through the city council an ordinance that required the council to approve future demolitions.

Businesses won on the demolition of public housing, the construction of mixed-income housing complexes, and the decision not to replace each public housing unit with a new one. HRI won when it got to build on the site of the former St. Thomas housing project. This developer won again when the city council agreed to provide it with additional finances in exchange for shared revenue from the sale of private houses on the St. Thomas site.

By contrast, those who had benefited from HANO's patronage lost in the pre-Katrina period. The federal takeover of HANO took away jobs, contracts, and money from many local actors. Some public housing residents also lost. The homes where many of them lived were destroyed, and HANO would not guarantee replacement. Iberville residents won when HANO decided not to demolish or reconstruct that complex. The extent to which the city was able to determine the fate of its public housing diminished toward the end of the pre-Katrina period, a loss for local government.

We have seen how a public-private chasm opened up over the issue of public housing in New Orleans. Businesses and developers, led primarily by whites, wanted to end public housing in New Orleans. A black mayor and a majority-black electorate opposed those moves until Nagin took office.

Race was not the only—or even the predominant—dividing line in pre-Katrina housing policy. Black legislators in New Orleans East opposed Section 8 housing in their part of the city, fearing that it would lower housing values and change the nature of their community. This divide centered on class, not race. Class divisions hardened when wealthy business leaders, developers, and even legislators changed the living arrangements for poor residents.

The federal government essentially ruled over public housing in pre-Katrina New Orleans. It removed local control from the housing authority that had governed this policy. As was the case in economic development and education, an extra-local entity, HUD, stripped a local institution, HANO, of its authority. As in the other instances we have discussed, this local institution had misspent funds, was plagued by corruption, and delivered substandard services. These characteristics discredit institutions and leave them open to a loss of authority.

Even before Katrina, those with the resources and/or authority began to establish a loose coalition. The federal government and city council enacted many of the policies preferred by businesses and developers. The electorate muted some of this coalition's force, but it could not stop the changes to public housing. HUD made a legitimate choice to change the governance of HANO and set an agenda favored by business. The demolition of public housing was a national phenomenon at the time; HUD and HANO made this policy a reality in pre-Katrina New Orleans.

Housing in the Post-Katrina Era

When a natural disaster strikes, the most socially vulnerable—racial minorities, the poor, the elderly, and the undereducated—are slower to evacuate than other citizens, sustain the greatest degree of damage, possess fewer resources for recovery, and take more time to rebuild. Disasters thus exacerbate patterns of inequality that existed prior to the event. After a disaster, property vacancy and abandonment are most likely to occur in neighborhoods already on the decline.[29]

Disasters exert their most negative effects on African Americans, who in many locations live in less well constructed homes, possess fewer resources to rebuild, maintain lower levels of insurance, and have more limited savings. The Small Business Administration is less likely to approve loans for African Americans than for others, and FEMA is less likely to provide grants to African Americans than to others. The standard of living drops for African Americans and low-income residents after disasters.[30]

The federal government and, to a lesser extent, states fund housing recovery after a disaster. Local governments plan the location of temporary housing, deal with damaged properties, grant rebuilding and repair permits, and decide whether to rezone their jurisdiction.[31]

New Orleans followed domestic and foreign precedents as the most socially vulnerable residents sustained the greatest damage from Katrina and recovered slowly from the disaster. Blacks were most likely to be displaced, and they were the last and the least likely to return to the city after the storm. Hurricane Katrina severely damaged 150,000 homes and seriously damaged another 50,000 owner-occupied homes and 51,000 rental homes in New Orleans. The city lost 43,000 rental units. Less than a year after Katrina, rents had increased by 39 percent in the city.[32]

After the storm, HUD and HANO closed the city's public housing, installed steel doors on the buildings, and built fences around them. Former residents and their advocates marched, protested, broke into public housing to retrieve personal belongings, occupied the B. W. Cooper project and delayed its demolition, crossed police barriers, occupied the area around public housing, and were arrested for trespassing.[33] They filed a number of lawsuits to prevent the demolition of public housing and demanded one-for-one replacement.

HANO and HUD argued that the damage to public housing was too extensive and too expensive to repair, though there was disagreement about this. HANO's recovery adviser and board chairperson claimed that renovation of the Big Four housing projects—St. Bernard, B. W. Cooper, C. J. Peete, and Lafitte—would cost $745.2 million, compared with $597 million for demolition, though according to Loyola University New Orleans law professor Bill Quigley, HANO's internal documents indicated that rebuilding would cost tens of millions more than repairing the buildings. In addition, HANO officials stated that former residents did not want to return to New Orleans's vacant public housing; a HUD-sponsored survey of public housing families displaced by Katrina supported this claim.[34]

Public housing residents and their advocates, who included U.S. Representatives William Jefferson of New Orleans and Maxine Waters of Los Angeles, demanded an immediate reopening of public housing and one-for-one replacement of any demolished public housing unit. Mary Landrieu, Democratic senator from Louisiana, a native of New Orleans and daughter of Moon Landrieu, co-wrote the Gulf Coast Housing Recovery Act, which sought to replace every demolished public housing unit in New Orleans. Waters sponsored this legislation in the House,

which passed the bill, 302–125. The bill never made it out of committee in the Senate, however. HANO, HUD, the city council, the mayor,
and the planning commission favored demolition of damaged housing,
decreased density, and mixed-income living.

In December 2006, sixteen months after the hurricane, HANO approved
a plan to demolish the Big Four housing complexes and replace them with
mixed-income communities.[35] At the city council meeting a year later to
decide whether to grant the permits, an overflow crowd filled the council chambers. Police locked out protesters and then pepper-sprayed and
arrested them. The city council approved the demolition permits, 7–0.

Amid protest from some UN human rights experts in February 2008,
the city council released a statement to explain its support for demolition: "The past model of public housing in New Orleans has been a
failed one—years of neglect and mismanagement left our public housing
developments in ruin. These are critical times in our city's history—we
can choose to continue on the path of progress and positive change or we
can choose to maintain the status quo."[36]

Mayor Nagin signed three of the four demolition permits but with-
held permission for the demolition of the Lafitte housing project in the
Treme neighborhood to ensure that HUD met certain requests from the
city council and his office. In March, after he and the council agreed that
HUD had honored its promises, he authorized the demolition of Lafitte.
Before approving the demolitions, the city council waived property taxes
for the developers of the former public housing sites and scattered-site
housing.[37]

At the meeting to authorize the demolition of the Big Four, the Rev-
erend Torin Sanders, a Baptist minister and the former president of the
OPSB, argued, "People, simply because they are poor, are being locked
out of our city."[38] Protesters referred to the demolitions as genocide.
Mayor Nagin believed that the demolitions represented progress.[39]

HUD and public housing advocates expressed opposing views on the
effects of post-Katrina housing plans on homelessness. Orlando Cabrera,
an assistant secretary of HUD, told a U.S. Senate committee that four
hundred public housing apartments remained vacant in New Orleans
because former residents would not return to them. The executive director of the Greater New Orleans Fair Housing Action Center said that
the assistant secretary was "frankly wrong."[40] Senator Bob Menendez, a
Democrat from New Jersey, asked Cabrera why HUD could not find tenants even as homelessness was on the rise—to as high as twelve thousand.

Cabrera replied: "I don't know enough about the issue of homelessness post-storm. I can't answer the question honestly."[41]

HUD and HANO awarded close to $100 million in Community Development Block Grant (CDBG) money and $34 million in Gulf Opportunity (GO) Zone tax credits to national developers and local nonprofit organizations to redevelop the Big Four projects. Developers agreed to build a mix of public housing, affordable housing, and market-rate single-family housing at each site. According to HUD, "This concept of affordable housing has eliminated concentrations of poverty in cities like Atlanta, Washington, D.C., and Boston."[42]

Coalitions of private resource providers teamed up to redevelop former public housing sites in New Orleans. Columbia Residential of Atlanta, the Baton Rouge Area Foundation, and the Fore! Kids Foundation, a New Orleans–based nonprofit founded in 1958, partnered to create the Bayou District Foundation (BDF). The BDF redeveloped the St. Bernard Housing project into Columbia Parc at the Bayou District, a $440 million development complete with mixed-income housing, a championship golf course, a K–8 charter school, and a new high school. Serving as a model for BDF was Atlanta's East Lake Village, which had transformed a public housing development into a residential community with a professional golf course and a charter school. The United Way, Literacy Alliance of New Orleans, Goodwill Industries, Volunteers of America, and Via Link provided services for residents of Columbia Parc and former residents of St. Bernard living off-site with the use of housing vouchers. Similar teams of developers and nonprofits planned and provided public services for the B. W. Cooper, C. J. Peete, and Lafitte complexes.[43]

Then there was Iberville, the last of the New Deal public housing projects in New Orleans. Although Iberville had received only minor damage, the city council voted unanimously in May 2013 to demolish it, claiming that the demolition would facilitate economic development on Canal Street and in the central business district. This meeting did not resemble the beehive environment that had accompanied the December 2007 meeting in which the council agreed to demolish the Big Four. As part of the redevelopment, the city and HANO would build 2,446 apartments and replace each of the 821 public housing units lost. They planned to preserve and renovate fourteen of the complex's original brick buildings.[44]

To redevelop Iberville, HANO selected HRI and McCormack Baron Salazar, which had turned St. Thomas and C. J. Peete, respectively, into mixed-income communities. The Choice Neighborhood Initiative paid for $30.5 million of the redevelopment, while the Louisiana Housing Corporation allocated $15 million in low-income housing tax credits. The total redevelopment, "Iberville-Treme," which extends three hundred blocks beyond the Iberville footprint, cost about $660 million and included apartments above retail stores, cafés, and targeted services such as education and medical care.[45]

HANO relocated about 350 families as a result of this demolition. Its representatives addressed residents' questions about displacement and a potential return to Iberville at each meeting held on the redevelopment. Urban Strategies, the social services arm of McCormack Baron Salazar, provided case management of Iberville residents who stayed onsite and those who relocated as the redevelopment took place. Mayor Landrieu supported the transformation of Iberville and touted it in his 2013 State of the City address.[46]

Public housing residents and their advocates won concessions from HANO, HUD, and the city council. Amid pressure from residents, activists, and local clergy, HUD agreed to reopen one thousand additional public housing units in New Orleans. HUD raised the value of its rental vouchers to landlords by 35 percent. It spent $2.7 million to renovate ninety-four units at Lafitte even though it still planned to demolish those facilities in March of the following year. According to Donna White, a spokesperson for HUD, "While it has cost the Housing Authority of New Orleans a lot to fix these units, HUD was committed to building consensus among elected officials, housing activists, and residents." Council member Jacquelyn Brechtel Clarkson referred to the one-for-one replacement of apartments in Lafitte, one of the Big Four complexes, as "the compromise."[47]

At the Desire housing complex, residents changed HANO's plans for the use of federal stimulus money. The preliminary plan had called for the construction of new rental units. After a seven-hour meeting with resident leaders, HANO agreed to use that money to rehabilitate existing projects.[48]

In late May 2014, HUD Secretary Shaun Donovan and Mayor Landrieu announced that HANO would return to local control. The seven-member board would consist of five people selected by the mayor and two public housing residents who would be chosen from a list provided by the Citywide Tenants Council. Secretary Donovan declared, "I truly believe New Orleans is as strong as it has ever been and now is the right time for the agency to come home."[49]

The Road Home

Federal, state, and local officials needed to decide what to do with the 200,000 houses severely damaged by Hurricane Katrina. After Congressman Baker was unable to get Congress to agree on a plan to purchase damaged homes and the state legislature rejected a similar plan by Governor Blanco, she and the Louisiana Recovery Authority (LRA) announced what would become the Road Home. Governor Blanco issued an executive order to create the LRA on October 17, 2005. A thirty-three-member board of gubernatorial appointees, the LRA established short- and long-term rebuilding goals, planned and coordinated rebuilding efforts, represented Louisiana's funding priorities to the federal government, and allocated federal dollars to localities damaged by the storm. Blanco referred to the LRA as the board of directors of the recovery. On the basis of a directive from the LRA, the twenty-three parishes most affected by hurricanes Katrina and Rita would have to devise rebuilding plans to get their share of $200 million in federal recovery funds.[50]

The LRA created the Road Home, a housing assistance program that provided compensation to cover uninsured damages. It offered three options to homeowners: rebuild or reoccupy their homes within three years; agree to own land somewhere else in Louisiana; or sell and either remain in Louisiana as a renter or move to another state. Those who sold under option three received 60 percent of the home's pre-storm value or the estimated cost of damage. The Road Home assessed a 30 percent penalty against owners of properties within the floodplain who lacked flood insurance. The awards were capped at $150,000 and were not to exceed the cost of reconstruction.[51]

Instead of providing direct payments, the Road Home established an escrow account for each homeowner; the money was allocated in increments. Louisiana paid $756 million to ICF International to administer the Road Home program. The state's Office of Community Development (OCD), which allocates CDBG money for Louisiana, monitored ICF's work. At first, the state did not include performance measures for ICF to reach.[52]

Applicants were required to go through as many as seventy-five verification steps, including thumbprinting, in order to receive Road Home compensation. LRA director Andy Kopplin attempted to avoid the mistakes made by FEMA, which had allocated more than $1 billion in fraudulent payments after Katrina. The decision to choose fraud protection over expediency frustrated some people. In a private meeting, state legislator Cedric Richmond from New Orleans told other legislators and the governor's staff, "You're treating homeowners like thieves and children."[53]

The state of Louisiana had received $6.2 billion in CDBG money for housing assistance. Congress waived the requirement that local governments contribute 10 percent of rebuilding costs, but Blanco insisted that the state needed another $4.2 billion to implement any housing plan. Upon the urging of Donald Powell, who served as the coordinator of federal support for the recovery and rebuilding of the Gulf Coast region, President Bush requested the $4.2 billion in a supplemental bill, which Congress approved. The state now had $10.4 billion to address housing needs. Of that total, $7.6 billion went to homeowner grants, $1.5 billion for hazard mitigation/elevation grants, and $869 million to landlords to rebuild rental properties.[54]

The Louisiana housing plan was typical of previous post-disaster programs in that it concentrated on owner-occupied properties. Renters received neither direct subsidies nor money to replace lost possessions such as furniture. When asked why the Road Home focused on home-owners even though New Orleans had a high percentage of renters, the LRA's chief of staff said, "The recovery hinges on getting homeowners back to the area, so the decision to move first for homeowners—I think everyone would say that has been critical." The state estimated that the $869 million earmarked for landlords would repair only 18,000 of Louisiana's 82,000 damaged rental properties. This shortage drove rental prices up by 46 percent in the first two years after Katrina.[55]

When Congress passed the bill to appropriate the additional $4.2 billion, Blanco said, "We have all the funding we need to run our full program." Less than a year later, however, she was warning that the Road Home would go bankrupt if it continued to operate at its current pace. Her administration's initial estimate was that the program needed another $3 billion. That figure soon rose to between $4 and $5 billion. At the time, it appeared that fifty thousand eligible homeowners would not receive Road Home funds unless the federal government agreed to allocate more money to the program. The state concluded that lower-than-expected insurance payments to homeowners were contributing to the shortfall. FEMA had predicted that 123,000 homeowners would sign up for Road Home assistance, but the program received more than 145,000 applications. At the same time, higher-than-expected construction costs and

Louisiana's decision to provide additional $50,000 loans to low-income homeowners contributed to the Road Home shortfall.[56]

Congress allocated another $3 billion to Louisiana, but Blanco had to agree to spend $1 billion in state money to address the gap in Road Home funds. To make that $1 billion contribution, the LRA board reallocated $577 million in federal blocks grants to the Road Home for infrastructure repairs and cut funds to the rental housing program and infrastructure and economic development improvements.[57]

Money was not the Road Home's only problem. ICF International expected 6,000 calls per day when it set up its call centers, but received 32,000 in the first three days of operation. Within six days of opening the phone centers, the firm had to shut down its phones because the number of applicant callers was overwhelming its system. ICF employed too few operators at its call centers and not enough interviewers at its visitor centers. Its computer system broke down. In its first attempts to distribute money, ICF made mistakes in about one-quarter of the five thousand award letters it sent. In September 2007 a legislative audit revealed that one-third of the Road Home payments were inaccurate. ICF also provided inaccurate information about how to transfer grant awards.[58]

By early October 2006, ICF had distributed less than 1 percent of Road Home funds. By the end of February 2007, only 782 of the 108,751 Road Home applicants had received their final payments. Blanco referred to this process as "unacceptable" and "maddening."[59]

ICF verified each applicant's income and confirmed the benefits each participant received. It could not figure out, however, how to appraise homes or expedite appeals. The process for challenging an award became so cumbersome and long that many began to refer to it as "the black hole." Grant recipients waited a median of 238 days to get their Road Home money.[60]

The Louisiana House of Representatives passed a resolution, by a vote of 97–1, to demand that Blanco cancel ICF's contract. Representative Charmaine Marchand of New Orleans camped out on the capitol grounds to protest the performance of ICF and Governor Blanco. Other representatives from New Orleans, including Democrat J. P. Morrell and Republican Peppi Bruneau, condemned ICF. In Washington, U.S. Representative Maxine Waters called the Road Home "a joke." Blanco, however, refused to fire ICF and would not entertain Mayor Nagin's idea of allowing New Orleans to run its own Road Home program.[61]

Under pressure from the federal government and program applicants, the Road Home cut the number of verification steps to forty-two. In an attempt to eliminate the black hole effect, the LRA and OCD agreed to explain their decisions in writing. The Road Home hired ACORN Housing and Southeast Louisiana Legal Services to expedite applications and funding decisions. The state added performance measures and penalties for failure to meet them to ICF's contract.[62]

Some of the changes came as the result of pressure from the Citizens' Road Home Action Team (CHAT) and the Jeremiah Group (Jeremiah), a New Orleans faith-based community organization. A group of New Orleans professionals formed CHAT to condemn the Road Home process and suggest changes to the program. Jeremiah, an Industrial Areas Foundation affiliate which had existed in New Orleans since the late 1990s, assumed the role of Road Home watchdog in the post-Katrina period. CHAT recommended enabling homeowners to use post-storm appraisals in their application. Both CHAT and Jeremiah demanded a formal review of the Road Home process, and the LRA granted this request. The LRA added members of each group to its housing task force. After Jeremiah persuaded the LRA to reduce the amount of money it planned to cut from rental assistance, the LRA invited Jeremiah members to help it lobby Congress. In his assessment of CHAT's influence, the director of ICF's Road Home team said, "We've had a good dialogue, and we've been able to take some of their ideas and do them right away."[63]

In the middle of March 2007, HUD informed Governor Blanco that Louisiana's escrow account system violated federal regulations. HUD told Louisiana to eliminate the accounts and distribute the money in lump sums. Only applicants without mortgages had been receiving lump-sum payments. The Road Home switched to direct compensation to comply with HUD regulations. At the same time, Blanco announced that she would not seek reelection.[64]

On August 16, 2010, a federal judge ruled that the Road Home had discriminated against blacks when it used pre-storm home value as part of its post-storm award calculation, basing the grant on the lower of either pre-Katrina housing value or the cost of rebuilding after the storm. He ordered the OCD not to provide any more awards based on the pre-Katrina value of a home. Two fair housing organizations and five New Orleans homeowners had brought the suit on behalf of about twenty thousand black homeowners. The formula was found to be discriminatory because the cost of rebuilding turned out to be the same regardless of the neighborhood in which the homeowner lived. Consequently, wealthy, predominantly white homeowners received more Road Home funding than poor, predominantly black homeowners.[65]

Less than a year after this judgment, the OCD and the plaintiffs reached a compromise in which the state would distribute $62 million of its $100 million in surplus Road Home funds to 1,460 homeowners in Orleans, St. Bernard, Plaquemines, and Cameron parishes—the four hit hardest by hurricanes Katrina and Rita. These homeowners had already received Road Home money but needed more aid to rebuild their homes. An earlier study had also concluded that Road Home did not pay enough for people to rebuild their homes, especially if the property was located in a neighborhood with low housing values.[66]

Blight

Katrina exacerbated New Orleans' blight problem. The city was home to about 26,000 blighted properties before the storm; that number skyrocketed to approximately 50,000 afterward. Despite various post-Katrina programs and efforts, New Orleans had more blight than any other city in the country in 2008. One of every three properties was blighted in New Orleans; 30 percent of properties were blighted in Detroit, which finished just behind New Orleans in that category. Katrina explained a good portion of the city's problem, but blight, like other post-storm issues, had plagued New Orleans before August 29, 2005.[67]

Mayor-elect Mitch Landrieu promised to decrease blight in the city. In the time between his victory and the day he took office, Landrieu's task forces on housing and blight listened to residents' suggestions and heard that the city needed to address blight immediately. The task force was led by the senior vice president for programming at the Greater New Orleans Foundation and the executive director of Tulane's Public Law Center.[68]

When he outlined his anti-blight strategy, Landrieu told a predominantly black audience of one thousand at a New Orleans East church that he wanted to talk about race. Saying that the reaction to his decision to demolish hazardous and abandoned property was likely to be met by the charge, "Why don't you want the brothers and sisters to come home, Little Mr. Mitch, looking the way you do?" Landrieu asked his audience, "Is it about race, or is it about the city?" He referred to demolition as a tough issue that meant some people would not be returning to New Orleans. Landrieu then asked for "just a show of hands, how many people think that day is sooner rather than later for the city to start enforcing that? Because as soon as that door closes, people are going to say we don't want people to come back home."[69] The crowd demanded demolition as soon as Landrieu could deliver it.

Less than three months later at his budget address, Landrieu said: "I am putting owners of blighted property on notice: Get your property up to code because we are beginning strict code enforcement on Nov. 2. Enough is enough. Nov. 2 is the day."[70]

The Landrieu administration created BlightSTAT. A system similar to COMPSTAT, in which police use statistics to identify crime hot spots, BlightSTAT allows city government to locate blighted properties and track the progress it makes on these sites. BlightSTAT starts with a complaint about a property. After an inspection, the owners of the property in question receive a notice about ordinance or health code violations, and a hearing follows. At the hearing, owners can show that they have now complied with the code. If owners are found guilty of continuing to violate inspection codes, there are three final options: a sheriff's sale, demolition, or lot clearing. BlightSTAT tracks each of these steps. On a monthly basis, various city agencies report the Blight-STAT figures.[71]

When he announced his anti-blight strategy, Mayor Landrieu said that he wanted to decrease the total of 43,755 blighted properties in New Orleans by 10,000 by the end of 2013. The number of blighted buildings in New Orleans decreased from 34 percent of the city's homes in 2008 to 21 percent in 2012. In August 2012, the Greater New Orleans Data Center reported that New Orleans (21 percent) now ranked behind two Michigan cities, Flint (27 percent) and Detroit (24 percent), for the percentage of blighted properties in its housing stock. On January 9, 2014, the mayor announced that the city had reached its goal. An independent survey found that New Orleans had cut blight by 30 percent since Landrieu announced an aggressive anti-blight policy.[72]

The city's blight reduction strategy included stronger code enforcement capabilities, an assistance program for first-time homebuyers, demolition of property, collection of foreclosure liens, selling former Road Home properties, and more than $30 million in federal funds to reinvest in blighted neighborhoods. The city created over a dozen public, private, and nonprofit partners for the implementation of various elements of the city's anti-blight strategy. Harvard University's Ash Center for Democratic Governance and Innovation at the John F. Kennedy School of

Government gave a 2012 Bright Idea in Government award to the city of New Orleans for its anti-blight program.[73]

The Post-Katrina Political Arrangement for Housing

Public housing reform was already under way in New Orleans before disaster hit. After Katrina, HUD and HANO continued to use their authority to demolish and reconstruct the rest of the city's public housing complexes. The governing arrangement coalesced into a concentrated arrangement that exercised considerably stronger policy fidelity. Business interests and developers supported mixed-income public housing and commercial activity on the sites of former public housing complexes. Neither HUD, HANO, the city council, the mayor, the LRA, nor Congress rushed to get public housing residents back in their homes.

HUD and HANO enacted the demolition of public housing and the closing of public housing units. The city council approved demolition permits once HUD agreed to its terms. CDBG dollars and GO Zone tax credits paid for the reconstruction of the Big Four public housing projects. HUD, HANO, FEMA, and the state allocated money to redevelop the C. J. Peete complex. The federal government's Choice Neighborhood Initiative and low-income housing tax credits from the Louisiana Housing Corporation paid for the redevelopment of Iberville.

Governor Blanco used an executive order to enact the Road Home program. CDBG funds, Congress, and President Bush and "recovery czar" Donald Powell made certain that the LRA had enough money to execute the Road Home. A private company implemented the Road Home, and Louisiana's Office of Community Development monitored it. Federal regulations forced the governor and the state to change from incremental to lump sum payments. Federal judges allowed the city council to issue demolition permits, punished HANO and HRI for renting spaces reserved for former public housing tenants to employees of HANO, and changed the Road Home financial allocation process.

Developers won. They built on the sites of former public housing complexes. The city council waived property taxes for the developers of former public housing and scattered-site housing. Businesses won. HUD and HANO executed most of the housing policies that businesses had championed before the storm.

Residents of public housing could not return to their old homes because HUD and HANO closed or destroyed most of them and these governing entities would not guarantee one-for-one replacement. Former residents of the St. Thomas housing project lost when HANO and HRI rented apartments intended for them to management employees of HANO. Former public housing residents did secure at least one victory, however, when HANO and HUD ruled that nonprofits needed to provide services to them in the redeveloped housing at each of the former Big Four locations.

Black residents of New Orleans lost. Their property was most likely to be damaged by Katrina, they were most likely to be displaced because of changes to public housing, and the Road Home's funding process discriminated against them.

Local control lost in the post-Katrina era. Most of the decisions about housing were made by extra-local actors. In the implementation of the housing reconstruction, however, HANO and HUD allowed for and incorporated public and resident feedback. They provided concessions to organized groups and public housing residents, activists, and local clergy. To say that local actors were completely shut out of the housing reconstruction would be an exaggeration. But to say that public housing residents fared the worst in the post-Katrina era would not be hyperbole.

Homeowners won and renters lost in the post-Katrina era. The Road Home program applied to homeowners, not renters. The LRA cut funds to the rental housing program as well in order to provide additional funding to the Road Home.

Former and current public housing residents, their advocates, and some clergy wanted restoration of traditional public housing, the immediate reopening of the city's public housing stock, and the maintenance of garden-style housing. They fought HUD and HANO, which pursued a plan that included demolition of damaged complexes and the construction of mixed-income housing, scattered-site housing, and commercial activity on the site of former public housing complexes. Businesses and developers advocated these housing policy options.

In the case of the Road Home, the pre-Katrina fragmentation reemerged. Mayor Nagin wanted local control of the program, which Governor Blanco denied. The Louisiana House of Representatives asked Blanco to fire ICF; she did not. Governor Blanco and the LRA fought with FEMA over lump sum payments to Road Home recipients; FEMA won. Blanco and the state legislature disagreed over how to handle damaged properties. The legislature rejected Blanco's plan, which the governor carried out without legislative approval. This fragmentation prevented smooth implementation of the Road Home.

Public housing in post-Katrina New Orleans looks like the plans that were envisioned by businesses and developers. Mixed-income and scattered-site housing along with commercial development have replaced the old public housing complexes in the city. Public housing residents won some concessions in this period, but public housing policy does not reflect their preferences.

To summarize, HUD, FEMA, the LRA, Governor Blanco, the city council, the mayor, foundations, and business interests made housing policy decisions, set the agenda, and enacted housing policies after the storm. The political arrangement in post-Katrina New Orleans favored extra-local actors as well as businesses and developers. The pre-Katrina arrangement had been moving in that direction. The state government assumed a prominent position in the post-Katrina arrangement. The governor and the LRA dictated the terms of the Road Home, and Governor Blanco rejected Mayor Nagin's plea for local control over this housing assistance program. Some organized interests became part of the decision-making processes of several housing initiatives. One major change from the pre- to post-Katrina era was the incorporation of public input into housing decision making. Resident feedback became a central part of the process to redevelop the Big Four and manage the Road Home.

6

Public Safety or an Unsafe Public?

The head of any organization faced trouble when Mike Wallace, from CBS's *60 Minutes* came to investigate. Joseph Orticke, superintendent of the New Orleans Police Department (NOPD), found himself in that position in the fall of 1994. When Orticke said that New Orleans was "no different than any other major city in the United States," Wallace interrupted and said: "No different? If I may, no different except that you are number one—according to the Department of Justice, number one in the nation in police brutality."[1] Orticke agreed with Wallace and said, "We have a problem in the New Orleans Police Department."

Wallace heard eyewitness accounts of police brutality toward tourists and cabbies. In one instance, a local civil rights advocate told Wallace that three men had jumped into a cab and started to pistol whip the driver. When the passengers yelled for the police, the assailants said, "We are the police."

The NOPD's problems were not limited to police brutality. A former member of the NOPD told Wallace that he had made close to $100,000 a year by robbing banks, extorting drug dealers, looting, and protecting illegal gambling while he was on the force. When Wallace told him that he sounded more like a gangster than a police officer, the bank-robbing ex-cop asked, "What's the big deal?" and said that his actions were just part of being a cop. To which Wallace asked, "In New Orleans?" Wallace's report ended with the former officer's answer: "Yes."

The police department has embodied the racial division that characterized New Orleans over time. The city has a history of police brutality against blacks, and to varying degrees, the department has never been able to shake this reputation, as instances of racially motivated police brutality dot New Orleans's history. One example of the racial tensions associated with the NOPD occurred in 1980, when a white officer, Gregory Neupert, was killed at a housing project where he uncovered a drug deal. In the course of investigating Neupert's murder, police officers killed four African Americans. These murders led to protests by blacks and the resignation of the superintendent of the NOPD. All members of the department were cleared of murder charges, but three were convicted for violating the civil rights of suspects, some of whom they had beaten or illegally jailed in order to obtain information about the Neupert murder.[2]

Blacks have also faced discrimination within the department. The NOPD hired its first black officer in 1950. In 1980, when African Americans made up a plurality of the city's residents, they constituted less than 2 percent of the police force. In 1987 the NOPD entered into a consent decree, agreeing to end practices that discriminated against African Americans in both hiring and promotion.[3]

The previous chapters afforded an opportunity to take stock of the policy arena both before and after Katrina. When the storm struck and the city flooded, residents left their homes, and schools and businesses closed. Policing is different; the NOPD continued to provide services throughout the disaster, never having the opportunity to reset afterward, as the other policy areas did.

Reforming Policing in Pre-Katrina New Orleans

Marc Morial—along with all of the other candidates for mayor in New Orleans in 1994—ran on a public safety and police reform platform. He referred to the NOPD as a "completely dysfunctional agency."[4] Four years later, Morial said, "We had the three towers of dysfunction: crime and corruption and brutality. Other cities, like New York, maybe had a crime problem, or they had a brutality problem, or they had a corruption problem. They didn't have all three at the same time."[5]

Unimpressed with the results of a national search for a new superintendent of police, Morial followed a friend's suggestion and turned to a D.C. assistant chief of police who was credited with reforming that department. After he appointed Richard Pennington, Morial did not interfere with his superintendent, but he supported the NOPD before the city council when necessary.[6]

On October 13, 1994, the day Pennington was sworn in as superintendent of the NOPD, the FBI informed him that Len Davis, a member of the force who had been under surveillance for running a cop-led cocaine ring, had just ordered a hit on Kim Groves, a woman who had reported to NOPD internal affairs that she had seen Davis pistol-whip a teenager less than twenty-four hours earlier. An FBI tape recording revealed that Davis had ordered the hit and gloated after the hit man indicated he had killed Groves. The FBI investigation into the Davis cocaine operation resulted in the conviction of eleven officers who worked with and for drug dealers.[7]

The FBI also briefed Pennington on an armed robbery case. On March 5, 1995, NOPD officer Antoinette Frank and her boyfriend robbed a Vietnamese restaurant in New Orleans East and murdered two owners and the off-duty cop hired to guard the place. Frank and the off-duty officer had partnered on occasion. Frank returned to the restaurant later under the guise of responding to a call on the police radio. As Frank walked into the restaurant, employees who had hidden during the robbery identified her as the murderer; Frank was taken to the police station, was later convicted, and now sits on death row in the state of Louisiana. It was against this backdrop that Pennington began his mission to reform the New Orleans Police Department.[8]

According to Pennington, the NOPD suffered from the city's status as the murder capital of the nation, as well as gang violence and corruption within the department. In 1994 New Orleans set a city record for murders with 421. Despite the murder rate, Pennington's immediate concern was to clean up the NOPD.[9]

Five years after he took over, about one-third of the officers who had been there when Pennington began were gone. Eighty-five of those officers had been arrested, one hundred were fired, two hundred left during or after being disciplined, and the rest retired. Pennington closed the department's internal affairs office and created a unit called the Public Integrity Division (PID), which monitored police activity and investigated complaints. The PID included two FBI special agents. In addition, Pennington instituted an early warning system, designed to identify potential problem officers before their behavior became egregious.[10]

Pennington capped off-duty hours at twenty per week, decentralized the department's 250 detectives, and, on the advice of consultants from

New York City, implemented COMPSTAT, a management and account-ability tool that uses a computer system to identify hot spots of crime. He then created substations in crime hot spots. According to Jack Maple, who designed the system in New York and brought it to New Orleans: "Where all the dots on the map are, that's where you send the cops. You go get the scumbags."[11]

Pennington helped create important partnerships when he asked local businesses to get involved in public safety. At Pennington's suggestion, forty local business leaders created the New Orleans Police Foundation (NOPF), a nonprofit organization that advocates for the NOPD and provides financial resources so that the department can accomplish its goals. By 1998, one hundred companies had contributed a total of $1.5 million a year to the foundation. By 2002, the New Orleans Police Foundation employed seven and had a twenty-three-member board. Terry Ebbert, NOPF's executive director, explained their goal: "We're trying to bring a business approach to policing, that you've got to maintain and train people. The only difference is, in business you want to make money. Here, you want to reduce the total crimes committed. This is something the business community understands."[12]

The New Orleans Police Foundation paid for consultants from New York to advise the NOPD on how to replicate that city's success in crime reduction and police reform. It funded a $400,000 advertising campaign to recruit officers and improve relations with the public. The foundation also secured hundreds of thousands of dollars in grant money to, among other things, communicate details of a federal program designed to reduce violent crime, contribute to the Community Oriented Police Services for Kids Program, and integrate law enforcement technology and information sharing.[13]

Along with Morial and Pennington, the foundation made up a new arrangement that governed policing in New Orleans. It helped frame the policing problem in New Orleans. Foundation leaders linked crime and the image of police to economic development. They believed that increasing crime and NOPD's poor reputation for public safety was hurting tourism. As policy entrepreneurs, they advocated increased pay for police, a larger force, and more promotions. For the most part, the foundation got its wishes granted any time it lobbied the city council and the mayor. Pennington and the Police Foundation argued that low salaries contributed to corruption. After they lobbied for action, police salaries increased by 53 percent during the first three years after the creation of the NOPF. In a two-year span, the NOPD hired 500 police officers, increasing the force at one point from 1,250 officers to 1,700. The city council approved $1.4 million for 645 promotions two months after an NOPF report criticized the lack of promotions.[14]

By most accounts, the new political arrangement produced a safer New Orleans. Two years after the city set a local record for murders with 421, the number of murders was down by 70. From 1994 to 1997, homicides decreased by 40 percent. In seven years, the murder rate dropped by 62 percent. In 1998, the police closed 78 percent of their cases. The positive trends subsided over time. Soon after Pennington ran for mayor in 2002 and lost to Nagin in the runoff, Atlanta hired him as its police chief. That year, homicides had increased by 22 percent in New Orleans. The next, New Orleans was once again the murder capital of the nation. The 275 murders in 2003 were the most in the city since 1996. Complaints about the use of excessive force by the police also increased after Pennington left.[15]

While effective during his tenure, Pennington failed to institutionalize reform at the NOPD. His successes in dealing with corruption, brutality, and overall public safety came during an era when crime was decreasing across the nation. The inability to make reforms stick left the door open for a return to the NOPD's old ways.

Policing Hurricane Katrina

During the immediate response to Hurricane Katrina, the three other areas on which we have focused—housing, economic development, and public education—temporarily shut down. Policing could not. The NOPD needed to maintain order and coordinate rescue operations. The actions of its officers during the crisis became an important part of the fabric of the department.

Amidst the aftermath of the storm and the flooding, the NOPD faced problems with communications, coordination, resources, and mission priorities. Deficiencies in any one of these areas would pose serious problems for just about any police department. The combination of all of them at once produced a policing disaster.

The NOPD lost communication capacity as the floodwaters rose in the city. The transmission tower lost power, and without the tower, radios could not function. The police did not have satellite phones, and while random telephone lines and cellular phones provided intermittent communication, they could not replace the department's radio system.

A command and control police department, used to instant responses from its officers, found itself incapable of communicating, rendering the chain of command useless in many situations. Instead, the department relied on small groups of officers, working blindly, to address the impact of the storm. Technology, or rather the failure of technology, made itself strongly felt.

Another problem with communications came with the arrival of other public safety agencies. Police departments that sent volunteers to New Orleans provided those officers with their own department radios, most of which did not match the frequencies employed by the NOPD. When communications eventually came back online, Assistant Superintendent Warren Riley told an interviewer, "We have moved from chaos to organized chaos and now we are better organized."[16]

The first priority of law enforcement is the provision of public safety. To that end, the NOPD immediately started search and rescue missions. Along with the Coast Guard and volunteer armadas, the department used available resources to search for survivors of the storm. In some instances, those who needed rescue included officers. "'This was the ultimate enemy,' Riley said of the flooding. 'What do you do when the enemy has cut off your supply routes, your food, your water and puts you in a situation where your rescuers had to be rescued? Nothing prepares you for this.'"[17]

The Superdome, which housed 35,000 city residents, and the Convention Center, holding 20,000 more, presented another challenge for the NOPD. Neither site prepared very well for the catastrophe, and while the Superdome offered some medical care, when it lost electricity, many life-saving devices no longer operated. This also left the shelter seekers without provisions. Additionally, citizens at the two sites were told repeatedly throughout the week that buses would arrive to take them away, but without result, making it difficult to maintain order. The media reported serious criminal activity at the two sites, reports spurred on by comments from both Mayor Nagin and Police Superintendent Eddie Compass. Many of the reports of atrocities turned out to be false, but they reinforced the image of a city out of control. Indeed, as more carefully researched studies on Katrina have reached publication, the more stunning fact may be the relative lack of violence perpetrated by those housed at the two sites. Some authors found that the police and National Guard preserved that order.[18]

As people began to venture from their homes and shelters, another issue, looting, rose to the forefront. The looting posed a problem for the department, but also, in some instances, it included the department. Some of the police looting mirrored that of citizens in need, as police officers took vital supplies such as food and water. Other officers, however, participated in looting of a different variety, seizing high-end electronics, jewelry, and hundreds of vehicles from a Cadillac dealership. Those officers involved in looting contributed heavily to the worsening reputation of the NOPD.[19]

Initial reports indicated that one-third of the police force deserted during Katrina. That number dropped over time, as police officials better accounted for officers who had been unable to contact their precincts because of the communication disruptions.[20] Still, between looting and desertion, the NOPD suffered a blow to its reputation. Various news accounts heralded the actions of individual officers, but for the department as a whole, the immediate response to Katrina could at best be characterized as problematic.

The department was also reeling from the loss of two of their own through suicide. One of the officers killed himself in the midst of fellow officers, reportedly distraught over officer looting and desertion.[21] The department's public information officer drove out of town to commit suicide.

Just like everyone else in the city, officers worried about their families and homes. Staying on the job meant putting aside other responsibilities, and for some of the deserters, the task proved impossible. One NOPD commander used the words "psychologically devastating" to describe the effect of Katrina on the city's police officers.[22] The officers became exhausted after working around the clock. Nagin recognized the need for officer relief. In the words of a news account, "The officers had been under incredible pressure: long hours, impossible communications, little food, some shot at and finding bodies they had no means to recover."[23]

The department's leader, Eddie Compass, came under serious criticism as the crisis continued. At first, in some media reports, including CBS's *60 Minutes*, Compass received praise as a compassionate leader, one who joined in the efforts and supported his force. That coverage waned when some of Compass's public comments, most notably his seemingly unstable appearance on *Oprah* where he spoke of babies being raped, proved untrue. A clearer picture of Compass started to emerge, one that included stories about his absence from the city during part of the emergency. That did not bode well for the commander of a department in which many other officers abandoned their posts.

New Orleans waited a long time for a federal response to Hurricane Katrina. Many scholars have criticized the slow response time and the lack of coordination in the disaster response.[24] The White House wanted Governor Blanco to sign her power over National Guard troops to the federal government. Blanco, sensing that such an agreement was meant to target a Democratic governor in the Republican South, never signed the document. Governor Haley Barbour of Mississippi, a Republican, would federalize his troops, but he was never asked to sign or approve an agreement.

On Thursday, September 1, Nagin made an appearance on WWL radio with host Garland Robinette, who remained on the air throughout much of the disaster. The mayor argued against further press conferences by public officials until outside help arrived in New Orleans. In a speech laced with profanity, Nagin blasted federal officials. The appearance brought increased attention to the plight of New Orleanians while at the same time causing some to question the stability of the mayor. The *Times-Picayune* ran an editorial that began with the words "New Orleans needs a show of force. Now."[25] By week's end, thousands of troops were providing security across the city and engaging in search and rescue missions. They accomplished a lot of good during this period, leaving open the question of how much more they could have achieved if they had arrived in the city earlier.

About 240 police officers went missing during Hurricane Katrina. After the storm, sixty-two officers resigned, forty-six abandoned the force never to return, eighteen left while under investigation, eleven were fired for neglect, and another eleven retired; three died during Katrina, including the two who committed suicide. In response to the number of officers who did not show up for duty or left their posts never to return, Superintendent Compass expressed his opinion of them bluntly: "I've called individuals who have shirked their responsibility and duty cowards. . . . Not only are they cowards, they're less than a coward."[26]

Some members of the NOPD—and Superintendent Compass himself—added to the chaos in the aftermath of Katrina. MSNBC cameras caught four NOPD officers taking clothing and other items from a New Orleans WalMart. When asked by a reporter what she was doing, an officer responded, "Looking for looters," and stormed away.[27] The NOPD cleared the officers of stealing because, it announced, all four "had received permission from their commanders to get clothing for fellow officers who were soaking wet. They did not steal anything." The NOPD did suspend the officers for ten days each for not trying to stop others from looting the store. The officer who gave the terse response to MSNBC received an additional three-day suspension for her "discourteous" answer.

About forty officers even went so far as to steal cars from a Cadillac dealership in Metairie. The officers—and the department for that matter—claimed that the officers took the cars, many of which were the popular Escalade, to patrol the streets. Jed Horne disputes this claim in *Breach of Faith*, stating that instead, many officers used the cars to abandon their posts and leave the city.[28]

Some evacuees attempted to take Superintendent Compass hostage at the convention center in the belief that he could get them out of New Orleans. Compass's security team, which consisted of three members of the NOPD and two from the National Guard, fought off the assailants, whom Compass identified as a group of about fifteen "gangsters from the city . . . [who] command the street crimes."[29] Ed Bradley of CBS asked Compass if he had ever thought that things would get to that point. Compass replied, "No one in the world could ever imagine it would get to that."[30]

Compass stepped down as superintendent of police a month after Katrina. He claimed he was forced out when reports surfaced that he had fabricated stories about rapes and murders in the Superdome during and after the hurricane, though he also said he would take the reasons for his resignation "to my grave. I was trying to be helpful, and they tried to make it look like I was embellishing."[31]

The NOPD and NOPF tried to put the spotlight on the 1,200 officers who'd stayed in New Orleans and saved thousands. Warren Riley, who took over for Compass as superintendent of police, stated that as many as eighty members of the force who failed to show up for duty had been trapped on rooftops or in their attics,[32] some for as much as three or four days. Riley particularly wanted people to know about this because the media had made it seem as if all the officers who were not on duty had abandoned their posts. Furthermore, owing to the lack of radio communication, some officers were on duty and helping the public even though they were not in their assigned areas of the city. Ultimately, Hurricane Katrina left 80 percent of NOPD officers without a home.

In the end, 239 officers were disciplined for desertion, with their punishments ranging from suspension and demotion to being fired from the force. An internal investigation revealed that the four officers who had been filmed by the MSNBC crew had in fact been gathering appropriate clothing and supplies, and did so at the behest of a supervisor.

Policing in the Post-Katrina Era

The calm that existed during the concluding months of 2005 resulted from the significant depopulation of the city. Once citizens began to return, the crime rate rose.

By year's end, an examination of violent crime found that the numbers were half what the city had experienced in 2005, but since New Orleans now had less than half its previous population, the crime rate had actually risen during 2006.

As residents returned and the city's population continued to grow, in 2007 New Orleans was once again the "murder capital" of the United States (see table 15). That distinction accompanied increases in all types of crime in the city. By the end of 2008, crime appeared to be headed downward, but the crime rate still outpaced that of most of the rest of

TABLE 15
Violent crime rates and homicide rates: U.S. and New Orleans, 2000–2012

	Violent crime		Homicide	
	U.S.	New Orleans	U.S.	New Orleans
2000	506.5	1063.6	5.5	42.1
2001	504.5	1213.5	5.6	44.0
2002	494.4	937.1	5.6	53.1
2003	475.8	967.3	5.7	57.7
2004	463.2	948.3	5.5	56.0
2005	469.0	*	5.6	*
2006	479.3	523.0	5.8	37.6
2007	471.8	1564.3	5.7	94.7
2008	458.6	1019.4	5.4	63.6
2009	431.9	777.0	5.0	51.7
2010	404.5	754.2	4.8	50.9
2011	387.1	792.0	4.7	57.6
2012	386.9	815.2	4.7	53.2

Source: Federal Bureau of Investigation, Uniform Crime Reports.
* No data reported for New Orleans in 2005. All rates are per 100,000 residents.

the country. And in 2009, the city's homicide rate again sat atop the FBI's annual Uniform Crime Report. At almost fifty-two murders per 100,000 residents, New Orleans produced a murder rate higher than in St. Louis, Detroit, or Baltimore.

In 2010 the violent crime rate dipped to its lowest point since 2006, but it was still almost double the rate for the nation as a whole, and the homicide rate continued to be more than ten times the national average. This pattern was to persist throughout the next two years, leaving citizens of the city wary of violent crime, and much more susceptible to homicide than their fellow citizens elsewhere in the country.

In order to help the NOPD with the increase in crime in 2006, Governor Blanco sent in the National Guard in June of that year. Guard troops were armed, and were authorized to shoot and to make arrests, although they were discouraged from doing so. (Given the uncertainty of the length of their deployment, they might not be around for the criminal proceedings.) The NOPD and the Guard worked out procedures so that the police department ran investigations on serious cases, but the influx of the Guard troops had an immediate impact on the city's criminal justice system. Arrests quickly rose, and hot spots could again be targeted by the department. In addition to the National Guard, fifty state troopers were assigned to New Orleans.[33]

Despite the additional personnel, the NOPD could do little to stem crime. Certainly the department faced vast challenges, as district station houses and headquarters required rebuilding, and the reconstituted patrol fleet was composed in large part of donated out-of-service vehicles from police agencies across the country. With a much smaller population, however, the NOPD had a significant edge in police strength (the ratio of police to citizens in a jurisdiction), yet Superintendent Riley seemed unable to deploy those officers in a way that reduced crime.

One frequent question was how long the Guard would stay in the city. Blanco would call for the removal of the Guard at six-month intervals, only to extend their stay. Her successor, Governor Jindal, followed in Blanco's footsteps, keeping the Guard in place after he assumed office. Finally, in late February 2009, the Guard made its last patrol of the city and turned over all police functions to the NOPD.[34] In this instance, although intergovernmental relations had led to the allocation of extra resources, those resources remained under the direction of the NOPD, removing any possibility of cross-fertilization of ideas or strategies.

Reflecting on the decline in the total number of murders in 2008, Riley noted, "Certainly this is not a victory; there is no celebration."[35] As if to emphasize the fact that the victory had not yet been won, 2009 began with three firearms murders on New Year's Day.[36]

An analysis of murders in post-Katrina New Orleans indicated that approximately half of them were committed during daytime hours, an unusual occurrence for homicide. This indicated to the department that many of these murders could be considered executions. Describing these crimes as a "tide of violence," a *Times-Picayune* editorial went on to compare the failures and excuses presented by the NOPD with the successes that had occurred in the schools and the ability of the city to generate recovery funds for the reconstruction of New Orleans.[37]

Riley's successor, Ronal Serpas, who served as superintendent from May 2010 to August 2014, was disturbed by the continued high rate of homicides in the city, a rate that ran ten times higher than in the rest of the country. The U.S. Bureau of Justice Assistance compiled two reports on the city's homicide problem. The first found that the murders were occurring in concentrated areas of the city, that they predominantly involved black males, and that almost three-quarters of the murder victims had a criminal history. The second concluded that the NOPD was understaffed and relied on out-of-date training practices and technologies. On the basis of the second report, Serpas sent a request to the city council to secure additional resources for the homicide unit.[38]

Six months later, homicides continued to perplex the NOPD, which could not determine any significant patterns or develop suspects. Contrary to the finding from the Bureau of Justice Assistance report on homicide victims, many of the victims from the latter half of 2011 did not have criminal histories.[39]

Although the homicide rate decreased from 2010 to 2011, in absolute numbers more people were the victims of homicide in 2011. As part of the strategy for handling the city's violent crime problem, the federal government agreed to increase the activity of both the Bureau of Alcohol, Tobacco, and Firearms and the Drug Enforcement Administration in New Orleans. This was a direct result of requests from Mayor Landrieu to U.S. Attorney General Eric Holder.[40]

When asked by members of the city council in 2012 whether additional officers could guarantee a decrease in the homicide rate, Superintendent Serpas answered, "I don't think anybody could tell you that."[41] Serpas indicated that deep-seated societal problems were mostly to blame for the city's high homicide rate, and that until those issues of poverty, disadvantage, and failing public education were solved, the homicide rate would continue to be a serious issue. One black leader agreed with Serpas, saying, "We cannot police our way out of the problems we have." Serpas nevertheless requested from the city council an increase of more than 400 officers in order to grow the force to more than 1,700.

One of the final issues concerning crime in the city relates to the measurement of crime. For decades the FBI has compiled the Uniform Crime Reports, but the figures in those reports are subject to the truthfulness of the reporting law enforcement agencies. Pointing to these FBI reports, Superintendent Serpas in 2013, noted that aside from murder, the city of New Orleans was a very safe place to visit. This assertion was clearly related to the importance of tourism in the local economy. The fact is, however, that other types of violent crime, such as aggravated assault or serious sexual assault, are open to a greater degree of miscategorization. To say that the city is safe, with the exception of murder, fails to take into account the reality that the police department may downgrade certain crimes, for example, reducing incidents of aggravated assault to the category of simple assault. In fact, an internal NOPD audit revealed the downgrading of numerous types of crimes, from rape to assault, leading some to questions the city's violent crime statistics.[42]

A Myriad of Strategies

Throughout the post-Katrina era, the NOPD oscillated between enforcement tactics and community-friendly strategies. In early 2011 the department said it would increase traffic stops for targeted enforcement. Later that year it suggested that its plan was to increase community policing skills. The department began to utilize external experts, such as George Capowich of Loyola University New Orleans, in the generation of hot spots and targeted policing.[43]

But some of the aggressive policing tactics, especially those that appeared to emulate NYPD's stop-and-frisk policy, raised questions about racial profiling. Superintendent Serpas indicated that the data generated from traffic stops across the city was helping to build a critical database for use in the solving of crimes. This stop-and-frisk policy led to a meeting between Mayor Landrieu and local NAACP leader Danatus King to discuss the larger issue of racial profiling.[44]

The NOPD did make large numbers of arrests throughout the post-Katrina period, but the nature of those arrests, and the results of those arrests, caused some to question the street-level tactics of the department. Groups such as the Metropolitan Crime Commission criticized NOPD efforts to stem both violent crimes and property crimes. In report after report, the commission's leadership chastised the NOPD for focusing far too heavily on misdemeanors and for its poor investigation of serious felonies. The effect of the large number of misdemeanor arrests was to drive the department's arrest statistics to a high level while masking its low levels of success against the most serious violent crimes. The insufficient attention paid to felony arrests would, in many instances, lead to very low conviction rates for those serious crimes. After several years of Metropolitan Crime Commission reports, the NOPD appeared to be taking the criticism to heart, but the practice of encouraging arrests, especially for misdemeanors, was a key example of the ineffective tactics employed by the NOPD in the post-Katrina era.[45]

Since Katrina, NOPD officers have faced numerous allegations, as well as a plethora of convictions for corrupt or brutal behavior. As the NOPD attempted to build bridges within neighborhoods, the reputation of the police remained one of lawlessness and corruption. Even as the department was dealing with officers charged with crimes and departmental violations during Katrina, some of the first incidents of misconduct began to come to light. In the early months of 2006, one New Orleans police officer was indicted on a rape charge and two others were arrested, one for theft and one in a beating case. Residents, especially minorities, complained that they were subjected to abuses such as strip searches in public and unnecessary use of force. A videotaped incident that occurred in the French Quarter in late 2005 led to the indictment of three police officers on charges of beating a retired schoolteacher and assaulting an AP news producer.[46]

After a police officer's wife claimed that three NOPD officers had beaten her, the city council renewed calls for an independent monitor for the police department. The idea, initially proposed in 2002, would have created an independent monitor to investigate misdeeds by the department without being a part of the department.[47]

In succeeding years, the problems continued. In 2007, a lawyer for ACORN claimed he had been handcuffed and beaten by two officers in the French Quarter. The NAACP demanded an investigation into the incident. Though the officers denied the account, they were reassigned

while the case was being investigated. Other incidents that year included
an officer being charged with incest, another entering a guilty plea for
shaking down suspects he arrested, officers fired for brutality and fight-
ing in a bar, and an officer arrested for a high-speed chase on the Lake
Pontchartrain Causeway. In 2008 an NOPD officer was accused of using
text messages to warn drug dealers of surveillance. The district attorney's
office was forced to drop charges in thirty-seven drug offense cases when
the arresting officer was himself arrested.[48]

In the latter half of 2010, three New Orleans police officers were
convicted of committing and covering up a murder; two other police
officer defendants were acquitted. Throughout 2011–12, and during the
first half of 2013, the department continued to suspend or fire officers
accused of misconduct. Money was found to be missing from the department property division. An officer was accused of being a predatory sex
offender. Multiple officers were involved in an investigation of a brawl
at a second line party. And several officers in multiple trials were found
guilty of assault and murder.[49]

The most significant event relating to the police department in
post-Katrina New Orleans was the Danziger Bridge affair. On September
4, 2005, just days after Katrina struck, New Orleans police officers went
to the bridge in response to a call for officer assistance, with an indication
that an officer had been injured. The responding police noted in their
reports that as they arrived in a rental truck, they were taking fire from
civilians. At that point the officers opened fire, wounding four and killing
two. Months later, seven of the officers were indicted at the state level
for the shootings. Later, however, the internal investigation conducted
by the NOPD was found to be severely lacking in key evidence, leading
prosecutors eventually to drop the state-level charges.[50]

In October 2008, the Department of Justice opened an investigation
into the shootings on the Danziger Bridge. According to FBI agents, the
accounts given by the officers involved in the shooting did not match, and
significant information appeared to be missing from the official reports.
After a lengthy trial, jurors determined that the officers had violated the
civil rights of the civilians on the bridge, leading to the conviction of
the officers. At a pre-sentencing hearing, the judge delivered a pointed
editorial on the conduct of the prosecution during the case, and also laid
the blame for the incident at the feet of the NOPD leadership. And the
case did not end there. In September 2013 the judge granted a defense
motion for a new trial on the grounds of prosecutorial misconduct. At

this writing the most pivotal case in the post-Katrina history of the city remains unresolved.[51]

It should be clear at this point that the post-Katrina NOPD had fully reverted to its pre-Pennington behavior. While every U.S. police department has its corrupt or brutal officers, this litany of offenses far outpaces the experience of the typical city. What could New Orleans do to stem the double-headed issue of crime and police misconduct? It appeared that the strongest possibility was to mimic the policy arenas of housing and education by looking to those outside the city for assistance. Thus the Department of Justice began a lengthy review in anticipation of a consent decree, with an eye toward cleaning up the mess that was the NOPD.

The early conversations between Mayor Landrieu and Attorney General Holder, which led to the Bureau of Justice Assistance reports on the NOPD, started the dialogue. Those initial discussions later led Landrieu and Holder to agree to a far more detailed Justice Department investigation of the NOPD, with an eye toward crafting a federal consent decree for the operation of the department. In July 2012 the details of the federal investigation and the draft of a consent decree were made public. Holder and Landrieu held a joint press conference to announce the 492-point plan, which would be enforced by the federal courts. The aim of the decree was the full overhaul of the New Orleans Police Department. This would include significant changes to many of the policies and practices it employed. There would be a cost for implementing the decree, initially estimated to be $11 million per year.[52]

The decree was welcomed by Superintendent Serpas and received praise from the community. The *Times-Picayune* called it a "blueprint for police reform." The Fraternal Order of Police, which did not have input during the crafting of the decree, wanted to be able to weigh in on the agreement. A federal judge quickly ruled against the police union. But the union's initial negative reaction to the decree would soon be shared by city officials. An additional question was the future role of the police monitor, with some suggesting that the decree, and federal court oversight, would remove the need for a separate, independent police monitor.[53]

Six months after the joint announcement with Attorney General Holder, Mayor Landrieu indicated that he was having second thoughts about the decree. His concerns were financial; implementing the decree would cost more than the city could afford. With that in mind, the mayor's office filed an appeal in the federal courts to postpone implementation of the decree, in the hope of modifying the agreement. The Justice

Department, which had worked closely with Landrieu during the crafting of the decree, opposed the mayor's decision. A federal judge ruled against Landrieu's motion, and the Justice Department claimed that the mayor had acted in bad faith.[54]

Landrieu's new position was that the city did not need the consent decree, and that the department was already well on its way to reform. But at the same time, a number of consulting firms were beginning to prepare their bids for the contract to monitor the consent decree. Tied to the reforms listed in the agreement was the long-standing issue of off-duty work among NOPD officers. As Landrieu and the Department of Justice continued submitting filings in federal court over the consent decree, city council considered a bill that would overhaul the off-duty detail program. As the city moved closer to finalizing new rules for paid details, the police union again filed a challenge to the changes in off-duty employment. This left both the consent decree and the closely related work detail issues unresolved.[55] Eventually, the federal government moved ahead with the implementation of the consent decree, with police officials providing regular updates to the federal monitor and a federal judge.

A consent decree is a major undertaking for any police department. But in most instances, the parties that requested the consent decree do not attempt to back out of the agreement. Mayor Landrieu had the opportunity to begin the reform process for the NOPD but moved slowly. In October 2014, Landrieu appointed Michael S. Harrison as superintendent, and Harrison began restructuring the department in response to consent decree requirements. While city residents awaited meaningful change in the realm of policing, the city's inspector general reported in November 2014 that hundreds of sex crime cases had been mishandled over several years, leaving yet another impression of dysfunction at the NOPD.[56]

The Post-Katrina Political Arrangement for Policing

In New Orleans, the closed arena of public safety policy has been overseen by a very small group of actors. The mayor and police superintendent remained the prominent agenda setters and enactors of policing policies. A concentrated governing arrangement has exercised strong policy fidelity, but as with the strong and concentrated arrangement in pre-Katrina public education, the policies have been ineffective. Others who were not heard, at least in any meaningful way, included neighborhood groups, religious groups, the business community, external critics (such as the Metropolitan Crime Commission), the city council, and the citizens of the city. During the political era of policing, from roughly the 1840s to the 1920s, external actors (especially political machines) used the police to do their bidding. As a result, the larger reform movement in the United States called for, and won, a stricter separation of the police from local politics. The result was the disconnection of police from many local controls, which led to police chiefs across the country gaining significant increases of internal authority.

After Katrina, the only actors with regular, sustained, and meaningful oversight of the NOPD were the mayor and the police superintendent. But neither mayors Nagin and Landrieu nor police superintendents Riley and Serpas could control the officers or policies of the NOPD. Both superintendents left office with meager claims of reform, and Serpas's departure came just days after he issued a public apology for a police shooting.[57] Countless shifts in policy, numerous scandals, and attempts at additional controls have all failed to reform the NOPD. In some ways the question of policy enactment in the public safety arena is moot, but the failure to implement policy rests at the feet of the post-Katrina mayors and superintendents.

There was a time, under Richard Pennington, when the Police Foundation played a critical role in modernizing the department. The foundation brought consultants in to assist the NOPD in implementing the COMPSTAT management model and improved the quality of life for officers by lobbying for pay increases and promotions. In the post-Katrina era, the Metropolitan Crime Commission tried to serve as a voice for the citizenry in the area of public safety, but the lack of unified political allies, and of significant resources, blunted the effect of the commission.

The strategic policy option choices for the NOPD were fairly basic, especially in contrast to the myriad choices available in economic development, public education, and housing. First, the NOPD was required to rebuild its personnel and physical infrastructure. Beyond those immediate and pressing concerns, the choice was essentially whether to continue operating the department as it was under Eddie Compass or to attempt to reinstitute reforms enacted under Pennington. The reform efforts of the past were hard-fought battles, and they occurred at a time when the city was not facing the massive challenges of rebuilding. Continuing in its most recent form was the easiest path for the NOPD to follow, especially in light of the fact that the mayor did not have the ability to turn his full focus on the department, leaving the management of the police to the chief.

External groups like the Metropolitan Crime Commission and the Vera Institute lobbied for the reform route.[58] They wanted to see modern policing tactics employed by an upstanding, corruption-free department. With the exception of the National Guard patrols—and even they came under the command of the NOPD—no external actors provided resources to effect such change. Outsiders rushed in to transform New Orleans's public schools, but no such corollary existed for public safety.

The New Orleans Police Department was corrupt, brutal, and ineffective before the storm. The arrival of Pennington, and the reforms that he initiated, led to temporary improvements in the department. He won substantial pay raises for officers, making corrupt practices less tempting. Pennington weeded out many of the worst officers and created programs, like the early warning system, to detect bad behavior. He invited experts, such as New York's Jack Maple, to design and implement new tactics and technology. The department benefited, too, from the nationwide decrease in crime.

Pennington's departure for Atlanta, and the subsequent promotion of Compass to superintendent, put the department in a position to revert to form. The role of local culture is critical in understanding why corruption occurs in some departments and not others, and is also important for explaining why corruption may be more acceptable in some jurisdictions. New Orleans, located in the state that produced Huey Long, Edwin Edwards, and William Jefferson, among many others, has a long-standing tradition and culture of both corruption and toleration of corruption. The city and state have come to typify what Martin Shefter termed "rapacious individualism," leading to acceptance of corrupt behavior.[59]

This deeply embedded culture, one that accepts corruption, blocked Pennington's attempts to institutionalize his reforms sufficiently. As long as he ran the NOPD, he could personally account for the misdeeds of his officers and deal with them swiftly. But once he left, regression to the old ways quickly occurred. Instead of embarking on the lengthy and difficult course of reform, Warren Riley chose to tinker in a piecemeal fashion. He regularly rolled out media-friendly programs that were more public relations than substance.

There are easily identifiable losers in the failure to produce adequate public safety in New Orleans. Certainly the citizens of the city suffer. They cannot depend on the police to be effective at their work, nor can they count on them to be fair, honest, and lawful. But the public at large is not the only group that is injured; those officers who are fair, honest, and lawful suffer as well. William K. Muir reminds us that the practice of law enforcement puts the police officer's soul at risk.[60] Officers' moral framework is a product of both their personal development and their organization, and when an organization such as the NOPD incubates corruption and brutality, it is the officers who suffer.

So, unlike in the other policy areas, there really are no winners in the realm of public safety. One could surmise that the mayor and police chief are nominal winners, in that they remained the sole decision makers in the policy arena; but with the dismal record of the NOPD, winning is not really winning. Instead, the city is left with a broken public safety policy, whereby everyone loses.

Under Pennington, the department and the city were divided between reformers and champions of the status quo. The tight span of control in policing, the backing of the mayor, and the support of the Police Foundation provided Pennington with the tools and resources he needed to effect change in the NOPD, but only temporarily. Those who remained patient during the Pennington years, and who were eager for a return to the old NOPD, had only to wait until Pennington moved on from his post. As his hard-won reforms melted away under the Nagin-Compass regime, those who supported the institutionalization of reforms saw that hope slip away.

Another key division in public safety policy in New Orleans exists between the police and the public. In the early nineteenth century, Sir Robert Peel, the father of modern policing, emphasized the interconnectedness among all residents of the city, but his adage "the police are the public, and the public are the police" fails to capture the New Orleans experience. The poor, minorities, and even tourists express fear of the NOPD. And with good reason. Officers have repeatedly engaged in brutal behavior, including deadly violence, against those they have sworn to protect. The blue wall of silence exists in almost every city in the United States. In New Orleans, this division between the police and the public lessens public trust and further demoralizes the honest and hardworking officers of the department.[61]

A final division rests with the geography of the city. Some residents feel safe, or at least safer, from violent crime in their homes and neighborhoods. These neighborhoods most often correlate with the wealthier sections of the city. This class division leaves those in the poorer neighborhoods feeling a greater potential exposure to violent crime. And it leaves the impression that public safety is a benefit for only some of the citizenry.

There has been no substantial change between the pre- and post-Katrina NOPD. Pennington brought a brief glimmer of hope to the department, but the lengthy history of the NOPD before Katrina, and its performance since the storm, have been far from optimal.

Public policy arenas exist on a spectrum of permeability. While some policy areas may come close to reflecting the full degree of Robert Dahl's original pluralism, other areas become what biologists would term "semi-permeable membranes."[62] Only certain actors gain access to these more closely controlled policy areas. And policing remains stubbornly closed to most policy entrepreneurs.

In studying the conditions necessary to reform corrupt police departments, Lawrence Sherman finds that there must be both external and internal control, and both sets of controls must favor reform.[63] In New Orleans, those controls failed to favor reform, opting instead for the status quo. Under Pennington, the second condition—internal control—existed to a high degree, yielding a temporary change in the police department's behavior. But after the storm, neither external nor internal controls emerged in the service of reform.

Before and after Katrina, the mayor and the police chief remained the key decision makers, agenda setters, and enactors of public safety policy. This political arrangement was temporarily expanded to include the Police Foundation during the Pennington era, but that expansion was short-lived, and its effect was temporary. Of all the policy areas detailed here, policing is the one that remains tightly controlled by a small group. The implications of this closed group for responsiveness, innovation, and flexibility have been tremendous. The NOPD remains mired in scandal, unable to reform, a disappointment to the citizenry.

While breaking into this tight policy arena has been next to impossible in the years since Katrina, the potential for external control may remain the city's best hope. The consent decree does enlarge the scope of influence on the department, bringing the federal government's supervisory capacity to bear. The mayor's initial reluctance to follow the terms of the decree seemed to be based mainly on budgetary concerns. Thus, the hope for reform in policing lies with the introduction of a new actor in the public safety policy agreement. The question remains: Can the federal government succeed where countless others have failed? Can the federal government replicate the success of the Road Home or imitate the state's impact on public education? The citizens of New Orleans hope so.

Conclusion

The Effects of Sudden Shocks on Governance, Politics, and Policy

Considerable political change took place in New Orleans after Katrina. The arrangement that governed the city changed from one focused on patronage and corruption to one dedicated to reform. Various actors used their resources and/or authority to capture the innermost position within the political arrangement (see table 16).

A new political arrangement formed to eliminate machine-style politics and replace those who used these tactics. It altered the governing structures of economic development, public education, and housing. Only the area of policing remained relatively untouched by reform, and even there, the current consent decree holds the promise of change.

Before the storm, local resources and authority allowed patronage to occur. Some locally elected and appointed actors, along with people who worked with, for, and under them, used their positions of authority and access to resources to enrich themselves and others. After Katrina, a shift in resources and authority moved certain actors into the core of the arrangement and others farther outside. The poor sit consistently on the outside. Civic elites and local business entities organized and created a narrative that governmental reform needed to take place. Their fiscal resources and ability to find partners with authority and additional resources produced change.

The new political arrangement had an extra-local flavor. State- and federal-level actors set rules and allocated resources in the post-Katrina

TABLE 16

A comparison of the political arrangement in pre-Katrina and post-Katrina New Orleans

Position	Roles and function of each position	Pre-Katrina arrangement	Post-Katrina arrangement
Inner Core	Agenda setters	Elected and appointed officials	Federal government, state government, civic elite, business leaders, national foundations
Outer core	Implement, support, and/or benefit from the agenda	Government employees, relatives of elected and appointed officials, close associates of elected and appointed officials and government employees; city government–centric	Local government, reform-oriented public and private actors and organizations, middle class of all races
Beyond the core	Core alternatives, attempts to influence or redirect agenda	Business leaders, civic elite, state- and federal-level actors, reform-oriented elected officials, neighborhood and community organizations	Neighborhood and community-based organizations, practitioners of corruption and mismanagement
Outer ring	Rarely set, support, enact, and benefit from the agenda; pay costs	Poor minorities and the poor in general	Poor, promulgators of corruption, leaders and supporters of previous government arrangement

period. The governor, state legislature, and Louisiana electorate enacted reforms that stripped authority from patronage-producing positions. The federal government allocated money to bring about more charter schools and fewer levee boards. National foundations paid for some education reforms and defined the conditions under which New Orleans planned its recovery. Extra-local players employed their resources and/or authority to assume a direct role in the governance of the city. As cities continue to operate with scarce resources, extra-local resource providers will use that context to set and implement their agendas.

Public-private partnerships emerged in the new political arrangement. Reform-oriented members of the city council and a new mayor established a formal public-private partnership and championed an increased role for private leadership over the city's recreation department. By their nature charter schools are public-private partnerships, and they exploded in number after Katrina. Developers continued to assume an important role in New Orleans's political arrangement. They benefited from post-disaster housing policies. Meanwhile, the city's business organizations ruled over and benefited from economic development, education, housing, and policing policies in the post-Katrina era.

Extra-local and private actors were able to set the agenda, enact policies, and assume prominent positions in the political arrangement because they possessed resources and authority sufficient to accomplish their agenda. In many instances, either local actors had lost their authority or scarce resources diminished their span of control. They lacked the kinds of resources necessary to carry out the reconstruction of public policies.

A governing coalition developed after the storm. It concentrated on governmental reform, market-based policies, and an attack on patronage. This kind of unity was absent before the disaster. The new political arrangement changed governmental structures and accelerated policies adopted pre-Katrina in education and housing. If the pre-disaster political arrangement blocked reform, the new one championed change.

The structures that governed schools, levees, assessors, sheriffs, the master plan, and housing, among others, changed after the storm. State- and federal-level actors, in addition to reform-minded local officials and organizations and national foundations, discredited and displaced embedded interests. Before Katrina, however, every major office in the city was held by a black person. After the storm, a white person won every major position, including mayor.

A market-driven reform agenda ruled New Orleans post-Katrina. The city's pre-storm entrenched interests paid the price and lost. The poor still did not have a public agenda that focused on them.

Thus, New Orleans moved from its prior position in our categorization of cities (see table 1). The city, previously characterized by diffuse political arrangements and weak agenda fidelity, still exhibits substantial diffusion among policy arenas, but among those arenas we identify much stronger agenda fidelity. This transitional period in New Orleans may be leading to an eventual placement in the concentrated and strong position, as groups like Citizens for 1 Greater New Orleans continue to push for a single unified arrangement centered on clean government.

New Orleans started in the most disadvantaged position in the matrix. It was unable to provide fundamental services on a sustained basis. The ability of those who supported alternatives to the pre-storm agenda to penetrate the core and place their stamp on the post-Katrina agenda has helped New Orleans move toward more responsible city governance.

Lessons for Cities Hit by Disaster

Natural disasters do not have to lead to significant changes in government. The easiest path after a disaster is simply to return to normal. The particulars of a disaster and the political context before the shock matter. In the case of New Orleans, the severity of Katrina, combined with nascent reform efforts, expanded governmental, political, and policy changes afterward.

New Orleans is a special city, one that was dysfunctional before the hurricane but had experienced some change. It is difficult to use New Orleans or any area to produce a generic understanding of the politics of disaster response, but post-Katrina New Orleans provides lessons for cities subject to a sudden shock:

- Resources and authority determine political change after a disaster.
- Reform policies take hold.
- Recovery agenda is set from the top down; neighborhood rebuilding is accomplished from the bottom up.
- Post-disaster recovery limits local control.

Other principles apply specifically to the case of New Orleans:

- Decision makers and collaboration change.
- Structural, physical, and electoral change take hold.
- Racial divide narrows; social divide persists; public-private partnerships increase.
- Civic elite, developers, business, and state government win; machine-style politics and the poor lose.
- The Big Easy was reformed, but . . .

Resources and Authority Determine Political Change after Disaster

One key lesson that post-Katrina politics can teach cities hit by disaster is that resources and authority affect the degree to which politics, governance, and policy change. If the pre-disaster entrenched interests retain their resources and authority, they continue to rule. If not, those with resources and authority set the agenda, make strategic choices, and enact policies.

In post-Katrina New Orleans, the longtime political machine lacked the resources to maintain its agenda, while reformers of all sorts possessed the resources they needed to push through long-desired plans. In the aftermath of Hurricane Katrina, New Orleans's government lost almost all of its resources, and it lacked the money to operate its services. This loss of resources diminished the city's authority. Mayor Nagin acknowledged in congressional testimony on October 18, 2005: "We have really had some struggles, and as a result of my total economy being collapsed, I have no revenues coming in at the moment to run city government. I have already laid off half of my work force, which is about 3,000 workers, in the City of New Orleans, because we have no revenues coming in."[1] Demographer Gregory Rigamer testified before a congressional committee that New Orleans had seen a "complete cessation of governmental and business activities" as a result of Hurricane Katrina.[2]

As the city's resources became depleted and municipal authority waned, a new coalition of actors with resources and authority set the public agenda and enacted policies they preferred. The storm neutered those at the top of the arrangement that governed pre-Katrina New Orleans, and a new political arrangement emerged, one dominated by extra-local and nongovernmental actors, focused on governmental reform and continued policy change.

Disasters are windows of opportunity when they affect resources and authority. When sudden shocks deplete local resources, diminish local authority, or require higher levels of authority to make decisions, then political change is likely. In the case of Hurricane Katrina, all three of these conditions applied to New Orleans's government.

To understand post-disaster governance, politics, and policies, one must identify the actors who control the resources and authority necessary to set the agenda and enact policy. In the aftermath of Hurricane Katrina, reform-oriented actors who possessed resources and/or authority formed a coalition to set the post-disaster agenda and enact public policies. That agenda allowed non-local and private actors to control education and housing policies. Structural changes limited machine-style politics. Post-disaster policies emphasized market-centered strategies.[3] A new political arrangement developed because reformers had the resources and authority to carry out their agenda. The leaders under the old arrangement lost the resources and authority necessary to maintain the status quo.

If the poor, displaced residents, patients at Charity Hospital, residents of public housing, and advocates of these four groups had controlled resources and possessed authority, the agenda would have focused on the immediate reopening of schools, Charity Hospital, and public housing. Instead, those with the resources and authority chose to close Charity and public housing. They waited to reopen schools and made certain that charters were the primary option.

Those who set the public agenda claimed that the city *had to* pursue these policies or New Orleans would perish. They also implied that their agenda allowed everyone to win. In reality, those with resources and authority chose to set an agenda that benefited them. Their actions produced clear winners and losers. For the most part, coalitions with resources and authority won in the post-disaster period. Those without resources and authority lost.

Years of corruption and mismanagement had discredited the exercise of authority by various governmental bodies in New Orleans. In many instances, post-Katrina reforms continued what had already begun before the disaster as various actors stripped elements of local control from authority holders. The dysfunction in the city made the case easier for higher levels of government to create new systems of authority. These systems emphasized extra-local and private actors and displaced members of the political machine from privileged positions in the New Orleans political arrangement.

Being widely discredited, authority was therefore easily modified to create a new political arrangement. Neither the state nor the federal government responded well to the emergency, but the local arrangements were conspicuously inadequate in every regard. It was easy to focus blame on agents who were already discredited.

Reform Policies Take Hold

In the United States, state-level and private actors use their resources and/or authority to rule urban policies when city-level actors lack the resources necessary to accomplish their agenda. These new actors diminish local control and craft urban policy in ways that the president, Congress, federal departments, governors, state legislators, and private resource providers favor. In post-Katrina New Orleans, these preferences included limited government, more privatization, market-centered policies, government reform, and attacks on patronage.

As the state and federal governments assume authority over more and more distressed and resource-poor cities, and national foundations allocate more resources, the larger national agenda will become more prominent in urban areas. Post-Katrina New Orleans fits a national trend in which market-driven policies and extra-local control dominate.

Even before Detroit declared bankruptcy, an emergency manager, who was appointed by the governor, controlled that city's finances. The emergency manager consulted with the governor to declare Chapter 9 bankruptcy and developed a financial restructuring plan. The Michigan state legislature allocated $194.8 million to the so-called grand bargain fund to help Detroit settle its bankruptcy. Ford, GM, and Chrysler pledged $26 million to this fund, and the United Autoworkers (UAW) promised a $5 million contribution.[4]

In takeovers of urban school districts, local-level actors, such as the school board and the teachers' union, lose control over education policy. State-level players and businesses use their resources and/or authority to pursue school choice, charters, privatization, and other reforms that they favor. Governors have also used their resources and authority to dictate urban economic development policies.[5]

One lesson from New Orleans, Detroit, and other cities subject to a loss of resources and authority is that the federal and state governments and private resource providers will dictate urban public policy. In the case of New Orleans, that agenda focused on good-government reforms, market-centered policies, and an attack on patronage.

Recovery Agenda Is Set from the Top Down

Social capital—or civic cooperation—did not determine the recovery agenda. A top-down agenda prevailed because it had powerful backing. The bottom-up agenda failed to take hold because its backing lacked the power to guide a remaking effort. The top-down agenda is likely to succeed after disasters because those who espouse it possess the resources and authority necessary to set and implement it.

New Orleans saw an explosion of neighborhood and community groups after the storm. According to one researcher: "Since Katrina, the region has found its social capital mojo! Citizens are highly engaged in civic issues and have become very knowledgeable of public issues, actively shaping public decisions. Many new coalitions have formed to call for the end to the status quo and advocating for new reforms. New neighborhood organizations and nonprofit developers have created new capacity to rebuild their own communities in ways that are more equitable and opportunity-rich."[6]

The number of neighborhood and community groups and the level of engagement among citizens did rise after Katrina. In some instances, such as the issuance of building permits and the location of FEMA trailers, those who had higher levels of social capital won individual policy victories. The social capital of neighborhood and community organizations, among other groups, did not enable them to set the public agenda in post-Katrina New Orleans. Even though public feedback became a part of the policy process, it did not guarantee governmental responsiveness to issues raised by neighborhood and community groups.[7]

Nevertheless, although social capital did not always influence post-Katrina governance, politics, or policies, it did play an important role in the rebuilding of New Orleans. Community and civic organizations reconstructed neighborhoods. It is unlikely that many community-based projects and whole neighborhoods of the city would exist today if it were not for their social capital. When it comes to setting the public agenda, however, social capital was not in the most privileged position in the post-Katrina political arrangement.

Post-Disaster Recovery Limits Local Control

The rebuilding of New Orleans is a story of the role of democracy in decisions that affect people's lives. How much say, if any, do or should residents have in rebuilding and over the basic policies that govern their lives? In the New Orleans case, coalitions of various state and federal actors made important decisions about housing and schooling without input from residents, many of whom had yet to return. The mayor and city council supported these choices.

The new political arrangement muted the elected Orleans Parish School Board and cut the number of appointed boards and positions. It continued to limit local control over housing. Education leaders expressed disdain for democratic participation in their policy area. They wanted the experts—themselves—to decide. Policing was already the least democratic of the policy areas and remained so after the storm.

Some of the post-Katrina changes occurred via democratic means. Voters enacted a number of reforms through constitutional amendments or changes to the city charter. The newly elected reformers on both the city council and the school board enacted reforms as well. The head of the state's department of education claimed that the participation of charter school boards in New Orleans education exemplified democracy in action.

Contrary to what Robert D. Putnam argued about the positive connections between reform and democracy, opponents of New Orleans's reforms often appealed to democracy to argue against policy and institutional change. Sudden shocks limit local control over policy. Without the resources necessary to rebuild, local actors gave way to outside resource providers and authority holders. Local elected officials did not pay for the recovery—and in some instances were given limited access to funds—but they wanted to continue to rule the city. The federal and state governments, in addition to foundations, dictated how the local government and other entities were to spend their dollars.

Some black legislators inside and outside New Orleans, among others, used democracy, or the lack thereof, as the core of their argument against reform and policy change. State Senator and future U.S. Congressman Cedric Richmond wanted displaced residents to return to the city before any decisions about governmental change or reform were made. A black state representative referred to the legislature's reform agenda as an effort to dismantle New Orleans.

State government maintains responsibility over police powers, those policies that protect and promote the health, welfare, education, safety, and morality of the citizenry. Local governments are created by the state to implement those police powers.[8] If local entities, like those in New Orleans, fail to carry out their policy duties, then the state government can relieve them of their duties and implement policies in some other way. Local control does not permit New Orleans to imperil its citizens' health, welfare, education, or safety. When New Orleans schools failed, the state had the constitutional authority and responsibility to take over. As the police department continues to be plagued by ineffectiveness and corruption, the federal government is in the process of stepping in via consent decree. Furthermore, if cities do not have the resources to address their problems, state government can use its finances to assume a prominent place in a city's political arrangement.

Many of the post-Katrina decisions came from outside the city. The governor, state legislature, state boards, secretaries of state agencies, and the Louisiana electorate made almost all of the changes to the educational system. The governor, state legislators, and the statewide electorate cut the number of levee boards and assessors; the governor and legislature slashed the Orleans Parish court system. The HUD-controlled Housing Authority of New Orleans decided the fate of public housing. Congress and the U.S. Department of Education used fiscal resources to dictate changes to the levee board and increases in the number of charter schools.

Local elites and business organizations demanded governmental reform after Katrina. They got it. They supported charter schools and choice. They got it. They wanted the demolition of public housing to continue. They got it. A public-private partnership placed the creation of an inspector general's office on the agenda. It got it. A reform-oriented organization championed a binding master plan. It got it.

The state and federal roles extended beyond the setting of rules and allocation of resources. Instead, state- and federal-level actors governed education and economic development in post-Katrina New Orleans. Business organizations advocated and enacted market-centered policies.

Hurricane Katrina did not sweep away New Orleans's past. It shifted the playing field. As a result of the disaster, the rulers of the pre-Katrina political arrangement moved down while those in the middle moved up. Both groups remained in post-Katrina New Orleans. One was wounded by the storm, the other emboldened.

While the case of New Orleans demonstrates that widespread policy change is possible in the wake of a disaster, it is critical to keep the counter-example in mind. Disasters themselves do not bring about this sort of change, but they do have the potential to create conditions under which change can take place.

As noted in the introduction, cities like San Francisco and Waco rebuffed reforms after disasters. Entrenched interests have the potential to remain in power and continue to dictate the agenda. In other cities from Galveston to Mexico City to Aceh, disasters created opportunities for change in the local political arrangements.

Reform-minded actors should be mindful of the potential for change in a disaster recovery period. But any such actors would need to acquire the requisite resources and authority to set the agenda and implement reform policies. And perhaps just as important, reform-minded actors must take careful account of the resources and authority possessed by the pre-disaster entrenched interests. If the pre-disaster coalition continues to hold the requisite resources and authority, it may be difficult for the reform-minded to take hold.

Decision Makers and Collaboration Change

Moving from the general to the specific, we now highlight the key lessons that apply in particular to post-Katrina New Orleans. There is a tendency to think about governance in terms of in- and out-groups. The in-group makes decisions; the out-group does not. The in-group benefits from decisions; the out-group does not. Power is not an all-or-nothing proposition. In the case of pre-Katrina New Orleans, those who practiced machine-style politics held the resources and authority necessary to rule *most of the time*. Even though the machine dominated the political arrangement and benefited from it, the machine did not always possess the resources or authority to enact its agenda. In some instances, higher levels of government overruled locally controlled institutions and used their resources and authority to enact policies they preferred. They planted the seeds for post-Katrina reform.

Several kinds of governance can occur at once. New Orleans's pre-Katrina arrangement produced patronage, corruption, and substandard services. Within that arrangement, however, reform-oriented federal, state, and local actors secured victories and started a trend toward reform. Post-Katrina New Orleans differs from pre-Katrina New Orleans, but it is not new. Alterations in the trajectory of governance, politics, and policy began before the disaster. Machine-style politics lost influence before Katrina and continued to lose influence afterwards. Reformers increased their influence after the storm.

Those who practiced machine-style politics lacked sufficient resources and authority to overcome the sudden shock of the disaster. In the aftermath of the storm, coalitions used their resources and authority to accelerate pre-Katrina reforms and enact changes they never dreamed possible before the hurricane. Without resources and authority, the leaders of the old arrangement now had no way to resist.

While it is debatable that an Atlanta-style regime formed after Katrina, it is possible to see much greater collaboration between public and private actors since the disaster. Civic elites and leaders of business organizations and private companies served on charter boards, endorsed and participated in the city's first formal public-private partnership, helped lead the new recreation department, and collaborated with the governor, city council, and new mayor on a variety of reforms. Private companies worked with federal, state, and local governments to redevelop public housing sites and implement the Road Home program. Civic elites and business organizations had a shared purpose: to change governance in New Orleans and undo what they regarded as the mistakes in the past. They framed an agenda to accomplish these purposes and pursued the general goal of governmental and policy reform over particular benefits.

Structural, Physical, and Electoral Change Took Hold

The changes to the levee boards, number of assessors, Orleans Parish courts, the master plan, and the Office of Inspector General now have the force of the state constitution, city charter, gubernatorial executive orders, and public resources behind them. Voters in New Orleans supported changes to the levee boards, assessors, and recreation department, the creation of an inspector general, and the establishment of a binding master plan. They elected a mayor and members of the city council who supported and championed reform. The state and federal governments, along with national and local foundations and teaching organizations, have also used their resources and authority to ensure that the charter school movement has taken hold in post-Katrina New Orleans.

Physical changes also took hold in post-Katrina New Orleans. Resource providers and authority holders continued to eliminate public housing and institute mixed-income housing and commercial development on the site of former public housing complexes. The mega–medical complex will change the landscape of the central business district and has the potential to change the job mix in the region.

The first post-Katrina election ended twenty consecutive years of black-majority rule on the city council, which went from a majority of five black members before Katrina to a majority of five white members after October 2007. In 2006 Stacey Head defeated incumbent Renee Gill Pratt to become the first white person to represent District B in thirty-one years. When council president Oliver Thomas had to resign and went to prison, whites occupied both at-large seats on the city council. The unwritten rule that whites and blacks would each hold one at-large seat fell; it had existed since 1976. After Katrina, the election of Mitch Landrieu ended thirty-two consecutive years of black mayors. Post-Katrina voters also elected a white district attorney and majority-white school board.[9]

Yet the political narrative of post–Hurricane Katrina rebuilding is not as simple as blacks lost and whites won. The evidence suggests that black voters won substantive representation even while descriptive representation dissipated. In October 2006, 61 percent of black residents in New Orleans approved or strongly approved of the job that Ray Nagin was doing as mayor. Twenty-three percent of white residents approved (18 percent) or strongly approved (5 percent). Mitch Landrieu was elected by a majority of black as well as white voters, and in late November of the new mayor's first term, 78 percent of white residents and 72 percent of black residents approved or strongly approved of their new mayor. Blacks were not as enthusiastic about reform as whites, but most supported change.[10]

Racial Divide Changed, Social Divide Persisted, More Public-Private Partnerships

Patronage and corruption, racial and social divides, and a lack of engagement by civic elites and local businesses characterized the dysfunction of New Orleans's pre-Katrina political arrangement. The new arrangement cut patronage and continued to punish corruption. Racial and social divides persisted after the storm, but white and black residents alike stood on the same side of many issues. Social division was most apparent in post-Katrina public policies.

When he released the findings from his survey of New Orleans residents, James Carville noted that black and white residents were not as divided as everyone had claimed. His poll numbers supported his case. Black and white voters agreed on most post-Katrina issues. Both favored the creation of the Office of Inspector General, the consolidation of levee boards and the number of assessors, and changes to the city's recreation department. Black and white residents voted for and approved the performance of a new white mayor.

Leaders within the black community and black elected officials opposed changes to a greater extent than black voters. They claimed that these changes violated local control and democratic principles. For the most part, however, black voters in the city of New Orleans endorsed reform.

Class divisions persisted after Katrina. Almost none of the governmental reforms had any bearing on the quality of life of the poor, but other policy changes mattered greatly. The changes to public housing exerted the greatest burdens on the poor residents who lived there. A rich-poor divide in the educational system became even more prominent in post-Katrina New Orleans. The poor lost medical care when Charity Hospital closed.

Governmental fragmentation decreased after Hurricane Katrina. Local actors allied with the governor, the state legislature, state-level agencies, and the federal government to promote and execute housing and education policies along with reform and economic development. This kind of cooperation was limited before the storm; after Katrina, actors with resources and authority realized that they had a common purpose: to limit patronage in the city, change the governance and politics of New Orleans, and accelerate pre-Katrina reforms.

Before the storm, Republicans inside and outside New Orleans opposed the manner in which the city governed itself. They advocated reform, but machine-style politics, supported by local control and endorsed by local voters, limited their success. After the storm, Louisiana Republicans formed coalitions with local civic elites, business organizations, and the governor to carry out their pre-Katrina policy preferences.

Civic Elite, Developers, Business, and State Government Win; Machine-Style Politics and the Poor Lose

The so-called two-tier school system favored whites and the wealthy; the poor and blacks continued to attend the lowest-performing schools. The demolition of public housing displaced predominantly black and poor residents. The housing compensation plan focused on homeowners and gave less attention to renters. The teachers' union and those who served in patronage positions also lost in the post-Katrina era.

Developers benefited because of HUD's and HANO's emphasis on mixed-use housing over traditional public housing. The organizations that supplied new teachers to New Orleans's schools won. Business organizations favored changes to the city's governmental structures, which state-level intervention helped streamline. Business, tourists, and white upper-class families won as a result of the rebuilding of New Orleans. Displaced black families did not.[11] And in public safety, no one has won yet; not the public, not the elected officials, and not the honest members of the NOPD.

Uptown elites, local business and good-government organizations, reformers, the owner of the New Orleans Saints, developers, homeowners, new teachers' organizations, charter schools, and elite students won as a result of post-Katrina policies. The governor and state legislature, national foundations, Congress, and state and federal agencies used their fiscal resources and authority to make winners of these groups.

Leaders of this intergovernmental political arrangement decided not to pursue one-for-one replacement of public housing, the immediate opening of traditional schools and public housing, and the renewal of the teachers' union contract. The poor and some black elected officials and clergy supported these options. The wealthy and middle class did not. The new political arrangement did not work to bring back displaced residents as quickly as possible. The choice to pursue reform over other options meant that some of the poor and working class had no place to live or send their children to school.

The list of winners and losers provides additional support to claims that reform is not neutral. Whites, the wealthy, business organizations, developers, and homeowners either were beneficiaries of change or were unaffected by the post-Katrina policy agenda. In almost every instance, either the poor and/or blacks bore the brunt of change.

The Big Easy Was Reformed, But . . .

Hurricane Katrina provided an opportunity for actors with resources and authority to change the city's dysfunctional political arrangements. To accomplish this goal, they created a new educational system, cut patronage positions and government boards, implemented oversight of city agencies, continued attempts to improve the governance of public housing, and attacked corruption. By these measures, governance appears to be much more functional in the post-Katrina period than it was prior to August 29, 2005.

The Big Easy was reformed after Katrina. Used in this context, "reform" refers to an output, not an outcome. The new political arrangement instituted reforms and pursued corruption to a greater extent than before. These actions mark a change from the pre-Katrina period, but they do not mean that the city is better off. The city's governing structures are different, and elected officials are focused on anti-corruption measures. New Orleans's public services have improved but are far from first-rate.

The longer-term question is whether the new political arrangement, and the changes it made, produced better jobs, streets, housing, and schools. Charter school advocates claim that rising test scores demonstrate significant improvement for all students. Evidence suggests that schools have improved for those fortunate enough to attend the best of these institutions; the educational changes meant that the poor, many minorities, and the disabled attend substandard schools. The housing changes displaced some but provided better living conditions for its residents.

New Orleans continues to attract tourists' dollars, and the new medical complex has the opportunity to improve the economic foundation of the city and region. The city still struggles with crime, especially murder, and police corruption. The next ten years will help determine whether reforms persist and bring about the substantive policy changes that will help make New Orleans a better and safer place to live, work, and raise children. The rage against the machine has started, but the long-term benefits are yet to be fully reaped or seen.

Notes

Introduction

1. U.S. Department of Justice, Federal Bureau of Investigation, "C. Ray Nagin, Former New Orleans Mayor, Convicted on Federal Bribery, Honest Services Wire Fraud, Money Laundering, Conspiracy, and Tax Charges," press release, February 12, 2014, http://www.fbi.gov/neworleans/press-releases/2014/c.-ray-nagin-former-new-orleans-mayor-convicted-on-federal-bribery-honest-services-wire-fraud-money-laundering-conspiracy-and-tax-charges (accessed August 22, 2014).

2. Lawrence J. Vale and Thomas J. Campanella, "Introduction: The Cities Rise Again," in *The Resilient City: How Modern Cities Recover from Disaster*, ed. Lawrence J. Vale and Thomas J. Campanella (New York: Oxford University Press, 2005), 12; Daniel P. Aldrich, "Fixing Recovery: Social Capital in Post-Crisis Resilience," *Journal of Homeland Security* 6 (2010): 1–10; Alice Fothergil, Enrique G. M. Maestas, and JoAnne DeRouen Darlington, "Race, Ethnicity, and Disasters in the United States: A Review of the Literature," *Disasters* 23, no. 2 (1999): 156–73.

3. For the reader's convenience, in paragraphs with multiple citations, all are combined in a note at the end of the paragraph (with the exception of those citing direct quotes). For more on disasters as political phenomena, see Richard Stuart Olson, "Toward a Politics of Disaster: Losses, Values, Agendas, and Blame," *International Journal of Mass Emergencies and Disasters* 18, no. 2 (2000): 265–87; Mark Pelling and Kathleen Dill, "Disaster Politics: Tipping Points for Change in the Adaptation of Sociopolitical Regimes," *Progress in Human Geography* 34, no. 1 (2010): 21–37, esp. 22; J. M. Albala-Bertrand, *Political Economy of Large Natural Disasters: With Special Reference to Developing Countries* (Oxford: Clarendon Press, 1993); Mark Pelling and Kathleen Dill, "Disaster Politics: From Social Control to Human Security," Environment, Politics and Development Working Paper Series, paper no. 1, Department of Geography, King's

College, London, 2008; Christopher Arnold, *Reconstruction after Earthquakes: Issues, Urban Design, and Case Studies,* report to National Science Foundation, San Mateo, CA, Building Systems Development, 1993; Robert P. Wolensky and Kenneth C. Wolensky, "Local Government's Problem with Disaster Management: A Literature Review and Structural Analysis," *Review of Policy Research* 9, no. 4 (1990): 703–25, esp. 722; Philip Fradkin, *The Great Earthquake and Firestorms of 1906: How San Francisco Nearly Destroyed Itself* (Berkeley: University of California Press, 2005); Harry Estill Moore, *Tornadoes over Texas: A Study of Waco and San Angelo in Disaster* (Austin: University of Texas Press, 1958); Robert B. Olshansky, "How Do Communities Recover from Disaster?" paper presented at the annual meeting of the Association of Collegiate Schools of Planning, Kansas City, 2005.

4. Russell R. Dynes and E. L. Quarantelli, "A Brief Note on Disaster Restoration, Reconstruction and Recovery: A Comparative Note Using Post-Earthquake Observations," University of Delaware, preliminary paper no. 259, 2008; J. Birkmann et al., "Extreme Events and Disasters: A Window of Opportunity for Change? Analysis of Organizational, Institutional, and Political Changes, Formal and Informal Responses after Mega-Disasters," *Natural Hazards* 55 (2010): 637–40; Pelling and Dill, "Disaster Politics: Tipping Points"; USAID, "Windows of Vulnerability and Opportunity. Foreign Aid in the National Interest: Promoting Freedom, Security and Opportunity, 2002, http://www.usaid.gov/fani/ch04/windows.htm. For more on how existing leaders used a disaster to push through changes that failed before the disaster, see Naomi Klein, *Shock Doctrine: The Rise of Disaster Capitalism* (New York: Picador, 2007); David W. Edgington, *Reconstructing Kobe: The Geography of Crisis and Opportunity* (Vancouver: University of British Columbia Press, 2010); Jamie Peck, *Constructions of Neoliberal Reason* (New York: Oxford University Press, 2010); Clyde Woods, "Les Misérables of New Orleans: Trap Economics and the Asset Stripping Blues, Part I," *American Quarterly* 61, no. 3 (2009): 769–96; Diane E. Davis, "Reverberations: Mexico City's 1985 Earthquake and the Transformation of the Capital," in Vale and Campanella, *The Resilient City,* 255–80; John Edward Weems, "The Galveston Storm of 1900," *Southwestern Historical Quarterly* 61, no. 4 (1958): 494–507; Birkmann et al., "Extreme Events and Disasters," 644; Pelling and Dill, "Disaster Politics: Tipping Points."

5. Jeremy Pais and James R. Elliott, "Places as Recovery Machines: Vulnerability and Neighborhood Change after Major Hurricanes," *Social Forces* 86, no. 4 (2008): 1415–53; Robert K. Merton, foreword to *Communities in Disaster: A Sociological Analysis of Collective Stress Situations,* by Allen H. Barton (New York: Doubleday, 1969); Dynes and Quarantelli, "A Brief Note on Disaster Restoration"; Stephanie Farquhar and Noelle Dobson, "Community and University Participation in Disaster-Relief Recovery," *Journal of Community Practice* 12, no. 1–3 (2005): 210; Caroline L. Clarke and Mohan Munasinghe, "Economic Aspects of Disasters and Sustainable Development: An Introduction," in *Disaster Prevention for Sustainable Development: Economic and Policy Issues,* ed. Caroline L. Clark and Mohan Munasinghe (Washington, DC: The World Bank, 1995), 2; Fothergil, Maestas, and DeRouen Darlington, "Race, Ethnicity, and Disasters in the United States"; Robert Bolin and Lois Stanford "Shelter, Housing, and Recovery: A Comparison of U.S. Disasters," *Disasters* 15, no. 1 (1991):

24–34; Joanne M. Nigg, "Disaster Recovery as a Social Process," University of Delaware Research Center, preliminary paper no. 219, 1995.

6. Eric Klinenberg, *Heat Wave: A Social Autopsy of Disaster in Chicago* (Chicago: University of Chicago Press, 2003); Eric Klinenberg, letter to the editor, "Review of *Heat Wave: Social Autopsy of Disaster in Chicago*," *New England Journal of Medicine* 348, no. 7 (2003): 666–67.

7. Marc Poumadere et al., "The 2003 Heat Wave in France: Dangerous Climate Change Here and Now," *Risk Analysis* 25, no. 6 (2005): 1483–94.

8. Wolensky and Wolensky, "Local Government's Problem," 720; Philip R. Berke, Jack Kartez, and Dennis Wenger, "Recovery after Disaster: Achieving Sustainable Development, Mitigation, and Equity," *Disasters* 17, no. 2 (1993): 96; Richard Francaviglia, "Xenia Rebuilds: Effects of Pre-Disaster Conditioning on Post-Disaster Redevelopment," *Journal of the American Institute of Planners* 44 (1978): 13–24; Fothergil, Maestas, and DeRouen Darlington, "Race, Ethnicity, and Disasters in the United States"; Robert Bolin, *Household and Community Recovery after Earthquakes* (Boulder: Institute of Behavioral Science, University of Colorado, 1993); Brenda D. Phillips, "Cultural Diversity in Disasters: Sheltering, Housing, and Long-Term Recovery," *International Journal of Mass Emergencies and Disasters* 11, no. 1 (1993): 99–110.

9. Pais and Elliott, "Places as Recovery Machines," 1430–32.

10. We use multiple methods to identify agenda setters, strategic alternatives among policy options, and enactment. News accounts, stakeholder interviews, congressional testimony, scholarly and popular books and articles, survey data, votes by citizens and elected officials, analyses and reports by consultants and private think tanks, census data, and government reports, among other data, allow us to identify elements of the political arrangement.

11. For examples, see the Urban Colloquy in *Urban Affairs Review* that includes Katherine B. Hankins, "Regime Politics in Geography," first published November 28, 2014, as doi: 10.1177/1078087414559606; Michael Jones-Correa and Diane Young, "Whose Politics? Reflections on Clarence Stone's *Regime Politics*," *Urban Affairs Review*, first published November 27, 2014, as doi: 10.1177/1078087414558949; Joel Rast, "Urban Regime Theory and the Problem of Change," *Urban Affairs Review*, first published November 27, 2014, as doi: 10.1177/1078087414559056; Clarence N. Stone, "Reflections on *Regime Politics*: From Governing Coalition to Urban Political Order," *Urban Affairs Review*, first published November 23, 2014, as doi: 10.1177/1078087414558948.

1. Pre-Katrina New Orleans

1. Clarence N. Stone, *Regime Politics: Governing Atlanta, 1946–1988* (Lawrence: University Press of Kansas, 1989); Heywood Sanders, "The Politics of Development in Middle-Sized Cities: Getting from New Haven to Kalamazoo," in *The Politics of Urban Development*, ed. Clarence Stone and Heywood Sanders (Lawrence: University Press of Kansas, 1987), 182–98.

2. Morton Inger, *Politics and Reality* (New York: Center for Urban Education, 1969); Liva Baker, *The Second Battle of New Orleans: The Hundred-Year*

Struggle to Integrate the Schools (New York: HarperCollins, 1996); interview with a black political leader, New Orleans, June 25, 2014.

3. Edward Renwick, address to Emory University's Community Building Fellows Program participants, Loyola University New Orleans, May 16, 2007.

4. Rachel E. Luft, "Beyond Disaster Exceptionalism: Social Movement Developments in New Orleans after Hurricane Katrina," *American Quarterly* 61, no. 3 (2009): 499–527; Bruce Nolan, "ACORN's Roots in New Orleans Are Withering," *Times-Picayune*, September 20, 2009.

5. For example, see Gabriella R. Montinola and Robert W. Jackman, "Sources of Corruption: A Cross-Country Study," *British Journal of Political Science* 32, no. 1 (2002): 147–70; Mitchel A. Seligson, "The Measurement and Impact of Corruption Victimization: Survey Evidence from Latin America," *World Development* 34, no. 2 (2006): 381–404; Paolo Mauro, "Corruption and Growth," *Quarterly Journal of Economics* 110, no. 3 (1995): 681–712; quotation from Fahim A. Al-Marhubi, "Corruption and Inflation," *Economics Letters* 66, no. 2 (2000): 199–202.

6. Rebecca Menes, "Limiting the Reach of the Grabbing Hand: Graft and Growth in American Cities, 1880 to 1930," in *Corruption and Reform: Lessons from America's Economic History*, ed. Edward L. Glaeser and Claudia Goldin (Chicago: University of Chicago Press, 2006), 63–94.

7. Dick Simpson et al., "Chicago and Illinois, Leading the Pack in Corruption: Anti-Corruption Report Number Five," University of Illinois at Chicago and the Illinois Integrity Initiative of the University of Illinois Institute for Government and Public Affairs, February 15, 2012, http://cbschicago.files.wordpress.com/2012/02/leadingthepack.pdf (accessed August 24, 2014); Lauren McGaughy, "Louisiana's Rate of Public Corruption Convictions Highest in Nation, Report Says," *Times-Picayune*, September 4, 2013.

8. Mary Foster, Associated Press, "Corruption Cases on Upswing in New Orleans," *New Orleans City Business*, January 3, 2008; Adam Nossiter, "New Blow to New Orleans in Council Member's Plea," *New York Times*, August 14, 2007; U.S. Department of Education, Office of Inspector General, "Federal Grand Jury Indicts Eleven in Orleans Parish Schools Corruption Investigation," Investigative Reports, December 16, 2004, http://www2.ed.gov/about/offices/list/oig/invtreports/la122004.html (accessed August 22, 2014); U.S. Department of Justice, Federal Bureau of Investigation, "Federal Judge Sentences Major Orleans Parish School Board Probe Figure," April 15 2000, http://www.fbi.gov/neworleans/press-releases/2009/no041509b.htm (accessed August 22, 2014) Foster, "Corruption Cases on Upswing in New Orleans."

9. Adam Nossiter, "New Blow."

10. Harold V. Savitch and Paul Kantor, *Cities in the International Marketplace: The Political Economy of Urban Development in North America and Western Europe* (Princeton: Princeton University Press, 2002), 86, 37. For East St. Louis, see Charles L. Lumpkins, *American Pogrom: The East St. Louis Race Riot and Black Politics* (Columbus: Ohio University Press, 2008); for Camden, New Jersey, see Chris Hedges, "City of Ruins," *Nation*, November 4, 2010, 15. For an example of political dysfunction in a so-called good-government city, see Steven P. Erie, Vladimir Kogan, and Scott A. MacKenzie, *Paradise Plundered: Fiscal Crisis and Governance Failures in San Diego* (Stanford: Stanford University Press, 2011).

11. "Former Orleans Parish School Board President Sentenced to 18 Months in Federal Prison," State News Service, March 11, 2010.

12. Edward F. Haas, "Political Continuity in the Crescent City: Toward an Interpretation of New Orleans Politics, 1874–1986," *Louisiana History: The Journal of the Louisiana Historical Association* 39, no. 1 (1998): 5–18; George M. Reynolds, *Machine Politics in New Orleans, 1897–1926* (New York: Columbia University Press, 1968), 6; Joseph B. Parker, *The Morrison Era: Reform Politics in New Orleans* (Gretna, LA: Pelican Publishing Company, 1974).

13. Edward F. Haas, *DeLesseps S. Morrison and the Image of Reform: New Orleans Politics, 1946–1961* (Baton Rouge: Louisiana State University Press, 1974); Haas, "Political Continuity," 13.

14. Haas, "Political Continuity,"; Matthew J. Schott, "The New Orleans Machine and Progressivism," *Louisiana History: The Journal of the Louisiana Historical Association* 24, no. 2 (1983): 143; "History of BGR," Bureau of Governmental Research, www.bgr.org/about/history (accessed February 12, 2013); "Profile," Bureau of Governmental Research, www.bgr.org/about/ (accessed February 12, 2013).

15. Rod Dreher, "Big Sleazy Sobers Up," *National Review*, July 31, 2002; Alan Sayre, "Discovery of Tape Led to Graft Investigation," Associated Press, July 23, 2002; "New Orleans Graft Investigation Spreading," Associated Press, July 25, 2002.

16. Drew Jubera, "New Orleans Embraces Nagin: First-Year Mayor Is All Business in War on Corruption," *Atlanta Journal-Constitution*, July 7, 2003.

17. Bob Edwards and Juan Williams, "Mayor Ray Nagin and His Campaign Promise to Fight Corruption and Crime in the City of New Orleans," National Public Radio, November 5, 2003; Jubera, "New Orleans Embraces Nagin"; Adam Nossiter, "New Mayor Tackles Corruption in Big Easy: Scandal-Weary Residents Optimistic as Laid-Back Official Shakes Up Status Quo," *Washington Post*, November 9, 2002,.

18. Edwards and Williams, "Mayor Ray Nagin"; Nossiter, "New Mayor Tackles Corruption in Big Easy"; Brett Martel, "Mayor's Task Is Big—And Not Easy: New Orleans' Nagin Trying to Fight Corruption, Budget Issues," *Washington Post*, July 20, 2003.

19. Amy Bridges, *Morning Glories: Municipal Reform in the Southwest* (Princeton: Princeton University Press, 1997); Jessica Trounstine, *Political Monopolies in American Cities: The Rise and Fall of Bosses and Reformers* (Chicago: University of Chicago Press, 2009); Robert D. Putnam, with Robert Leonardi and Raffaella Y. Nanetti, *Making Democracy Work: Civic Traditions in Modern Italy* (Princeton: Princeton University Press, 1994).

20. Robert K. Whelan and Alma Young, "New Orleans: The Ambivalent City," in *Big City Politics in Transition*, ed. Harold V. Savitch and John Clayton Thomas (Newbury Park, CA: Sage Publications, 1991); Baodong Liu and James M. Vanderleeuw, *Race Rules: Electoral Politics in New Orleans, 1965–2006* (Lanham, MD: Rowman & Littlefield, 2007), 57.

21. Huey L. Perry, "The Reelection of Sidney Barthelemy as Mayor of New Orleans," *PS: Political Science and Politics* 23, no. 2 (1990): 156–57; Whelan and Young, "New Orleans: The Ambivalent City"; Haas, "Political Continuity," 15; Monte Piliawsky, "The Impact of Black Mayors on the Black Community:

The Case of New Orleans' Ernest Morial," *Review of Black Political Economy* 13, no. 4 (1985): 5–23.

22. *Among Brothers: Politics in New Orleans*, VHS, produced and directed by Paul Stekler (New Orleans: Deep South Productions, 1986).

23. Lyle Kenneth Perkins, "Failing the Race: A Historical Assessment of New Orleans Mayor Sidney Barthelemy, 1986–1994" (MA thesis, Louisiana State University Agricultural and Mechanical College, 2005); Perry, "The Reelection of Sidney Barthelemy," 156–57.

24. Liu and Vanderleeuw, *Race Rules*, 68; Robert S. Montjoy and Edward E. Chervenak, "Race, Performance, and Change in Post-Katrina New Orleans," paper presented at the Annual Meeting of the Southern Political Science Association, Orlando, January 3–5, 2013.

25. Allan McBride and Joseph B. Parker, "'Chocolate City' Politics: Race and Empowerment in the First Post-Katrina New Orleans Mayoral Election," *Politics & Policy* 36, no. 3 (2008): 350–74.

26. Dreher. "Big Sleazy Sobers Up."

27. Ibid.

28. Darwin BondGraham, "Building the New New Orleans: Foundation and NGO Power" *Review of Black Political Economy* 38, no. 4 (2011): 279–309; Arnold Hirsch and Joseph Logsdon, eds., *Creole New Orleans: Race and Americanization* (Baton Rouge: Louisiana State University Press, 1992). For more on the Creole-black divide in New Orleans, see Kimberly S. Hanger, "Patronage, Property, and Persistence: The Emergence of a Free Black Elite in Spanish New Orleans," in *Against the Odds: Free Blacks in the Slave Societies of the Americas*, ed. Jane G. Landers (Portland, OR: Frank Cass, 1996); Verna M. Keith and Cedric Herring, "Skin Tone and Stratification in the Black Community," *American Journal of Sociology* 97, no. 3 (1991): 760–78; Montjoy and Chervenak, "Race, Performance, and Change"; Arnold Hirsch, "Simply a Matter of Black and White: The Transformation of Race and Politics in Twentieth-Century New Orleans," in Hirsch and Logsdon, *Creole New Orleans*, 262–319.

29. Edward J. Blakely, *My Storm: Managing the Recovery of New Orleans in the Wake of Katrina* (Philadelphia: University of Pennsylvania Press, 2011), 117.

30. Ibid; for more on New Orleans's geography, see Richard Campanella, *Time and Place in New Orleans: Past Geographies in the Present Day* (Grentna, LA: Pelican Publishing, 2002); Richard Campanella, *Geographies of New Orleans: Urban Fabrics before the Storm* (Lafayette: University of Louisiana at Lafayette Press, 2006); Richard Campanella, *Bienville's Dilemma: A Historical Geography of New Orleans* (Lafayette: Center for Louisiana Studies, University of Louisiana at Lafayette, 2008).

31. James Gill, *Lords of Misrule: Mardi Gras and the Politics of Race in New Orleans* (Jackson: University Press of Mississippi, 1997), 17; interview with Darran Simon, December 12, 2011.

32. Interview with a black political leader, June 25, 2014.

33. John Kendall. *History of New Orleans* (Chicago: Lewis Publishing Company, 1922).

34. Bruce Katz, "Concentrated Poverty in New Orleans and Other American Cities," Brookings Institution, August 4, 2006, http://www.brookings.edu/opinions/2006/0804cities_katz.aspx (accessed February 7, 2011); Alan Berube

and Bruce Katz. "Katrina's Window: Confronting Poverty across America," Brookings Institution, October 2005; Elizabeth Fussell, Narayan Sastry, and Mark VanLandingham, "Race, Socioeconomic Status, and Return Migration to New Orleans after Hurricane Katrina," *Population & Environment* 31, no. 1 (2010): 20–42.

35. Gill, *Lords of Misrule*, 17.

36. Ibid.; Coleman Warner and Stephanie Grace, "Longtime Activist Taylor, 72, Dies: Her Carnival Krewe Discrimination Fight Her Biggest Legacy" *Times-Picayune*, August 19, 2000; "The Krewes and the Parades," http://www.novareinna.com/festive/krewes.html (accessed August 18, 2014).

37. See Peter F. Burns and Matthew O. Thomas, "A New New Orleans? Understanding the Role of History and the State-Local Relationship in the Recovery Process," *Journal of Urban Affairs* 30, no. 3 (2008): 264; Joan B. Garvey and Mary Lou Widmer, *Beautiful Crescent: A History of New Orleans*, 10th ed. (New Orleans: Garmer Press, 2001); Wayne Parent, *Inside the Carnival: Unmasking Louisiana Politics* (Baton Rouge: Louisiana State University Press, 2006); Robert Crain, *The Politics of School Desegregation* (Chicago: Aldine Publishing Company, 1968).

38. Edward F. Renwick, T. Wayne Parent, and Jack Wardlaw, "Louisiana: Still *Sui Generis* Like Huey," in *Southern Politics in the 1990s,* ed. A. P. Lamis (Baton Rouge: Louisiana State University Press, 1999), 281.

39. For the information that follows, see Burns and Thomas, "A New New Orleans," 262.

40. Renwick, Parent, and Wardlaw, "Louisiana: Still *Sui Generis* Like Huey."

41. Peter Burns, "Race and Support for State Takeovers of Local School Districts," *Urban Education,* 45 no. 3 (2010): 274–92.

42. "1920: Leander Perez's Rise to Power in St. Bernard, Plaquemines," *Times-Picayune*, October 24, 2011; Morton Sosna, review of *Leander Perez: Boss of the Delta,* by Glen Jeansonne, *American Historical Review* 83, no. 3 (June 1978): 840–41; "National Affairs: Racist Leader," *Time,* December 12, 1960.

43. James Brandt and Robert K. Whelan, "New Orleans: Metropolis Against Itself," in *Metropolitan Governance without Metropolitan Government?* ed. Donald Phares (Burlington, VT: Ashgate Publishing Company, 2004), 135–53; Peirce F. Lewis, *New Orleans: The Making of an Urban Landscape,* 2nd ed. (Santa Fe, NM: Center for American Places, 2003), 68.

44. Whelan and Young, "New Orleans: The Ambivalent City."

45. Michael Peter Smith and Marlene Keller, "'Managed Growth' and the Politics of Uneven Development in New Orleans," in *Restructuring the City: The Political Economy of Urban Development,* rev. ed., ed. Susan S. Fainstein et al. (New York: Longman, 1986), 150–51.

46. Remarks by Governor Kathleen Babineaux Blanco, "Urban Conversations: Cities at Risk," Rockefeller Foundation, New York, April 6, 2006; Lawrence N. Powell, *The Accidental City: Improvising New Orleans* (Cambridge: Harvard University Press, 2012); Christopher Morris, "Impenetrable but Easy: The French Transformation of the Lower Mississippi Valley and the Founding of New Orleans," in *Centuries of Change: Human Transformation of the Lower Mississippi,* ed. Craig E. Colten (Pittsburgh: University of Pittsburgh Press,

2000), 22–42; U.S. Library of Congress, Congressional Research Service, *Hurricane Katrina: Social-Demographic Characteristics of Impacted Areas*, by Thomas Gabe et al., CRS Report RL33141 (Washington, DC: Office of Congressional Information and Publishing, November 4, 2005).

47. John R. Logan, "The Impact of Katrina: Race and Class in Storm-Damaged Neighborhoods," n.d., www.s4.brown.edu/katrina/report.pdf (accessed August 18, 2014). For full details of the flood of 1927, see John M. Barry, *Rising Tide: The Great Mississippi Flood of 1927 and How It Changed America* (New York: Simon and Schuster, 1997).

48. Statement of Larry G. Schedler, *Rebuilding Housing in the Aftermath of Hurricanes Katrina and Rita: Hearing before the House Committee on Financial Services' Subcommittee on Housing and Community Opportunity*, U.S. House of Representatives, 109th Cong., New Orleans, January 13, 2006.

49. Bruce Katz, Matt Fellowes, and Mia Mabanta, "Katrina Index: Tracking Variables of Post-Katrina Reconstruction" (Washington, DC: Brookings Institution, Metropolitan Policy Program, May 3, 2006), http://www.brookings.edu/metro/pubs/200605_KatrinaIndex.pdf (accessed August 18, 2014).

50. Ibid.

51. Robert P. Wolensky and Kenneth C. Wolensky, "Local Government's Problem with Disaster Management: A Literature Review and Structural Analysis," *Review of Policy Research* 9, no. 4 (1990): 718; Michael K. Lindell and Carla S. Prater, "Assessing Community Impacts of Natural Disasters," *Natural Hazards Review* 4, no. 4 (2003): 176–85; Lawrence J. Vale and Thomas J. Campanella, "Conclusion: Axioms of Resilience," in *The Resilient City: How Modern Cities Recovery from Disaster*, ed. Lawrence J. Vale and Thomas J. Campanella (New York: Oxford University Press, 2005), 342–44; Robert B. Olshansky, "How Do Communities Recover from Disaster? A Review of Current Knowledge and an Agenda for Future Research," Forty-Sixth Annual Conference of the Association of Collegiate Schools of Planning, Kansas City, 2005; Jeremy Pais and James R. Elliott, "Places as Recovery Machines: Vulnerability and Neighborhood Change after Major Hurricanes," *Social Forces* 86, no. 4 (2008): 1453; Christopher M. Weible, Paul A. Sabatier, and Kelly McQueen. "Themes and Variations: Taking Stock of the Advocacy Coalition Framework," *Policy Studies Journal* 37, no. 1 (2009): 121–40; Ian Burton, Robert W. Kates, and Gilbert F. White, *The Environment as Hazard* (New York: Guilford Press, 1993); J. Birkmann et al., "Extreme Events and Disasters: A Window of Opportunity for Change? Analysis of Organizational, Institutional, and Political Changes, Formal and Informal Responses after Mega-Disasters," *Natural Hazards* 55 (2010): 652–53.

2. Reform and Economic Development

1. Michael Peter Smith and Marlene Keller, "'Managed Growth' and the Politics of Uneven Development in New Orleans," in *Restructuring the City: The Political Economy of Urban Development*, rev. ed., ed. Susan S. Fainstein et al. (New York: Longman, 1986), 126–66; Robert K. Whelan, "New Orleans: Public-Private Partnerships and Uneven Development," in *Unequal Partnerships:*

The Political Economy of Urban Redevelopment in Postwar America, ed. Gregory D. Squires (New Brunswick, NJ: Rutgers University Press, 1991), 223, 234–35; Peirce F. Lewis, *New Orleans: The Making of an Urban Landscape*, 2nd ed. (Santa Fe, NM: Center for American Places, 2003), 70. For more on changes in Miami, see Manny Diaz, *Miami Transformed: Rebuilding America One Neighborhood, One City at a Time* (Philadelphia: University of Pennsylvania Press, 2012).

2. Smith and Keller, "Managed Growth"; Robert K. Whelan, "New Orleans: Public-Private Partnerships and Uneven Development," in Squires, *Unequal Partnerships*, 233.

3. Richard O. Baumbach and William E. Borah, *The Second Battle of New Orleans: A History of the Vieux Carré Riverfront Expressway Controversy* (Tuscaloosa: Published for the Preservation Press, National Trust for Historic Preservation in the United States, by University of Alabama Press, 1981); Robert K. Whelan, "New Orleans: Mayoral Politics and Economic-Development Policies in the Postwar Years, 1945–1986," in *The Politics of Urban Development*, ed. Clarence Stone and Heywood Sanders (Lawrence: University Press of Kansas, 1987), 216–29; Smith and Keller, "Managed Growth," 137.

4. For more on New Orleans and federal aid during this period, see Kent B. Germany, *New Orleans after the Promises: Poverty, Citizenship, and the Search for the Great Society* (Athens: University of Georgia Press, 2007); Whelan, "New Orleans: Mayoral Politics."

5. Germany, *New Orleans after the Promises*, 134–37.

6. Lewis, *New Orleans*, 74.

7. "Oil Jobs Down in New Orleans," *State-Times/Morning Advocate*, April 12, 2000; Lewis, *New Orleans*, 123; Kevin Fox Gotham, "Tourism Gentrification: The Case of New Orleans' Vieux Carré (French Quarter)," *Urban Studies* 42 (2005): 1099–1121; Jane S. Brooks and Alma H. Young, "Revitalising the Central Business District in the Face of Decline: The Case of New Orleans," *Town Planning Review* 64, no. 3 (1993): 264.

8. Bureau of Governmental Research, "On the Right Track? New Orleans Economic Development Investment in Perspective," New Orleans, November 2004, 11; Luis Miron, "Corporate Ideology and the Politics of Entrepreneurism in New Orleans," *Antipode* 24, no. 4 (1992): 270.

9. Robert K. Whelan and Alma Young, "New Orleans: The Ambivalent City," in *Big City Politics in Transition*, ed. Hank V. Savitch and John Clayton Thomas (Newbury Park, CA: Sage Publications, 1991), 135.

10. Lewis, *New Orleans*, 110; Anthony J. Mumphrey and Pamela H. Moomau, "New Orleans: An Island in the Sunbelt," *Public Administration Quarterly* 8, no. 1 (1984): 91; Robert K. Whelan, "An Old Economy for the 'New' New Orleans? Post-Katrina Economic Development Efforts," in *There Is No Such Thing as a Natural Disaster: Race, Class, and Hurricane Katrina*, ed. Chester W. Hartman and Gregory D. Squires (New York: Routledge, 2006), 215–31.

11. Lewis, *New Orleans*, 108–9; Smith and Keller, "Managed Growth," 143.

12. Whelan and Young, "New Orleans: The Ambivalent City"; Smith and Keller, "Managed Growth," 141; Lewis, *New Orleans*, 112.

13. Whelan and Young, "New Orleans: The Ambivalent City," 144.

14. Miron, "Corporate Ideology," 71; Rebecca Mowbray, "Business Council Steps Up to Plate: Group Taking More Active Role in N.O.," *Times-Picayune*,

November 4, 2007; Whelan, "New Orleans: Mayoral Politics"; "Arnof Will Lead Business Council," *Times-Picayune*, January 12, 1994; "Business Groups Want Schools' Search Restarted," *Times-Picayune*, December 12, 1998; Bruce Eggler, "City's Finances Deemed 'Critical': Review Finds Litany of Fiscal Problems," *Times-Picayune*, May 4, 2002.

15. Details about these state-led projects come from Peter F. Burns and Matthew O. Thomas, "The Failure of the Nonregime: How Katrina Exposed New Orleans as a Regimeless City," *Urban Affairs Review* 41, no. 4 (2006): 517–27.

16. Details of Edwards's conviction come from "National Briefing/South: Louisiana; Former Governor, Current Inmate," *New York Times*, October 22, 2002.

17. Bruce Eggler, "Edwards: NBA Team on the Horizon," *Times-Picayune*, June 16, 1993.

18. Interview with civic leader, January 7, 2014.

19. *Kudlow & Company*, November 29, 2005, CNBC News transcripts; interview with business leader, July 18, 2014.

20. Brett Martel, "Business Group Calls on Blanco to Overhaul Levee Board," Associated Press, November 16, 2005.

21. Anne Rochell Konigsmark, "Residents Push to Rid Levee Board of Politics," *USA Today*, December 23, 2005.

22. "Commentary: Business Leaders Demand Levee Reform," *New Orleans CityBusiness*, December 16, 2005; Martel, "Business Group"; "Business Groups Back Louisiana Officials on Levee Reform," *New Orleans CityBusiness*, February 7, 2006.

23. Doug Simpson, "Blanco Reverses Herself on Levee Board Reform," Associated Press State & Local Wire, December 16, 2005.

24. Doug Simpson, "Louisiana OKs Levee Boards' Overhaul," *Houston Chronicle*, October 1, 2006.

25. Interview with business leader, July 18, 2014.

26. "Business Council Demands Reform in Assessing Property Taxes Necessary for New Orleans Recovery and Prosperity," PR Newswire US, March 28, 2006; "The New Orleans Blanco Plan to Consolidate Tax Assessors Wins Approval," *New Orleans CityBusiness*, April 27, 2006; "Bureau of Governmental Research Study Raps N.O. Assessors," *New Orleans CityBusiness*, February 6, 2006.

27. "Business Council Demands Reform in Assessing Property Taxes."

28. Melinda Deslatte, "Blanco Tries Again to Streamline New Orleans Government," Associated Press State & Local Wire, April 13, 2006; "Louisiana Affairs Council Plan to Consolidate Assessors into Single Office Ranks," *New Orleans CityBusiness*, June 1, 2006; "Bureau of Governmental Research Study."

29. "Mayor Nagin, State Legislators, and Civic Groups Unify for Assessor Consolidation," *US State News*, June 12, 2006.

30. Doug Simpson, "N.O. Tax Assessor Measure Needs to Pass Two Voter Tests," Associated Press State & Local Wire, October 26, 2006.

31. Bruce Nolan. "Change Is Mantra of Citizen Group: 'Now We See a Way Forward' for N.O.," *Times-Picayune*, February 12, 2006.

32. Doug Simpson, "Katrina Disaster Seen as Chance to Fix New Orleans Bureaucracy," Associated Press State & Local Wire, February 9, 2006.

33. Melinda Deslatte, "Lawmakers Have Mixed Reviews of Session Agenda," Associated Press State & Local Wire, February 2, 2006.

34. Ibid.

35. Melinda Deslatte, "Louisiana Governor Abandons, for Now, a Push to Streamline New Orleans Government," Associated Press State & Local Wire, February 15, 2006.

36. Greg LaRose, "Consolidation Bills Pass Louisiana House Panel," *New Orleans CityBusiness*, April 13, 2006.

37. "La. Lawmakers Postpone New Orleans Courts Merger," Associated Press State & Local Wire, June 24, 2008.

38. David A. Marcello, "Systemic Ethics Reform in Katrina's Aftermath," in *Resilience and Opportunity: Lessons from the U.S. Gulf Coast after Katrina and Rita*, ed. Amy Liu et al. (Washington, DC: Brookings Institution Press, 2011), 82–98.

39. Bring New Orleans Back Commission, Government Effectiveness Committee, "Recommendations," March 20, 2006, https://repository.library.brown.edu/studio/item/bdr:65564/ (accessed August 18, 2014); Becky Bohrer, "Former Mass. Inspector General to Be Watchdog as New Orleans Rebuilds," Associated Press State & Local Wire, June 13, 2007; Marcello, "Systemic Ethics."

40. Michelle Krupa, "New Orleans City Council's Attempt to Override Ray Nagin's Veto Comes Up Short," *Times-Picayune*, February 19, 2009.

41. Jaime Guillet, "New Orleans Inspector General Finds 'Systemic Problem' in City Vehicles Usage," *New Orleans CityBusiness*, December 18, 2008.

42. Office of Inspector General, City of New Orleans, "2013 Annual Report," March 6, 2014, http://www.nolaoig.org/uploads/File/Annual%20Reports/2013%20Annual%20Report%20final%20140303.pdf (accessed August 18, 2014).

43. Frank Donze, "New Orleans Recreation Department Needs New Leadership Structure, Citizens Panel Says," *Times-Picayune*, August 29, 2009; Transition New Orleans, "Recreation Task Force, Task Force Members," www.transitionneworleans.com/taskforce/recreation_bios.html (accessed August 18, 2014); Marcia Froelke Coburn, "Valerie Jarrett & Desiree Rogers," *Chicago Magazine*, August 20, 2000.

44. "NORD Reform to Be Considered by City Council during Regular Meeting Tuesday," Targeted News Service, May 27, 2010.

45. Robert S. Montjoy and Edward E. Chervenak, "Race, Performance, and Change in Post-Katrina New Orleans," paper presented at the Annual Meeting of the Southern Political Science Association, Orlando, January 3–5, 2013; Citizens for 1 Greater New Orleans, "Community Initiatives: NORD Reform: Recreation-Reform Supporters Make Election-Week Push in Uptown," www.citizensfor1greaterneworleans.com/community/nord-reform.html (accessed August 18, 2014); "Mayor Landrieu Welcomes New Donations to NORD Foundation," Targeted News Service, April 5, 2011; "Mayor Landrieu and City of New Orleans Applaud Successful 2012 for New Orleans Recreation Development Commission," State News Service, January 2, 2013.

46. Robert A. Collins, "No More 'Planning by Surprise': Post-Katrina Land Use Planning in New Orleans," in Liu et al., *Resilience and Opportunity,* 161–72.

47. Bruce Eggler, "Master Plan Given Force of Law: Zoning Moves Must Conform to Blueprint," *Times-Picayune*, November 5, 2008; Michelle Krupa, "Land-Use Anxieties Simmer in East N.O.: Residents Fear Plan Could Rub Them Out," *Times-Picayune*, November 15, 2008.

48. David Muller, "Developers Want More Specifics from Revised Zoning Laws in N.O.," *New Orleans CityBusiness*, June 29, 2009.

49. Information about increased participation comes from "Editorial: Ambitious Master Plan Had to Be Long," *Times-Picayune*, October 20, 2009; Bruce Eggler, "Final Planning Meeting Is Tonight: Council Prepares to Vote on Master Plan," *Times-Picayune*, April 7, 2010; Bruce Eggler, "Master Plan Nearly Ready for Council: Planning Panel OKs Hodgepodge of Edits," *Times-Picayune*, January 13, 2010.

50. Maria Nelson, Renia Ehrenfeucht, and Shirley Laska, "Planning, Plans, and People: Professional Expertise, Local Knowledge, and Governmental Action in Post–Hurricane Katrina New Orleans," *Cityscape* 9, no. 3 (2007): 23–52.

51. Bring New Orleans Back Commission, "Bring New Orleans Back Commission Meeting," October 31, 2005, http://www.bringneworleansback.org.

52. Details about the Bring New Orleans Back Commission also come from Burns and Thomas, "Failure of the Nonregime"; testimony by Mayor C. Ray Nagin, *A Vision and Strategy for Rebuilding New Orleans, Hearing before the Subcommittee on Economic Development, Public Buildings and Emergency Management and Subcommittee on Water Resources and Environment of the Committee on Transportation and Infrastructure*, U.S. House of Representatives. 109th Cong., 1st sess., Washington, DC, October 18, 2005 ; Robert B. Olshansky et al., "Planning for the Rebuilding of New Orleans," *Journal of the American Planning Association* 74, no. 3 (2008): 276.

53. Jeffrey Meitrodt and Frank Donze, "Plan Shrinks City Footprint: Nagin Panel May Call for 3-Year Test," *Times-Picayune*, December 14, 2005; Urban Land Institute, "New Orleans: A Strategy for Rebuilding," 2005, http://uli.org/wp-content/uploads/2012/11/NewOrleans-LA-05-v5.pdf.

54. Gary Rivlin, "Anger Meets New Orleans Renewal Plan," *New York Times*, January 12, 2006.

55. "Transcript of Nagin's Speech: New Orleans Mayor Ray Nagin Gave This Speech Monday during a Program at City Hall Commemorating Martin Luther King Jr.," *Times-Picayune*, January 14, 2006, http://www.nola.com/news/t-p/frontpage/index.ssf?/news/t-p/stories/011706_nagin_transcript.html (accessed December 29, 2010).

56. Brian J. Brox, "Elections and Voting in Post-Katrina New Orleans," *Southern Studies* 16, no. 2 (2009): 1–23; J. Celeste Lay, "Race, Retrospective Voting, and Disasters: the Re-Election of C. Ray Nagin after Hurricane Katrina," *Urban Affairs Review* 44, no. 5 (2009): 645–62.

57. Bureau of Governmental Relations, "Wanted: A Realistic Development Strategy," December 22, 2005, http://www.bgr.org/files/news/BGR_Reports_Realistic_Development_Strategy_12_22_05.pdf.

58. Olshansky et al., "Planning for the Rebuilding of New Orleans," 276.

59. Nicole Wallace, "Blueprint for Rebuilding," *Chronicle of Philanthropy* 19, no. 21 (2007): 32; Nelson, Ehrenfeucht, and Laska, "Planning, Plans, and People."

60. Nelson, Ehrenfeucht, and Laska, "Planning, Plans, and People."

61. Edward J. Blakely, *My Storm: Managing the Recovery of New Orleans in the Wake of Katrina* (Philadelphia: University of Pennsylvania Press, 2011), 43–54; Edward J. Blakely, "Citywide Strategic Recovery and Redevelopment

Plan," City of New Orleans, n.d., http://quake.abag.ca.gov/wp-content/documents/
resilience/New%20Orleans-FINAL-PLAN-April-2007.pdf. (accessed August 18,
2014); Jaime Guillet, "Blakely Has Grand Plan to 'Trigger' Rebuilding in N.O.,"
New Orleans CityBusiness, July 23, 2007.

62. Julie Bourbon, "Recovery Czar Rolls through the Wreckage: He'd Like to
See Real Progress in New Orleans by September," *Times-Picayune*, February 11,
2007; Becky Bohrer, "New Orleans Recovery Director Outlines $1.1 Billion Plan
to Give Developers Incentives," Associated Press, March 29, 2007.

63. Wallace, "Blueprint for Rebuilding," 32; Kristina Ford, *The Trouble with
City Planning: What New Orleans Can Teach Us* (New Haven: Yale University
Press, 2010).

64. "Editorial: Building a City for the Ages," *Times-Picayune*, May 10, 2013;
Bruce Eggler, "New Orleans Finishes 25 Capital Projects—52 Scheduled to be
Completed in 2013," *Times-Picayune*, January 4, 2013.

65. Interview with civic leader, January 7, 2014.

66. Bring New Orleans Back Commission, Urban Planning Committee,
"Action Plan for New Orleans: The New American City," 2006, http://uli.
org/wp-content/uploads/2012/11/NewOrleans-LA-05-v5.pdf (accessed August
18, 2014); Kristina Shevory, "A New Orleans Neighborhood Rebuilds," *New
York Times*, February 25, 2007; Nicole Gelinas, "The Big Easy Rebuilds, Bot-
tom Up," *City Journal* 18, no. 2 (2008); Anne Rochell Konigsmark, "New
Orleans' Recovery Slow and Slippery Process: Rebuilding Underway but in the
Same Flood-Prone Places," *USA Today*, August 23, 2006; Stephen Maloney,
"Moving Forward: Grassroots Groups in New Orleans," *New Orleans City-
Business*, August 20, 2007; Rukmini Callimachi, "FEMA, City Council Get
Dunked in New Orleans to Raise Money for Rebuilding Efforts," Associated
Press, November 12, 2006; Rick Jervis, "Recovery in New Orleans Still Spotty:
Six Years after Katrina Tragedy, Pockets of City Still Languishing," *USA Today*,
August 26, 2011.

67. Douglas Ahlers and Rebecca Hummel, "Lessons from Katrina," Harvard University Belfer Center, 2007, http://belfercenter.ksg.harvard.edu/publi
cation/17815/lessons_from_katrina.html?breadcrumb=%2Fproject%2F54%2F
broadmoor_project (accessed August 21, 2014); Allen G. Breed, "Who's to
Blame for State of New Orleans?" Associated Press, August 19, 2006; Rochell
Konigsmark, "New Orleans' Recovery Slow and Slippery Process"6; "Harvard
Kennedy School Continues Leadership Development in New Orleans: 'Broadmoor Project' Brings Harvard to the Neighborhood," PR Newswire, April 3,
2008; "New Orleans Resurgent," International Business Times News, August 29,
2010; "Broadmoor, NO Museum of Art Plug into High-Tech Emergency Plan,"
New Orleans CityBusiness, November 5, 2006; Kristina Shevory, "Neighbor-
hood Goes to Work, Rebuilds in New Orleans," Chattanooga Times Free Press,
March 4, 2007; "New Orleans Celebrates Opening of Carnegie Corporation–
Funded Rosa F. Keller Library and Community Center," States News Service,
March 13, 2012.

68. Nicole Wallace, "Fight for Survival Revives New Orleans," *Chronicle of
Philanthropy* 20, no. 14 (2008): 30; "School Officials, Broadmoor Community
Celebrate Andrew H. Wilson Groundbreaking," *US States News*, July 17, 2008;
"Broadmoor Group Seeks Out $1M for New Orleans Charter School," *New

Orleans CityBusiness, August 22, 2009; National Public Radio, "For One New Orleans School, an Uncertain Future," *All Things Considered*, May 17, 2007.

69. "New Orleans Celebrates Opening of Carnegie Corporation–Funded Rosa F. Keller Library and Community Center"; Gelinas, "The Big Easy Rebuilds"; Rochell Konigsmark, "New Orleans' Recovery Slow and Slippery Process.

70. Nicole Wallace, "Rebuilding Block by Block," *Chronicle of Philanthropy* 20, no. 14 (2008): 27; Adam Nossiter, "In Tale of Church vs. School, a New Orleans Dilemma," *New York Times*, December 19, 2006,; Maloney, "Moving Forward"; City of New Orleans, "Mayor Landrieu, City Council and New Orleans Redevelopment Authority Announce Lot Next Door Ordinance Revisions," February 27, 2013.

71. "Entergy New Orleans, Inc., Announces Joint Venture Neighborhood Partnership with Gentilly Civic Improvement Association," Targeted News Service, June 3, 2008; Clarence N. Stone, Robert Stoker et. al., *Urban Neighborhoods in a New Era: Revitalization Politics in the Post-Industrial City* (Chicago: University of Chicago Press, 2015).

72. Frederick D. Weil, "Rise of Community Organizations, Citizen Engagement, and New Institutions," in Liu et al., *Resilience and Opportunity*, 201–19. For more on civic organizations' sophisticated structure, see Pat Evans and Sarah Lewis, "A Reciprocity of Tears: Civic Engagement after a Disaster," in *Civic Engagement in the Wake of Katrina*, ed. Amy Koritz and George J. Sanchez. (Ann Arbor: University of Michigan Press, 2009), 44–58.

73. Kalima Rosa, "Community, Faith, and Nonprofit-Driven Housing Recovery," in Liu et al., *Resilience and Opportunity*, 4. Other information about NENA comes from "9th Ward Group Plans Service: Memorial Day Event Is to Honor the Dead," *Times-Picayune*, May 26, 2006.

74. Darran Simon, "$2 Billion Schools Plan OK'd: 1st Phase Creates, Rehabs 30 Campuses," *Times-Picayune*, November 7, 2008.

75. "Editorial: Lakeview Rebuilding in the Spotlight," *Times-Picayune*, May 20, 2006; "Editorial: Signs of Recovery; Evidence of Recovery Can Be Seen All Over the Metro New Orleans Area," *Times-Picayune*, July 5, 2008; Jeannie Paddison Tidy, "Beacon of Hope Gets $60,000 Donation," *Times-Picayune*, January 29, 2009.

76. Wallace, "Rebuilding Block by Block," 27; Christopher A. Airiess et al., "Church-Based Social Capital, Networks, and Geographical Scale: Katrina Evacuation, Relocation, and Recovery in New Orleans' Vietnamese American Community," *Geoforum* 39, no. 3 (2008): 1333–46; Emily Chamlee-Wright and Virgil Henry Storr, "Club Goods and Post-Disaster Community Return," *Rationality and Society* 21, no. 4 (2009): 429–58; Bruce Nolan, "How Two Churches Have Helped," *Regina Leader-Post*, August 12, 2006; Laura Grube and Virgil Henry Storr, "The Capacity for Self-Governance and Post-Disaster Resiliency," *Review of Austrian Economics* 27, no. 3 (2013): 1–24; "New Orleans Resurgent," *International Business Times News*, August 29, 2010; see also http://www. nolamusiciansvillage.org/ (accessed August 22, 2014).

77. U.S. Congress, "Landrieu Chairs Hearing on Progress Made and Remaining Challenges Five Years after Hurricane Katrina," Congressional Documents and Publications, August 26, 2010.

78. Interview with civic leader, January 7, 2014; interview with black political leader, June 25, 2014.

79. Weil, "Rise of Community Organizations"; Daniel P. Aldrich and Kevin Crook, "Strong Civil Society as a Double-Edged Sword: Siting Trailers in Post-Katrina New Orleans," *Political Research Quarterly* 61 no. 3 (2008): 379–89; Kevin Fox Gotham and Richard Campanella, "Toward a Research Agenda on Transformative Resilience: Challenges and Opportunities for Post-Trauma Urban Ecosystems," *Critical Planning* 17 (2010): 9–23; Rachel Morello-Frosch et al., "Community Voice, Vision, and Resilience in Post-Hurricane Katrina Recovery," *Environmental Justice* 4, no. 1 (2011): 71–80; Stephanie Gajewski et al., "Complexity and Instability: The Response of Nongovernmental Organizations to the Recovery of Hurricane Katrina Survivors in a Host Community," *Nonprofit and Voluntary Sector Quarterly* 40, no. 2 (2011): 389–403.

80. Cain Burdeau, "6 Years after Katrina, Lower 9th Ward Still Bleak," Associated Press, August 28, 2011.

81. See http://makeitright.org/ (accessed August 22, 2014).

82. Weil, "Rise of Community Organizations"; Frederick Weil, "Can Citizens Affect Urban Policy? Blight Reduction in Post-Katrina New Orleans," paper prepared for presentation at the Annual Meeting of the American Political Science Association, New Orleans, August 27–31, 2012, http://www.rickweil.com/Writings/Weil2012APSACanCitizensAffectUrbanPolicy.pdf (accessed August 8, 2014); Frederick Weil, "The Rise of Community Engagement after Katrina," in *The New Orleans Index at Five: Reviewing Key Reforms after Hurricane Katrina* (Washington, DC: Brookings Institution and Greater New Orleans Community Data Center, 2010).

83. City of New Orleans, "City Wins Judgment against Blighted Lake Terrace Shopping Center in Gentilly," January 8, 2013; Karen Gadbois, "Decrepit Strip Mall Financed by Taxpayer Money Avoids Wrecking Ball—For Now," *The Lens*, March 18, 2010, http://thelensnola.org/2010/03/18/strip-mall-financecd-by-taxpayer-money-avoids-wrecking-ball (accessed August 18, 2013).

84. Wade Rathke and Beulah Laboistrie, "The Role of Local Organizing: House to House with Boots on the Ground," in Hartman and Squires, *There Is No Such Thing as a Natural Disaster*, 255–70. For ACORN's pre-Katrina strategies, see Peter F. Burns, "Community Organizations in a Non-Regime City: The New Orleans Experience," in *Transforming the City: Community Organizing and the Challenge of Political Change*, ed. Marion Orr (Lawrence: University Press of Kansas, 2007), 56–83; J. Phillip Thompson, "Response to 'Post-Disaster Planning in New Orleans'," *Journal of Planning Education and Research* 28 (2009): 403–4; John Atlas, *Seeds of Change: The Story of ACORN, America's Most Controversial Anti-Poverty Community Organizing Group* (Nashville: Vanderbilt University Press, 2010); Fred Brooks, "One Hypothesis about the Decline and Fall of ACORN," *Social Work* 58, no. 2 (2013): 177–80; Bruce Nolan, "ACORN's Roots in New Orleans Are Withering," *Times-Picayune*, September 20, 2009; John Atlas, "ACORN Closes Its Last Door, Filing for Bankruptcy," *Huffington Post*, November 3, 2010, http://www.huffingtonpost.com/john-atlas/acorn-closes-its-last-doo_b_778047.html (accessed August 22, 2014).

85. Bruce Alpert, "ACORN Founder Saddened by Organization's Demise," *Times-Picayune*, March 24, 2010; Atlas, "ACORN Closes"; Kate Moran, "ACORN Board Clashes Over Probe: Two Members Asked to Rescind Lawsuit," *Times-Picayune*, October 21, 2008; "ACORN Founder Plans to Turn New

Orleans Coffeehouse into Community Activist Hub," *New Orleans Examiner*, September 18, 2011.

86. Rachel E. Luft, "Beyond Disaster Exceptionalism: Social Movement Developments in New Orleans after Hurricane Katrina," *American Quarterly* 61, no. 3 (2009): 499–527.

87. Whelan, "An Old Economy," 230.

88. Jaquetta White, "To Attract Businesses, Companies Say, New Orleans Needs to Change the Way It Deals with Them," *Times-Picayune*, November 25, 2007.

89. Bruce Eggler, "City's Business Policies Called 'Insane': Ineptitude, Cronyism Must End, Critics Say," *Times-Picayune*, August 15, 200.

90. Becky Bohrer, "New Orleans Council Backs Public-Private Approach to Economic Development," Associated Press, November 28, 2007; Jaime Guillet, "New Orleans Mayor Nagin Sets Economic Development Course," *New Orleans CityBusiness*, June 2, 2008.

91. Ben Myers, "New Orleans Mayor Tweaks Lineup of Economic Development Panel," *New Orleans CityBusiness*, June 2, 2010; Bruce Eggler, "Public-Private Panel Set Up as N.O. Looks for Jobs: Board Members Tapped for Group," *Times-Picayune*, August 14, 2010.

92. "Louisiana Lt. Gov. Mitch Landrieu Not Running for Mayor," *New Orleans CityBusiness*, July 8, 2009.

93. Campbell Robertson. "Louisiana: Lieutenant Governor to Run for Mayor," *New York Times*, December 9, 2009.

94. Jeff Crouere, "Commentary: Failed Mayoral Candidates Consider Political Future," *New Orleans CityBusiness*, February 23, 2010.

95. Vicki Mack and Elaine Ortiz. "Who Lives in New Orleans and the Metro Now?" The Data Center, New Orleans, September 26, 2013, http://www.datacenterresearch.org/data-resources/who-lives-in-new-orleans-now/ (accessed August 9, 2014).

96. Eggler, "Public-Private Panel Set Up as N.O. Looks for Jobs"; Frank Donze, "Business Alliance Gains Leader: Public-Private Push to Woo for N.O. Area," *Times-Picayune*. January 13, 2011; Myers, "New Orleans Mayor Tweaks."

97. Donze, "Business Alliance Gains."

98. "Mayor Landrieu Orders Sweeping Reforms of City Contracting," Targeted News Service, June 3, 2010; Marcello, "Systemic Ethics."

99. Forward New Orleans, "Fourth Progress Report," September 2013.

100. Ibid.

101. Ed Anderson, "80 percent of Dome's Roof Compromised: Superdome, Arena Appear Repairable," *Times-Picayune*, September 8, 2010; Scott Boeck, "Superdome Up, Running Again: But Work Continues at Damaged Stadium," *USA Today*, September 21, 2006; Mary Foster, "Temporary Repairs Scheduled to Begin at Superdome," Associated Press, October 14, 2005; Melinda Deslatte, "Lawmaker Questions Quick Pace for Starting Superdome Repairs," Associated Press, October 18, 2005.

102. Deslatte, "Lawmaker Questions."

103. Melinda Deslatte, "Blanco Says Superdome Repairs Will Help Symbolize Recovery," Associated Press, October 25, 2005.

104. Michelle Millhollon, "Houston Firm Picked to Design Superdome Job," *The Advocate*, October 20, 2005; Deslatte, "Blanco Says Superdome"; "Gov. Blanco Reopens Louisiana Superdome," *U.S. States News*, September 25, 2006.

105. "NFL Grant for Superdome Repairs Approved," Associated Press, July 14, 2006; Brett Martel, "Saints Payers Defend Decision to Restore Superdome," Associated Press, September 22, 2006; Cary O'Reilly and Curtis Eichelberger, "When the Saints Go Marching In . . . ," *Vancouver Sun*, September 23, 2006.

106. Wayne Curtis, "The Cost of Progress? Razing Entire Blocks for a Massive Hospital Complex in New Orleans Divided Residents and Decimated Parts of a Historic Neighborhood," *Preservation*, May–June 2011, http://www.preservationnation.org/magazine/2011/may-june/mid-city-new-orleans.html (accessed July 8, 2011).

107. Melinda Deslatte, "Charity Hospitals Face Accreditation, Money Woes," Associated Press State & Local Wire, March 13, 2005; "Past Cuts Could Cost Trauma Status for Charity Hospital's ER," Associated Press State & Local Wire, May 25, 2005.

108. Marsha Shuler, "Majority Favor Keeping State Charity Hospitals," *The Advocate*, January 12, 2005.

109. Edward Blakely, class presentation at Loyola University, New Orleans, October 30, 2008.

110. "Aftermath of Katrina: Wednesday's Developments," *Miami Herald*, October 5, 2005; National Trust for Historic Preservation, "Endangered Charity Hospital and Mid-City Neighborhood—And the Fight to Save Them," n.d., http://www.preservationnation.org/travel-and-sites/sites/southern-region/charity-hospital/endangered-charity-hospital.html (accessed July 8, 2011).

111. Darwin BondGraham, "Building the New New Orleans: Foundation and NGO Power," *Review of Black Political Economy* 38, no. 4 (2011): 299.

112. "Governor Blanco, Louisiana State University Announce Plans to Move Forward on LSU-VA Hospital in New Orleans," *U.S. States News*, February 21, 2007.

113. Curtis, "The Cost of Progress?"; "National Trust for Historic Preservation Files Motion for Preliminary Injunction in Lawsuit against VA and FEMA Relating to Siting of Hospitals in Mid-City New Orleans," Targeted News Service, March 30, 2010; Richard A. Webster, "Program to Move Homes from LSU-VA Hospital Site, Rehab Them, Remains in Disarray," *Times-Picayune*, November 24, 2012.

114. For more on the preservationists and politics, see Yue Zhang, *The Fragmented Politics of Urban Preservation: Beijing, Chicago, and Paris* (Minneapolis: University of Minnesota Press, 2013).

115. Lindy Boggs National Center for Community Literacy, "Recognizing the Underutilized Economic Potential of African American Men in New Orleans," June 2013, http://media.nola.com/politics/other/untapped%20resource.pdf (accessed August 18, 2014).

116. UNO Survey Research Center, "2013 Quality of Life Survey: Orleans and Jefferson Parishes," October 2013.

117. Ibid.

118. BondGraham, "Building the New New Orleans," 298.

119. Testimony of Mayor Mitch Landrieu, *Five Years Later: Lessons Learned, Progress Made, and Work Remaining from Hurricane Katrina: Hearing before the Ad Hoc Committee on Disaster Recovery of the Committee on Homeland Security and Governmental Affairs*, U.S. Senate, 111th Cong., 2nd sess., August 26, 2010.

120. Robert McClendon, "New Orleans' Credit Rating Surpasses Pre-Katrina Level as Local Economy Improves," *Times Picayune*, March 10, 2015.

3. Democracy versus Reform in Pre-Katrina Education

1. Dorothy Shipps, "Pulling Together: Civic Capacity and Urban School Reform, *American Educational Research Journal* 40, no. 4 (2003): 841–78; Wilbur C. Rich, *Black Mayors and School Politics: The Failure of Reform in Detroit, Gary, and Newark* (New York: Garland Publishing, 1996); Jeffrey R. Henig et al., *The Color of School Reform* (Princeton: Princeton University Press, 1999); Marion Orr, *Black Social Capital: The Politics of School Reform in Baltimore, 1986–1998.* (Lawrence: University Press of Kansas, 1999).

2. Shipps, "Pulling Together"; Dorothy Shipps, "Corporate Influence on Chicago School Reform," in *Changing Urban Education,* ed. Clarence N. Stone (Lawrence: University Press of Kansas, 1998), 161–83; Clarence N. Stone, "Introduction: Urban Education in Political Context," in *Changing Urban Education*, 1–22; Thomas Longoria Jr., "School Politics in Houston: The Impact of Business Involvement," in Stone, *Changing Urban Education*, 184–98.

3. Frank Donze, "Morial Charts School Reforms: Effort Patterned on NOPD Rescue," *Times-Picayune*, March 26, 1998; Rhonda Nabonne, "School Board Unveils Plan for Reform: Business Group Spearheads Push," *Times-Picayune*, February 9, 1999; Rhonda Nabonne, "Experts Visiting Schools in N.O.: Group to Assess Teaching Process," *Times-Picayune*, April 15, 1998.

4. Donze, "Morial Charts School Reforms."

5. Ibid.; Nabonne, "Experts Visiting Schools in N.O."; Rhonda Nabonne and Susan Finch, "N.O. Schools Waste Time, Report Says: One Day a Week Is Lost on Nonacademic Activity," *Times-Picayune*, August 14, 1998.

6. Nabonne, "School Board Unveils Plan"; Chris Gray, "Davis Denies He's Bailing Out: Group Lends Support Amid Speculation," *Times-Picayune*, November 30, 2000.

7. Rhonda Nabonne, "Deal Would Put Pressure on Educators," *Times-Picayune*, November 12, 1998.

8. Chris Gray, "School Board Split on Reforms: 3 Members Criticize Role of Foundation," *Times-Picayune*, February 11, 2001.

9. Lolis Eric Elie, "School Draft Needs Work," *Times-Picayune*, March 8, 1999.

10. Rhonda Bell, "Davis' Dad, Overtime to Be Investigated: School Board Looking at Janitor's Salary," *Times-Picayune*, December 18, 2001; "State Auditor Eyes Pay Controversy," *Advocate*, January 16, 2002; "Report into Overtime Blasted by Board," Associated Press State & Local Wire, January 8, 2002; "The Public Wants More," *Times-Picayune*, January 10, 2002.

11. "Working Day and Night," *Times-Picayune*, April 29, 2002.

12. Brian Thevenot, "Pair Set to Plead Guilty to Bribe Scheme: Deals May Give Lift to Corruption Probe," *Times-Picayune*, February 18, 2004; U.S. Department of Education, Office of Inspector General, "Federal Grand Jury Indicts Eleven in Orleans Parish Schools Corruption Investigation," Investigative Reports, December 16, 2004, http://www2.ed.gov/about/offices/list/oig/

invtreports/la122004.html (accessed August 22, 2014); U.S. Department of Justice, Federal Bureau of Investigation, "Federal Judge Sentences Major Orleans Parish School Board Probe Figure," April 15, 2000, http://www.fbi.gov/new orleans/press-releases/2009/no041509b.htm (accessed August 22, 2014); Mary Foster, "Corruption Cases on Upswing in New Orleans, " Associated Press, January 3, 2008.

13. Brian Thevenot, "Lawyer: Contractor to Admit Kickbacks: $4 Million in Repairs at N.O. Schools Probed," *Times-Picayune*, May 21, 2003; Coleman Warner and Gordon Russell, "Bribery Discussion Taped; Sources: Brooks-Simms Recorded Mose Jefferson," *Times-Picayune*, June 21, 2007; Brian Thevenot, "Schools Sue Over Business Contracts: System Alleges Misuse of Insurance Money," *Times-Picayune*, May 5, 2003; U.S. Department of Justice, "Federal Judge Sentences Major Orleans Parish School Board Probe Figure"; U.S. Department of Education, Office of Inspector General, "Federal Grand Jury Indicts Eleven."

14. Brian Thevenot, "Feds Open Investigation of School Payroll: Orleans Auditor Suspects Fraud," *Times-Picayune*, June 26, 2003; Gwen Filosa, "Three of Six Found Guilty in School Theft Probe: Ex-Williams Middle Employees Accused of Altering Payroll Sheets," *Times-Picayune*, October 12, 2007.

15. Brian Thevenot, "'It's Time': Schools Chief Davis to Leave," *Times-Picayune*, June 14, 2002; Aesha Rasheed, "School Board Picks Leader: Amato Received Credit in Hartford Turnaround," *Times-Picayune*, February 1, 2003.

16. Alan Wieder, "The New Orleans School Crisis of 1960: Causes and Consequences," *Phylon* 48, no. 2 (1987): 130.

17. Brian Thevenot, "Unintended Consequences: By the 1970s, Real Integration Had Come to New Orleans Public Schools, but as Middle-Class Families—Both Black and White—Fled, the Schools and the City Suffered," *Times-Picayune*, May 17, 2004.

18. Ibid.

19. Aesha Rasheed, "'I Can't Tell Where We Are Fiscally,'" *Times-Picayune*, March 26, 2003.

20. Brian Thevenot, "New Probe of N.O. Schools Is Launched: Six Laws Agencies Target Corruption," *Times-Picayune*, April 20, 2004.

21. Brian Thevenot, "System's Hunt for Answers Widens," *Times-Picayune*, June 30, 2003; Aesha Rasheed, "Schools Want More Time with Financial Advisers: Amato Asks Board for 90-Day Extension," *Times-Picayune*, December 5, 2003.

22. U.S. Department of Justice, United States Attorney's Office, Eastern District of Louisiana, "Former Orleans Parish School Board President Sentenced to 18 Months in Federal Prison," March 11, 2010.

23. Brian Thevenot, "School Auditor Reports Threats: Fraud Probe Elicits 'Hangman Letter,'" *Times-Picayune*, June 25, 2003; Lolis Eric Elie, "Board Can't See Error of Its Ways," *Times-Picayune*, July 25, 2003; James Gill, "School Accountability Starts at the Top," *Times-Picayune*, January 23, 2004; Rasheed, "Schools Want More Time."

24. Brian Thevenot, "Scale Tips Suddenly on Ousted President: Brooks-Simms' Allies Flip over Her Move on Superintendent," *Times-Picayune*, January

31, 2004; Susan Finch, "School Board Drops Consulting Company: Firm Found Myriad Financial Problems," *Times-Picayune*, December 16, 2003.

25. Louisiana Department of Education, "School Standards, Accountability, and Assistance: Louisiana's School, District, and State Accountability System," n.d., doa.louisiana.gov/osr/lac/28v83/28v83.doc (accessed August 18, 2014); Nelson Smith, "The Louisiana Recovery School District: Lessons for the Buckeye State," Thomas B. Fordham Institute, January 2012, http://files.eric.ed.gov/fulltext/ED528943.pdf (accessed August 18, 2014).

26. Louisiana Federation of Teachers, "Weekly Legislative Digest," April 4, 2003, http://www.lft-aft.org/ (accessed July 11, 2011).

27. Daniel Kiel, "It Takes a Hurricane: Might Karma Deliver for New Orleans Students What *Brown* Once Promised," *Journal of Law & Education* 40, no. 1 (January 2011): 125.

28. Louisiana State Senate, "Session Information: 2004 Regular Session Highlights," by Diane Burkhart, n.d., http://senate.legis.state.la.us/SessionInfo/2004/RS/Highlights/LinkShell.asp?s=k-12 (accessed August 22, 2014).

29. Ibid.

30. Brian Thevenot, "Judge: Hands Off of Amato: Politics Cited in Bid to Fire Schools Chief," *Times-Picayune*, August 4, 2004.

31. Brian Thevenot, "School Board's Unity Put to the Test," *Times-Picayune*, February 28, 2005. Election results available at http://electionresults.sos.la.gov/graphical.

32. Thevenot, "School Board's Unity Put to the Test."

33. U.S. Department of Education, Office of Inspector General, to Cecil Picard, February 16, 2005, http://www2.ed.gov/about/offices/list/oig/audit reports/a06e0008.pdf (accessed July 12, 2014); Ed Anderson and Robert Travis Scott, "Orleans Schools' Finances Focus of Meeting: Millions in Federal Funds May Be at Risk," *Times-Picayune*, February 15, 2005; "State Vows to Fix Finances in New Orleans: La. Schools Chief Crafts Agreement to Address Audit of Title I Spending," *Education Week*, March 9, 2005, 3; Coleman Warner and Susan Finch, "Feds Raise Pressure on Schools: Millions in Grants Hinge on Reforms," *Times-Picayune*, February 15, 2005; Coleman Warner and Susan Finch, "Feds Put Ball in State's Court: School Finances Leave Grants in Jeopardy," *Times-Picayune*, February 17, 2005.

34. "State Vows to Fix Finances in New Orleans: La. Schools Chief Crafts Agreement to Address Audit of Title I Spending," *Education Week*, March 9, 2005, 3.

35. Warner and Finch, "Feds Raise Pressure on Schools"; "Take the Help," *Times-Picayune*, February 20, 2005; "State Vows to Fix Finances in New Orleans," 3; Brian Thevenot, "La. Asks N.O. School Board to Cede Reins: It Wants Contractor to Control Finances," *Times-Picayune*, April 8, 2005.

36. Brian Thevenot, "School Board OKs Outside Managers: Members Approve $50 Million Loan to Ensure Meeting Payroll," *Times-Picayune*, April 12, 2005.

37. Deon Roberts, "Resignation of N.O. Public Schools Superintendent Amato Shakes Up Business Community," *New Orleans CityBusiness*, April 18, 2005.

38. Brian Thevenot, "Hatchet Men: The Company Hired to Solve New Orleans Public Schools' Financial Woes Is Proud of Its Rock-Ribbed Reputation,"

Times-Picayune, June 26, 2005; Brian Thevenot, "Power Struggle Leads to Power Sharing: Everyone, No One Ends Up in Charge." *Times-Picayune*, May 5, 2005.

39. Thevenot, "Hatchet Men"; Thevenot, "Power Struggle Leads to Power Sharing."

40. Thevenot, "Hatchet Men"; Thevenot, "Power Struggle Leads to Power Sharing"; Brian Thevenot and Aesha Rasheed, "Nagin Offers to Help Schools: City Could Assume Administrative Role," *Times-Picayune*, February 5, 2004.

41. Martha Carr and Brian Thevenot, "Nagin's Vision Faces Hurdles: Proposal for Schools Enormous Challenge," *Times-Picayune*, May 12, 2005.

42. Thevenot, "La. Asks N.O. School Board to Cede Reins."

43. Ibid.; April Capochino, "Orleans Parish School Board Moves Forward with Hiring of NY Accounting Firm," *New Orleans CityBusiness*, June 13, 2005.

44. Brian Thevenot, "Schools Give Up Financial Reins: Move Rends Board, Racism Is Alleged," *Times-Picayune*, May 24, 2005.

45. Thevenot, "Hatchet Men"; Thevenot, "Power Struggle Leads to Power Sharing."

46. Thevenot, "Schools Give Up Financial Reins."

47. Thevenot, "Hatchet Men"; Brian Thevenot, "Six Firms Bid to Manage Schools' Finances: One Did Similar Job for St. Louis System," *Times-Picayune*, April 19, 2005.

48. Thevenot, "Hatchet Men."

49. Ibid.

50. Ibid.

51. April Capochino, "Interview with Bill Roberti," *New Orleans CityBusiness*, April 1, 2005.

52. "Editorial: Beginning of a Turnaround?" *Times-Picayune*, July 31, 2005.

53. Stephanie Grace, "At Orleans Schools, Nowhere to Go but Up" *Times-Picayune*, July 31, 2005.

54. Capochino, "Interview with Bill Roberti"; "Orleans School Budget Cuts 800 Positions," Associated Press State & Local Wire, July 26, 2005; "Beginning of a Turnaround?"

55. "Louisiana News in Brief," Associated Press State & Local Wire, August 17, 2005.

56. Brian Thevenot, "Deeper Cuts in Line for N.O. Schools: Mass Layoffs Likely to Fill $48 Million Hole," *Times-Picayune*, August 9, 2005; "Beginning of a Turnaround?"

57. James Gill, "Are Schools Ready for Culture Change," *Times-Picayune*, July 27, 2005.

58. "Beginning of a Turnaround?"; Thevenot, "Deeper Cuts in Line for N.O. Schools."

59. Steve Ritea and Brian Thevenot, "Layoffs to Hit 150 in Orleans Schools: First Round of Cuts Planned for this Week." *Times-Picayune*, August 23, 2005.

60. Steve Ritea and Brian Thevenot, "First Day of Class Goes by the Book: Hotline for Principals Receives Only Four Calls," *Times-Picayune*, August 19, 2005; Brian Thevenot, "Lusher Faculty Approve Charter Proposal: Parents Next to Vote on Conversion Plan," *Times-Picayune*, August 18, 2005.

184 NOTES TO PAGES 79-83

4. The Most Reform-Friendly City in the Country

1. U.S. Library of Congress, Congressional Research Service, *Disaster Debris Removal after Hurricane Katrina: Status and Associated Issues,* by Linda Luther, CRS Report RL33477 (Washington, DC: Office of Congressional Information and Publishing, April 2, 2008); Eugene F. Provenzo and Sandra H. Fradd, *Hurricane Andrew, the Public Schools, and the Rebuilding of Community* (Albany: State University of New York Press, 1995).

2. Provenzo and Fradd, *Hurricane Andrew, the Public Schools, and the Rebuilding of Community,* 89.

3. Ibid., 93.

4. Ibid.

5. Louisiana Department of Education, "Louisiana Charter Schools At-a-Glance," n.d., http://www.louisianabelieves.com/schools/charter-schools (accessed August 18, 2014). According to the RSD's website, "Prior to Hurricane Katrina there were nine charter schools operating in Orleans Parish. Two were state charters: Milestone-Sabis Charter School and the International School; two were Type 1 charter (Orleans Parish School Board): Jim Singleton Charter School and New Orleans Charter Middle School; and five were Type 5 charters (Recovery School District): Pierre Capdau Charter School, Medard Nelson Charter School, Phillips (KIPP) College Prep, Sophie B. Wright Charter Middle, and Samuel Green Charter Middle School"; see http://www.rsdla.net/Resources/FAQs.aspx (accessed July 11, 2011).

6. U.S. Department of Education, "Louisiana Awarded $20.9 Million *No Child Left Behind* Grant to Assist Damaged Charter Schools, Create New Charter Schools: Funds to Be Used to Expand Classrooms for Students Displaced by Hurricanes," September 30, 2005, http://www2.ed.gov/news/pressre leases/2005/09/09302005.html (accessed August 23, 2014).

7. Steve Ritea, "School Health Coverage Revamped," *Times-Picayune,* October 15, 2005, 1; Catherine Gewertz, "Judge Calls Halt to New Orleans' Charter School Plan," *Education Week* 25 no. 9, October 26, 2005, 3.

8. Catherine Gewertz, Erik W. Robelen, and Michelle R. Davis, "Crescent Wrench," *Teacher Magazine* 17, no. 3 (November–December 2005): 20.

9. Steve Ritea, "Teachers Union Loses Its Force in Storm's Wake," *Times-Picayune,* March 6, 2006.

10. Steve Ritea, "Board Approves Charters for 20 Schools," *Times-Picayune,* October 29, 2005; Larry Carter, "Be Wary of Charter Schools: Opposing View: New Orleans Has Many, and They Are Shifting Problems Elsewhere," *USA Today,* August 24, 2009.

11. Cowen Institute for Public Initiatives, "Public Education through the Public Eye: A Survey of New Orleans Voters and Parents (2009)," Tulane University, http://www.coweninstitute.com/our-work/applied-research/public-education-through-the-public-eye-a-survey-of-new-orleans-voters-and-parents/ (accessed August 18, 2014).

12. Rick Jervis, "High Marks, New Starts in New Orleans: Charter Schools Revamp System 4 Years after Storm," *USA Today,* August 27, 2009; Stacy Teicher Khadaroo, "After Katrina, How Charter Schools Helped Recast New Orleans Education: New Orleans Has Become a Laboratory for Education Reform since Hurricane Katrina," *Christian Science Monitor,* August 29, 2010.

13. Susan Finch, "Orleans School Board Approves Lusher Charter Application: Unity Dissipates Quickly at First Post-Storm Meeting," *Times-Picayune*, September 16, 2005.

14. Catherine Gewertz, "Divided New Orleans Board Debates Reopening Schools," *Education Week*, September 28, 2005.

15. Louisiana Acts 2005, 1st Ex. Sess., no. 35, §1.Act 35 (La.R.S. 17:10.7); United Teachers of New Orleans, Louisiana Federation of Teachers, and American Federation of Teachers, "'National Model' or Flawed Approach," November 2006, http://www.coweninstitute.com/wp-content/uploads/2010/03/AFT NationalModelorFlawedApproach.pdf (accessed July 11, 2011).

16. Laura Maggi, "Senate Panel OKs School Takeover Bill—But Black Caucus, Unions Have Qualms," *Times-Picayune*, November 11, 2005; United Teachers of New Orleans, "'National Model' or Flawed Approach." The House vote is available at http://www.legis.la.gov/legis/ViewDocument.aspx?d=328672, and the Senate vote is available at http://www.legis.la.gov/legis/ViewDocument.aspx?d=328672.

17. Interview with education leader, May 21, 2012.

18. United Teachers of New Orleans, "'National Model' or Flawed Approach."

19. The findings from the polls in the discussion that follows come from Cowen Institute for Public Initiatives, "Public Education through the Public Eye."

20. *Written Testimony of Linda Johnson, President, Louisiana Board of Elementary and Secondary Education, Hearing of the United States Senate Subcommittee on Education and Early Childhood Development*, U.S. Senate, New Orleans, July 14, 2006.

21. Laurie Maggi, "Senate Panel OKs School Takeover Bill," *Times-Picayune* November 11, 2005; Ritea, "Teachers Union Loses Its Force in Storm's Wake"; Vaishali Honawar, "With Declining Membership Rolls, New Orleans Union Clings to Life," *Education Week* 26, no. 8 (October 18, 2006): 9; Darran Simon, "Teachers Union's Request Denied," *Times-Picayune*, April 25, 2007.

22. Steve Ritea, "Teachers Union Contract in Jeopardy," *Times-Picayune*, June 9, 2006; Darran Simon, "Teachers' Union Proposal Rejected: Incoming Members of Board Urged Delay," *Times-Picayune*, November 19, 2008.

23. Paul Tough, "A Teachable Moment," *New York Times*, August 17, 2008; "New Orleans Partners with Premier Education Program," *US States News*, March 4, 2007; Stephen Maloney, "State Officials Laud $17.5M Donation for N.O. Public Schools," *New Orleans CityBusiness*, December 13, 2007; Amber Bethel, "Teach Greater New Orleans Program Offers Professionals Chance to Become Teachers," *New Orleans CityBusiness*, April 14, 2003; The New Teacher Project, "Our History," n.d Tntp.org/about-tntp/our-history (accessed August 18, 2014); The New Teacher Project, "About," n.d., Tntp.org/about-tntp/ (accessed August 18, 2014); TeachNOLA, "TeachNOLA Master Teacher Corps," n.d., http://teachnola.ttrack.org/BecomeaMasterTeacher/ProgramOverview.aspx (accessed August 18, 2014).

24. Darwin BondGraham, "Building the New New Orleans: Foundation and NGO Power," *Review of Black Political Economy* 38, no. 4 (2011): 304–5.

25. Maloney, "State Officials Laud $17.5M Donation."

26. Ibid; "The Broad Foundation and U.S. Fund for UNICEF Announce $2.45 Million to Fund New KIPP Public Charter Schools in New Orleans," *Business Wire*, August 28, 2006.

27. "Capital One Announces Gifts Totaling $3 Million to Non-Profit Organizations in New Orleans and Across Louisiana," *Business Wire*, May 9, 2006; "Charitable Foundation Grants $355,000 to Teach for America in South Louisiana," Targeted News Service, December 6, 2011; "As Year Ends, Questions Remain for New Orleans," *Education Week* 27, no. 39 (June 4, 2008): 1; "Entergy, Nike Fund Solar Power Program for New Orleans Public Schools," *New Orleans CityBusiness*, September 30, 2009.

28. "Foundation Awards $500,000 Grant to Aid New Orleans Schools," *New Orleans CityBusiness*, April 20, 2006; "New Bush-Clinton Katrina Fund Grants Highlight Ongoing Recovery Effort," US Fed News, September 15, 2006; BondGraham, "Building the New New Orleans."

29. Lawrence J. Vale and Thomas J. Campanella, "Conclusion: Axioms of Resilience," in *The Resilient City: How Modern Cities Recovery from Disaster*, ed. Lawrence J. Vale and Thomas J. Campanella (New York: Oxford University Press, 2005), 340.

30. *Written Testimony of Scott S. Cowen, President, Tulane University, Hearing of the United States Senate Subcommittee on Education and Early Childhood Development*, U.S. Senate, New Orleans, July 14, 2006.

31. Rob Gurwitt, "Charter Changeover," *Governing Magazine*, September 2006, 28.

32. Ritea, "Board Approves Charters for 20 Schools."

33. "Louisiana, Tennessee Awarded $30 Million Innovation Grant to Transform Struggling Urban School Districts," States News Service, August 5, 2010. For a list of i3 awardees, see http://www2.ed.gov/programs/innovation/2010/i3hra-list.pdf; for a list of TIF awardees, see http://www2.ed.gov/programs/teacherincentive/apps/index.html.

34. "Board of Elementary and Secondary Education Names Paul Pastorek State Superintendent of Education," US Fed News Service, March 1, 2007; quotation from Greg Topo, "In New Orleans Schools, It's Like Starting Over," *USA Today*, June 7, 2007.

35. Mensah M. Dean, "Big Easy Clearing Path for Vallas?" *Philadelphia Daily News*, May 2, 2007; "Editorial: Getting Down to Basics," *Times-Picayune*, February 11, 2007; Steve Ritea, "Jarvis May Step Down at Recovery District," *Times-Picayune*, February 8, 2007; Larry Abramson, "New Orleans Hires Veteran to Run City Schools," National Public Radio, May 4, 2007, http://www.npr.org/templates/story/story.php?storyId=10011920 (accessed August 18, 2014).

36. Steve Ritea, "Vallas Takes Reins at N.O. Schools," *Times-Picayune*, May 5, 2007; quotation from Office of Senator Mary Landrieu, "Landrieu Comments on Paul Vallas, New Head of Recovery School District," May 4, 2007, http://landrieu.senate.gov/mediacenter/pressreleases/05-04-2007-1.cfm (accessed May 10, 2011); Steve Ritea and Darran Simon, "Educators Inspiring Others to Bring Their Skills to New Orleans," Associated Press State & Local Wire, June 2, 2007.

37. Elizabeth Useem, "Big City Superintendent as Powerful CEO: Paul Vallas in Philadelphia," *Peabody Journal of Education: Issues of Leadership, Policy, and Organizations* 84, no. 3 (2009): 300–317; Dale Mezzacappa, "Big Change at Districts, Less So in Classrooms," *Philadelphia Inquirer*, November 4, 2001; Linda Lenz, "Hard Knocks: Daley Takes a Tough Approach to Improving Chicago Schools," *St. Louis Post-Dispatch*, June 18, 2001.

38. Eva Travers, "Philadelphia School Reform: Historical Roots and Reflections on the 2002–2003 School Year under State Takeover" (Philadelphia: Research for Action, September 2003).

39. Dale Mezzacappa, "The Vallas Effect: The Supersized Superintendent Moves to the Superdome City," *Education Next* 8, no. 2 (Spring 2008): 30–37.

40. Ibid.

41. Abramson, "New Orleans Hires Veteran to Run City Schools."

42. Ibid.

43. Steve Ritea, "School Leader Reveals Ideas," *Times-Picayune*, May 9, 2007.

44. Caroline Hendrie, "Leadership Change Sparks Hope for Renewal," *Education Week*, May 16, 2007, 15.

45. Tough, "A Teachable Moment"; Paul Vallas, student forum at Loyola University, New Orleans, April 28, 2009.

46. Khadaroo. "After Katrina"; quotation from National Public Radio, "Obama's Trip to New Orleans to Focus Largely on Schools," October 14, 2009, http://www.npr.org/templates/story/story.php?storyId=113786050 (accessed August 22, 2014).

47. Paul T. Hill, Christine Campbell, and James Harvey, *It Takes a City: Getting Serious about Urban School Reform* (Washington, DC: Brookings Institution Press, 2000); Leigh Dingerson, "Dismantling a Community Timeline," *High School Journal* 90, no. 2 (2006): 13; Michelle Early Torregano and Patrick Shannon, "Educational Greenfield: A Critical Policy Analysis of Plans to Transform New Orleans Public Schools," *Journal for Critical Education Policy Studies* 7, no. 1 (2009): 320–40; Daniella Ann Cook, "Voices Crying Out from the Wilderness: The Story of Black Educators on School Reform in Post-Katrina New Orleans" (MA thesis, University of North Carolina, 2008); Paul Hill and Jane Hannaway, "The Future of Public Education in New Orleans," in *After Katrina: Rebuilding Opportunity and Equity into the New New Orleans* (Washington, DC: The Urban Institute, January 2006), http://www.urban.org/Upload edPDF/900913_public_education.pdf (accessed August 22, 2014).

48. Stephen Maloney, "Power Shift Proposal for School Boards in New Orleans," *New Orleans CityBusiness*, March 30, 2009.

49. Michelle Early Torregano. "Clean State: Making Sense of Public Education in the 'New' New Orleans" (PhD diss., Pennsylvania State University, 2010), 92; Adolph Reed Jr., "Class Inequality, Liberal Bad Faith, and Neoliberalism," *Neoliberalism Strategies in Disaster Reconstruction,* ed. Nandini Gunewardena and Mark Schuller (Lanham, MD: Rowman AltaMira, 2008), 147–54; Eric Ishiwata, "'We Are Seeing People We Didn't Know Exist: Katrina and the Neoliberal Erasure of Race," in *The Neoliberal Deluge: Hurricane Katrina, Late Capitalism, and the Remaking of New Orleans*, ed. Cedric Johnson (Minneapolis: University of Minnesota Press, 2011), 32–59; Geoffrey Whitehall and Cedric Johnson, "Making Citizens in Magnaville: Katrina Refugees and Neoliberal Self-Governance," in Johnson, *The Neoliberal Deluge*, 60–84; Aaron Schneider, "Privatization, Marketization, and Neoliberalism: The Political Dynamics of Post-Katrina New Orleans," *Perspectives on Politics* 10, no. 3 (2012): 718–20; Naomi Klein, *Shock Doctrine: The Rise of Disaster Capitalism* (New York: Picador, 2007); Kevin Fox Gotham, "Disaster, Inc.: Privatization and Post-Katrina Rebuilding in New Orleans," *Perspectives on Politics* 10, no. 3 (2012): 633–46;

Matt Sakakeeny, "Privatization, Marketization, and Neoliberalism: The Political Dynamics of Post-Katrina New Orleans." *Perspectives on Politics* 10, no. 3 (2012): 709–47; Loretta Pyles, "Neoliberalism, INGO Practices and Sustainable Disaster Recovery: A Post-Katrina Case Study," *Community Development Journal* 46, no. 2 (2011): 168–80; Christine L. Day, "Katrina Seven Years On: The Politics of Race and Recovery; Notes on a Roundtable Organized for the 2012 APSA Annual Meeting," *PS: Political Science & Politics* 46, no. 4 (2013): 748–52.

50. For example, see Kenneth J. Saltman, "Schooling in Disaster Capitalism: How the Political Right Is Using Disaster to Privatize Public Schooling," *Teacher Education Quarterly* (Spring 2007): 131–56.

51. Kristen L. Buras, "Race, Charter Schools, and Conscious Capitalism: On the Spatial Politics of Whiteness as Property (and the Unconscionable Assault on Black New Orleans)," *Harvard Educational Review* 81, no. 2 (2011): 296–331.

52. "Department Inviting Comments on Future Oversight of Recovery School District," *States News Service*, October 22, 2010.

53. The Council for a Better Louisiana, "New Orleans Voter Survey," August 27, 2009.

54. "Testing the Benefits, Burdens of School Choice," *Morning Edition*, National Public Radio, March 2, 2009.

55. "Pastorek Recommendation Guarantees Local Control of Schools," Targeted News Service, December 6, 2010.

56. Melinda Deslatte, "Education Board Panel Backs Plan for RSD Schools," Associated Press State & Local Wire, December 9, 2010.

57. United Teachers of New Orleans, Louisiana Federation of Teachers, and American Federation of Teachers, "Reading, Writing, Reality Check," October 2007, 10, http://la.aft.org/UTNO/index.cfm?action=article&articleID=eb05edfd-2efe-42b7–8753-dc4b84e3b504 (accessed July 12, 2011).

58. Ibid.

59. Ibid.

60. Institute on Race and Poverty at the University of Minnesota Law School, "The State of Public Schools in Post-Katrina New Orleans: The Challenge of Creating Equal Opportunity," May 15, 2010, 29.

61. Ibid., 30.

62. Interview with education leader, May 21, 2012.

63. Jed Kolko, "Where 'Back to School' Means Private School," *Trulia Trends*, August 13, 2014, http://www.trulia.com/trends/2014/08/private-vs-public-school/ (accessed August 22, 2014); Diana Samuels, "New Orleans Has Highest Percentage of Private School Students, Baton Rouge Is 4th," *Times-Picayune*, August 14, 2014; Danielle Dreilinger, "Private School Enrollment Falls 5% in Louisiana, Even More in New Orleans, Baton Rouge Areas," *Times-Picayune*, February 13, 2014.

64. Danielle Dreilinger, "Louisiana School Voucher Enrollment Opens for Fall 2014," *Times-Picayune*, January 15, 2014; Jessica Williams, "School Vouchers Are Distributed as Expanded Program Kicks In," *The Lens*, May 22, 2012, http://thelensnola.org/2012/05/22/vouchers-awarded/ (accessed August 22, 2014).

65. "A Response to the Institute on Race and Poverty's 'The State of Public Schools in Post-Katrina New Orleans: The Challenge of Creating Equal

Opportunity,'" Cowen Institute for Public Initiatives, May 2010, http://www. coweninstitute.com/wp-content/uploads/2010/05/CI-Response-to-IRP-Report. pdf (accessed August 22, 2014).

66. Leslie Jacobs, "After the Deluge, a New Education System," *Wall Street Journal*, August 30, 2010.

67. Ibid.

68. Arne Duncan, guest speaker at BGR's 2014 Annual Luncheon, New Orleans Marriott, December 11, 2014.

69. Charles J. Hatfield. "Have RSD Schools Really Improved Significantly since 2005?" Hatfield and Associates, April 1, 2011, http://theneworleansimper ative.files.wordpress.com/2011/02/hatfield-rsd-propaganda-2011.pdf (accessed August 22, 2014).

70. Interview with black political leader, June 25, 2014.

71. Sarah Carr, "Can School Reform Hurt Communities?" *New York Times*, June 15, 2013; see also Sarah Carr, *Hope Against Hope: Three Schools, One City, and the Struggle to Educate America's Children* (New York: Bloomsbury Publishing USA, 2014).

72. Luis Mirón, "Introduction. Education in Post-Katrina New Orleans: Where Are We Now and Where Might Imagination Take Us?" *Policy Futures in Education* 12, no. 8 (2014): 978.

73. Interview with civic leader, December 9, 2012.

5. From Mismanagement to Reform in Housing

1. U.S. Department of Housing and Urban Development, Secretary Henry G. Cisneros, "Letter to D. Michael Beard Regarding HANO," July 5, 1996, http://archives.hud.gov/offices/oig/reports/files/oig61802.pdf (accessed August 22, 2014); "HUD: New Orleans Housing Agency a Failure," Associated Press State & Local Wire, May 21, 2001; *Written Statement of Frank Nicotera, Executive Monitor, Housing Authority of New Orleans, Hearing of the Subcommittee on Oversight and Investigations, United States House of Representatives Committee on Financial Services*, U.S. House of Representatives, June 4, 2001; U.S. Department of Housing and Urban Development, Office of Inspector General, audit case no. 2001-FW-0001, May 11, 2001, 5.

2. Rhonda Bell, "Panel to Examine Overhaul of HANO: 8-Member Council Nationally Recognized," *Times-Picayune*, May 11, 2000.

3. U.S. Department of Housing and Urban Development, "Summary of the Quality Housing and Work Responsibility Act of 1998 (Title V of P.L. 105–276)," by Louise Hunt, Mary Schulhof, Stephen Holmquist, Rod Solomon, Senior Director Office of Policy, Program and Legislative Initiatives Office of Public and Indian Housing, December 1998; *Statement of the National Advisory Council of the Housing Authority of New Orleans Prepared for the Subcommittee on Oversight and Investigation's Hearing on the Operations of the Housing Authority of the City of New Orleans*, U.S. House of Representatives, June 4, 2001; *National Advisory Council of the Housing Authority of New Orleans,* U.S. House of Representatives, June 4, 2001; U.S. Department of Housing and Urban Development, Office of Inspector General, Gloria Cousar, "Audit Report on the

Housing Authority of New Orleans," May 11, 2001, http://archives.hud.gov/offices/oig/reports/internal/ig160001.pdf (accessed August 22, 2014).

4. "HUD Will Soon Control New Orleans Housing Agency," Associated Press State & Local Wire, December 20, 2001; U.S. Department of Housing and Urban Development, Office of Inspector General, audit case no. 2001-FW-0001.

5. Joan McKinney, "Baker Wants Takeover of N.O. Housing Agency," *The Advocate*, May 17, 2001; Dennis Persica, "HANO Takeover Talk Spurs Morial Protest: He Writes to HUD to Oppose Receivership," *Times-Picayune*, December 19, 2001; Lynne Jensen and Susan Finch, "Mayor's Plea to Halt HUD Plan Denied: Morial Wanted Court to Appoint Receiver," *Times-Picayune*, February 22, 2002; Lynne Jensen, "HUD Rebuffs Morial, Finishes Takeover: D.C. Man Appointed to Run Ailing HANO," *Times-Picayune*, March 1, 2002.

6. Gwen Filosa, "Guste Families Happy to Be Home: New Housing Is Attractive, Affordable," *Times-Picayune*, November 7, 2007.

7. *Dorothy Gautreaux v. The Chicago Housing Authority*, 296 F.Supp. 907 (7th Cir., 1969); *Hills v. Gautreaux* 425 U.S. 284 (1976); "Housing, Public, and Urban Policy: *Gautreaux v. Chicago Housing Authority*," *Yale Law Journal* 79, no. 4 (1970): 712–29; Susan J. Popkin et al., "The *Gautreaux* Legacy: What Might Mixed-Income and Dispersal Strategies Mean for the Poorest Public Housing Tenants?" *Housing Policy Debate* 11, no. 4 (2000): 911–42; Robert C. Ellickson, "The False Promise of the Mixed-Income Housing Project," *UCLA Law Review* 57 (2009): 983; Michael Darcy, "De-Concentration of Disadvantage and Mixed Income Housing: A Critical Discourse Approach." *Housing, Theory, and Society* 27, no. 1 (2010): 1–22; Joanna Duke, "Mixed Income Housing Policy and Public Housing Residents' 'Right to the City,'" *Critical Social Policy* 29, no. 1 (2009): 100–120; James Tracy, "Hope VI Mixed-Income Housing Projects Displace Poor People," *Race, Poverty & the Environment* 15, no. 1 (2008): 26–29; Susan J. Popkin, "A Decade of HOPE VI: Research Findings and Policy Challenges" (Washington, DC: The Urban Institute, 2004).

8. Robert J. Chaskin and Mark L. Joseph, "Building 'Community' in Mixed-Income Developments: Assumptions, Approaches, and Early Experiences," *Urban Affairs Review* 45, no. 3 (2010): 299–335; Mark L. Joseph, "Is Mixed-Income Development an Antidote to Urban Poverty?" *Housing Policy Debate* 17, no. 2 (2006): 209–34; James C. Fraser and Edward L. Kick, "The Role of Public, Private, Non-Profit, and Community Sectors in Shaping Mixed-Income Housing Outcomes in the U.S.," *Urban Studies* 44, no. 12 (2007): 2357–77; James E. Rosenbaum, Linda K. Stroh, and Cathy A. Flynn, "Lake Parc Place: A Study of Mixed-Income Housing." *Housing Policy Debate* 9, no. 4 (1998), 703–40; James Curtis Fraser et al., , "HOPE VI, Colonization, and the Production of Difference," *Urban Affairs Review* 49, no. 4 (2013): 525–56; Edward G. Goetz, "The Transformation of Public Housing Policy, 1985–2011,"*Journal of the American Planning Association* 78, no. 4 (2012): 452–63; Ellickson, "The False Promise."

9. Robert J. Chaskin and Mark L. Joseph, "Social Interaction in Mixed-Income Developments: Relational Expectations and Emerging Reality," *Journal of Urban Affairs* 33, no. 2 (2011): 209–37; Mark L. Joseph and Robert Chaskin, "Living in a Mixed-Income Development: Resident Perceptions of the Benefits and Disadvantages of Two Developments in Chicago," *Urban Studies* 47, no. 11 (2010): 2347–66; Chaskin and Joseph, "Building 'Community'"; Fraser et al., "HOPE

VI"; Erin M. Graves, "The Structuring of Urban Life in a Mixed-Income Housing "Community," *City & Community* 9, no. 1 (2010): 109–31; Ashley Brown Burns, "New Communities in Old Spaces: Evidence from HOPE VI" (PhD diss., Duke University, 2013); Darcy, "De-Concentration of Disadvantage," 1–22; Pauline Lipman, "Mixed-Income Schools and Housing: Advancing the Neoliberal Urban Agenda," *Journal of Education Policy* 23, no. 2 (2008): 119–34; Erin M. Graves, "Mixed Outcome Developments: Comparing Policy Goals to Resident Outcomes in Mixed-Income Housing," *Journal of the American Planning Association* 77, no. 2 (2011): 143–53; Edward G. Goetz, "The Politics of Poverty Deconcentration and Housing Demolition," *Journal of Urban Affairs* 22, no. 2 (2000): 157–73.

10. Rhonda Bell, "HANO Plan to Sell Surplus Lots Worries Neighbors: HANO Plans Raise Concerns," *Times-Picayune*, June 10, 2000.

11. Bruce Eggler, "Vote Expected Today on Wal-Mart Plan: Former St. Thomas Residents Set to Sue," *Times-Picayune*, October 17, 2002; Greg Thomas and Robert Scott, "Wal-Mart May Build Supercenter Uptown: St. Thomas Area Could be Revitalized," *Times-Picayune*. July 21, 2001; "HANO Welcomes Residents at River Garden Grand Opening," *US Fed News*, November 16, 2004.

12. Alexander J. Reichl, "Learning from St. Thomas: Community, Capital, and the Redevelopment of Public Housing in New Orleans," *Journal of Urban Affairs* 21, no. 2 (1999): 173–74.

13. "Commentary: Controversial St. Thomas Rehabilitation Project Should Move Forward," *New Orleans CityBusiness*, October 7, 2002; Christine C. Cook and Mickey Lauria, "Urban Regeneration and Public Housing in New Orleans," *Urban Affairs Review* 30, no. 4 (1995): 538–57.

14. Bruce Eggler, "Wal-Mart Critics Find Allies in D.C.: Federal Regulators See Snags in Plan," *Times-Picayune*, September 27, 2002.

15. Rob Nelson, "Senior Village Stands Poised to Receive Its First Occupant," *Times-Picayune*, July 15, 2003; Michelle Krupa, "N.O. Council May Seek Middle Ground on Demolitions," *Times-Picayune*, December 17, 2007.

16. For an award list see: http://portal.hud.gov/hudportal/documents/huddoc?id=DOC_10014.pdf; Rob Nelson, "HUD Chief Sounds Death Knell of Fischer Complex," *Times-Picayune*, April 25, 2003; Rob Nelson, "Grants Let HANO Destroy Units: Fischer Site One of 4 Targeted or Renewal," *Times-Picayune*, August 15, 2003.

17. Frank Donze, "Public Housing Overhaul Spat in N.O. Settled: City Will Allocate $14 Million, Deal Clears Way for Work to Begin," *Times-Picayune*, June 30, 2004.

18. Cook and Lauria, "Urban Regeneration," 540.

19. Katy Reckdahl, "Change Is in the Air at Iberville Complex: Last Traditional Public Housing Site in N.O. Could Get Revamp," *Times-Picayune*, September 10, 2010.

20. Cook and Lauria, "Urban Regeneration," 540.

21. Ibid., 552–53.

22. Quotation from Greg Thomas, "Favored Stadium Site Off-Limits, Morial Says," *Times-Picayune*, June 28, 2001; Bret Ladine, "Iberville Residents Say Plan for Stadium Is No Fair Game: Despite Its Many Problems, Area Is Home to Them," *Times-Picayune*, July 7, 2001.

23. U.S. Department of Housing and Urban Development, "Housing Choice Vouchers Fact Sheet," http://portal.hud.gov/hudportal/HUD?src=/topics/housing_choice_voucher_program_section_8 (accessed August 23, 2014); Bruce Alpert, "Feds Push City to Reform Section 8," *Times-Picayune*, March 28, 2000.

24. Gwen Filosa, "Housing Help: Wait Is Long, Price Is Right; Critics Say Program Invites Crime, Blight," *Times-Picayune*, May 31, 2005.

25. Popkin, "A Decade of HOPE VI."

26. Gwen Filosa, "Housing Blunders Admitted: Tenants, Families Were Hurt by Ousters," *Times-Picayune*, June 30, 2005.

27. Susan J. Popkin, *The Hidden War: Crime and the Tragedy of Public Housing in Chicago* (New Brunswick, NJ: Rutgers University Press, 2000); "A Place to Live," *Times-Picayune*, October 27, 2001; Rhonda Bell, "HANO Vows to Replace All Housing Units: Tenants Criticize Recent Policy," *Times-Picayune*, October 25, 2001.

28. Nora Goddard. "The Destruction of Public Housing in New Orleans," November 27, 2012, http://www.nolatourguy.com/public-housing/ (accessed August 22, 201); Rachel E. Luft and Shana Griffin, "A Status Report on Housing in New Orleans after Katrina: An Intersectional Analysis," in *Katrina and the Women of New Orleans* (New Orleans: Newcomb College Center for Research on Women, 2008), 50–53; R.W. Kates et al., "Reconstruction of New Orleans after Hurricane Katrina: A Research Perspective," *Proceedings of the National Academy of Sciences* 103, no. 40 (2006): 14653–60; Susan J. Popkin, Margery A. Turner, and Martha Burt, "Rebuilding Affordable Housing in New Orleans: The Challenge of Creating Inclusive Communities," After Katrina series (Washington, DC: The Urban Institute, 2006).

29. Shannon Van Zandt et al., "Mapping Social Vulnerability to Enhance Housing and Neighborhood Resilience," *Housing Policy Debate* 22, no. 1 (2012): 29–55; Yosuke Hirayama, "Collapse and Reconstruction: Housing Recovery Policy in Kobe after the Hanshin Great Earthquake," *Housing Studies* 15, no. 1 (2000): 111–28; Yang Zhang and Walter Gillis Peacock, "Planning for Housing Recovery? Lessons Learned from Hurricane Andrew," *Journal of the American Planning Association* 76, no. 1 (2009): 5–24; Anthony Oliver-Smith, "Post-Disaster Housing Reconstruction and Social Inequality: A Challenge to Policy and Practice," *Disasters* 14, no. 1 (1990): 7–19; Yang Zhang, "Will Natural Disasters Accelerate Neighborhood Decline? A Discrete-Time Hazard Analysis of Residential Property Vacancy and Abandonment Before and After Hurricane Andrew in Miami-Dade County (1991–2000)," *Environment and Planning, Part B: Planning and Design* 39, no. 6 (2012): 1084; Alice Fothergil, Enrique G. M. Maestas, and JoAnne DeRouen Darlington, "Race, Ethnicity, and Disasters in the United States: A Review of the Literature," *Disasters* 23, no. 2 (1999): 156–73; Enrico L. Quarantelli, "Patterns of Sheltering and Housing in U.S. Disasters," *Disaster Prevention and Management* 4, no. 3 (1995): 43–53; Rebekah Green, Lisa K. Bates, and Andrew Smyth, "Impediments to Recovery in New Orleans' Upper and Lower Ninth Ward: One Year after Hurricane Katrina." *Disasters* 31, no. 4 (2007): 311–35.

30. Lisa K. Bates, "Post-Katrina Housing: Problems, Policies, and Prospects for African-Americans in New Orleans," *The Black Scholar* 36, no. 4 (2006): 13–31. Bates reaches this conclusion by citing Robert C. Bolin and Patricia

A. Bolton, "Race, Religion, and Ethnicity in Disaster Recovery" (Boulder: Institute of Behavioral Science, University of Colorado, 1986), and F. Cooper and L. Laughy, "Managing Hazards in a Changing Multinational World," unpublished paper (1994). See also Fothergil, Maestas, and DeRouen Darlington, "Race, Ethnicity, and Disasters in the United States."

31. Jie Ying Wu and Michael K. Lindell, "Housing Reconstruction after Two Major Earthquakes: The 1994 Northridge Earthquake in the United States and the 1999 Chi-Chi Earthquake in Taiwan," *Disasters* 28, no. 1 (2004): 63–81.

32. David L. Brunsma, David Overfelt, and J. Steven Picou, *The Sociology of Katrina: Perspectives on a Modern Catastrophe* (New York: Rowman & Littlefield, 2010); James R. Elliott and Jeremy Pais, "Race, Class, and Hurricane Katrina: Social Differences in Human Responses to Disaster," *Social Science Research* 35, no. 2 (2006): 295–321; John R. Logan, "The Impact of Katrina: Race and Class in Storm-Damaged Neighborhoods," n.d., www.s4.brown.edu/katrina/report.pdf; Michel Masozera, Melissa Bailey, and Charles Kerchner, "Distribution of Impacts of Natural Disasters across Income Groups: A Case Study of New Orleans," *Ecological Economics* 63, no. 2 (2007): 299–306; Jonathan D. Stringfield, "Higher Ground: An Exploratory Analysis of Characteristics Affecting Returning Populations after Hurricane Katrina," *Population and Environment* 31, no. 1–3 (2010): 43–63; Christina Finch, Christopher T. Emrich, and Susan L. Cutter, "Disaster Disparities and Differential Recovery in New Orleans," *Population and Environment* 31, no. 4 (2010): 179–202; Rodney D. Green, Marie Kouassi, and Belinda Mambo, "Housing, Race, and Recovery from Hurricane Katrina," *Review of Black Political Economy* 40, no. 2 (2013): 1–19; Elizabeth Fussell, Narayan Sastry, and Mark VanLandingham, "Race, Socioeconomic Status, and Return Migration to New Orleans after Hurricane Katrina," *Population & Environment* 31, no. 1–3 (2010): 20–42; William P. Quigley, "Obstacle to Opportunity: Housing That Working and Poor People Can Afford in New Orleans since Katrina," *Wake Forest Law Review* 42 (2007): 393; Amy Liu, Matthew Fellowes, and Mia Mabanta, *Special Edition of the Katrina Index: A One Year Review of Key Indicators of Recovery in Post-Storm New Orleans* (Washington, DC: Brookings Institution, 2006).

33. Matthew Cardinale, "U.S. Public Housing Advocates Coordinate National Movement," IPS: Inter Press Service, August 30, 2007.

34. Jordan Flaherty, "Floodlines: Preserving Public Housing in New Orleans," *Race, Poverty & the Environment* 17, no. 2 (2010): 61–65; Gwen Filosa, "Nagin Wants to Run Road Home in N.O.: Congressional Panel Gets Earful on Public Housing," *Times-Picayune*, February 23, 2007; Richard Cole et al., "Housing Authority of New Orleans: Pre-Katrina Resident Survey," presented at the Annual Meeting of the Urban Affairs Association Meeting, Baltimore, April 23–26, 2008; Cain Burdeau, "HUD: Demolition Plan for New Orleans Housing Validated by Survey," Associated Press State and Local Wire, March 6, 2008.

35. "HANO OKs Razing of 4 Housing Complexes," Associated Press State & Local Wire, December 9, 2006.

36. John Moreno Gonzales, "UN Experts Criticize New Orleans Housing," Associated Press, February 29, 2008.

37. Katy Reckdahl, "Nagin OKs Razing of Lafitte Complex: HUD Has Addressed Concerns, He Says," *Times-Picayune*, March 25, 2008; Bruce

Eggler, "Council OKs Tax Waiver on HANO Shut Sites," *Times-Picayune*. March 9, 2007.

38. Gwen Filosa and Coleman Warner, "Council Majority Backs Demolition: Public Housing Vote Set for This Morning," *Times-Picayune*, December 20, 2007.

39. Gwen Filosa, "Their Hearts' Desire: New 9th Ward Complex Is Hailed as the Future of Public Housing in New Orleans," *Times-Picayune,* June 7, 2007.

40. Testimony by Orlando Cabrera, *Two Years after the Storm: Housing Needs in the Gulf Coast, Statement to the Senate Committee on Banking, Housing and Urban Affairs*, U.S. Senate, September 25, 2007, http://www.hud.gov/offices/cir/test070925.cfm (accessed August 10, 2014); Bill Walsh, "Feds Oppose Full Replacement of N.O. Public Housing Units: HUD's Stance Takes Landrieu by Surprise," *Times-Picayune*, September 26, 2007.

41. Testimony by Cabrera.

42. Tram Nguyen, "Pushed Out and Pushing Back in New Orleans," *Color Lines: News for Action*, April 7, 2010, http://colorlines.com/archives/2010/04/pushed_out_and_pushing_back_in_new_orleans.html (accessed August 22, 2014); Steve Viuker, "Special Report: Rebuilding New Orleans," *Multi-Housing News*, September 2007; quotation from U.S. Department of Housing and Urban Development, "Housing Authority of New Orleans Board Approves Firms to Plan the Redevelopment of St. Bernard, C. J. Peete, B. W. Cooper," HUD News Release 07–030, March 28, 2007.

43. Darwin BondGraham, "Building the New New Orleans: Foundation and NGO Power." *Review of Black Political Economy* 38, no. 4 (2011): 280–304; Katy Reckdahl, "HUD Chief Ushers in New N.O. Units: Donovan Announces Partnership on Services," *Times-Picayune*, April 13, 2010.

44. Richard A. Webster, "New Orleans City Council Approves Demolition of Iberville Housing Development," *Times-Picayune*, May 16, 2013; Danny Monteverde, "N.O. Council OKs Demolition at Iberville Housing Project," *The Advocate,* May 22, 2013.

45. Katy Reckdahl, "Developers Picked to Revamp Housing: HUD Grant Sought to Remake Iberville," *Times-Picayune*, September 30, 2010; Webster, "New Orleans City Council Approves Demolition"; Monteverde, "N.O. Council OKs Demolition"; Katy Reckdahl, "HANO Gets $30.5 Million to Re-Do Iberville Public-Housing Complex," *Times-Picayune*, August 31, 2011.

46. Monteverde, "N.O. Council OKs Demolition"; Richard A. Webster, "HANO Begins Iberville Overhaul: Families to Move for the Construction," *Times-Picayune,* January 16, 2013; Reckdahl, "HANO Gets $30.5 Million."

47. Michelle Roberts, "HUD to Reopen More New Orleans Housing," Associated Press, June 14, 2006; White quoted in Katy Reckdahl, "HUD Pours Millions into Lafitte, but Complex Will Be Razed in March," *Times-Picayune*, August 27, 2008; Clarkson quoted in Gwen Filosa and Coleman Warner, "Council Majority Backs Demolition: Public Housing Vote Set for This Morning," *Times-Picayune*, December 20, 2007.

48. Katy Reckdahl, "Stimulus Money Reslated for Repairs: HANO Rethinks Focus on New Construction," *Times-Picayune*, May 2, 2009.

49. Richard A. WebsterThe Times-Picayune, "Mayor Landrieu, HUD Secretary Donovan Sign HANO Back to Local Control," *Times-Picayune*, May 28, 2014.

50. Laura Maggi, "Governor's Housing Trust Bill Dies: Blanco Seeks New Way to Aid Homeowners," *Times-Picayune*, February 18, 2006; State of Louisiana, Governor Katherine Blanco, Executive Order KBB 05–63, http://www.doa.la.gov/osr/other/kbb05–63.htm (accessed August 12, 2014); Robert B. Olshansky et al., "Planning for the Rebuilding of New Orleans," *Journal of the American Planning Association* 74, no. 3 (2008): 276; Marla Nelson, Renia Ehrenfeucht, and Shirley Laska, "Planning, Plans, and People: Professional Expertise, Local Knowledge, and Governmental Action in Post–Hurricane Katrina New Orleans," *Cityscape* 9, no. 3 (2007): 23–52; Robert K. Whelan, "An Old Economy for the 'New' New Orleans? Post-Katrina Economic Development Efforts," in *There Is No Such Thing as a Natural Disaster: Race, Class, and Hurricane Katrina*, ed. Chester W. Hartman and Gregory D. Squires (New York: Routledge, 2006), 215–31; testimony of Governor Kathleen Blanco, *A Vision and Strategy for Rebuilding New Orleans, Hearing before the Subcommittee on Economic Development, Public Buildings and Emergency Management and Subcommittee on Water Resources and Environment of the Committee on Transportation and Infrastructure*, U.S. House of Representatives, 109th Cong., 1st sess., October 18, 2005; Louisiana Recovery Authority, "The Road Home Housing Programs Action Plan Amendment for Disaster Recovery Funds" n.d., http://archives.hud.gov/news/2006/pr06–058.pdf (accessed August 18, 2014); Bruce Eggler, "UNOP Citywide Plan Wins Approval," *Times-Picayune*, June 14, 2007.

51. Gwen Filosa and Laura Maggi, "'Road Home' Brings Blanco to N.O.: Some Residents Say Proposal Isn't Enough," *Times-Picayune*, April 13, 2006; Karen Turni Bazile, "Official: Grants Aren't Lagniappe: Road Home to Cover Uninsured Damages," *Times-Picayune*, April 30, 2006.

52. Coleman Warner, "Group Pushing for Smooth Road Home: Grass-Roots Organization in N.O. Gaining Clout with State Officials," *Times-Picayune*, December 25, 2006; Jeffrey Meitrodt, "Understaffed and Overwhelmed: The Firm Administering Louisiana's Road Home Program Has Consistently Underestimated the Magnitude of the Task, Records Show," *Times-Picayune*, January 28, 2007.

53. Bruce Alpert, "Senate, President Approve Funds for Recovery: State to Ramp Up Road Home Effort," *Times-Picayune*, June 16, 2006; David Hammer, "Every Step Bumpy for Road Home: Crescendo of Gaffes Sets Stage for Shortfall," *Times-Picayune*, June 29, 2007.

54. Filosa and Maggi, "'Road Home' Brings Blanco to N.O"; David Hammer, "Governor to Ask Feds for Up to $4 Billion: She Hopes to Persuade Congress to Cover Road Home Gap," *Times-Picayune*, June 16, 2007; Laura Maggi, "Company Chosen to Take the Wheel for Road Home: Program to Be Run by ICF International," *Times-Picayune*, June 10, 2006.

55. Bates "Post-Katrina Housing"; Gwen Filosa, "On a Hard Road: The Much-Vaunted Road Home Relief Program Is Off to a Slow Start, to Put It Mildly," *Times-Picayune*, November 6, 2006; Bruce Nolan, "Blanco Tries to Light Fire under Road Home Plan: Thousands of Families Waiting for Applications to Be Processed," *Times-Picayune*, November 7, 2006; David Hammer, "Relief Far Off for La. Rental Owners: Their Road Home Paved with Red Tape," *Times-Picayune*, January 4, 2007; Luft and Griffin, "A Status Report on Housing"; David Hammer, "Rental Road Home Gets Rolling: Officials Promise It Will Work Quickly," *Times-Picayune*, January 31, 2007; "Fewer Homes for

Katrina's Poorest Victims: An Analysis of Subsidized Homes in Post-Katrina New Orleans," PolicyLink, December 2007, 9, http://www.policylink.org/documents/nola_fewerhomes.pdf (accessed August 22, 2014).

56. Coleman Warner, "Road Home Gets Full Funding: Congressional OK Arrived Last Week," *Times-Picayune*, July 12, 2006; David Hammer, "Road Home Going Broke, Blanco Aide Says," *Times-Picayune*, May 2, 2007; Hammer, "Every Step Bumpy for Road Home"; David Hammer, "Blowing in the Wind: Federal Officials and the Louisiana Recovery Authority Disagree on What Caused a Projected $3 Billion Shortfall in the State's Road Home Program," *Times-Picayune*, May 24, 2007; David Hammer, "Governor to Ask Feds for Up to $4 Billion: She Hopes to Persuade Congress to Cover Road Home Gap," *Times-Picayune*, June 16, 2007.

57. Michelle Krupa, "LRA Feeds Road Home Kitty: $1 Billion Figure is Key for Congress," *Times-Picayune*, June 26, 2007.

58. Gwen Filosa, "Nagin Wants to Run Road Home in N.O.: Congressional Panel Gets Earful on Public Housing," *Times-Picayune*. February 23, 2007; Valerie Faciane, "Applicants Overwhelm Road Home Web Site: Also, Glitch Made Private Data Public," *Times-Picayune*. August 28, 2006; Jeffrey Meitrodt "Understaffed and Overwhelmed: The Firm Administering Louisiana's Road Home Program Has Consistently Underestimated the Magnitude of the Task, Records Show," *Times-Picayune*, January 28, 2007; "Editorial: Road Home Woes Go On," *Times-Picayune*, September 12, 2007; David Hammer, "Policy Snarl Adds to Road Home Detours Officials Do About-Face on Transfer of Grants from Owners to Buyers," *Times-Picayune*, February 27, 2007.

59. Michelle Krupa, "Road Home Isn't Easy Street: Residents Complain of Slow Pace, Red Tape," *Times-Picayune*, October 7, 2006; Filosa, "Nagin Wants to Run Road Home."

60. Bill Barrow, "ICF May Let Cash Flow as Appeals Ironed Out: Ideas for Improving Road Home Aired Out at Governor's Mansion," *Times-Picayune*, December 20, 2006; Stephanie Grace, "Disconnect on the Road Home," *Times-Picayune*, December 24, 2006; Green, Kouassi, and Mambo, "Housing, Race, and Recovery," 1–19; David Hammer, "Disputes over Awards Add to Road Home Headaches: New Steps to Resolve Challenges Urged," *Times-Picayune*, March 13, 2007; Gulf States Policy Institute, "Road Home Program Leaves Many Homeowners Waiting" (Santa Monica, CA: RAND Institute, 2008), http://www.rand.org/content/dam/rand/pubs/research_briefs/2008/RAND_RB9355.pdf (accessed August 22, 2014); Michelle Krupa, "Road Home Waits Vary: People Selling Homes Faced Longer Delay," *Times-Picayune*, March 19, 2008.

61. Jeffrey Meitrodt, "State Blasts Road Home Firm—But Top Exec Defends ICF's Performance," *Times-Picayune*, December 24, 2006; Barrow, "ICF May Let Cash Flow"; Bill Walsh, "Hearing Blasts La.'s Housing Recovery: Road Home 'a Joke,' Congresswoman Says," *Times-Picayune*, February 7, 2007; Filosa, "Nagin Wants to Run Road."

62. Hammer, "Every Step Bumpy for Road Home"; David Hammer, "La. Road Home Makes Changes: Decisions in Writing Have Been Key Issue," *Times-Picayune*, December 22, 2007; David Hammer, "Many Early Applicants Waiting on Road Home: Homeowners Blamed for Some Delays," *Times-Picayune*, January 23, 2008; David Hammer, "Road Home Claims Major Strides: Penalties against ICF Bring Results," *Times-Picayune*, September 19, 2007.

63. Warner, "Group Pushing for Smooth Road"; Peter F. Burns, "Community Organizations in a Non-Regime City: The New Orleans Experience," in *Transforming the City: Community Organizing and the Challenge of Political Change*, ed. Marion Orr (Lawrence: University Press of Kansas, 2007); Hammer, "Every Step Bumpy for Road Home"; David Hammer, "LRA Hires Company to Review Road Home," *Times-Picayune*, August 24, 2007; David Hammer, "Road Home Deadline Today," *Times-Picayune*, July 31, 2007.

64. David Hammer, "Huge Roadblock for Road Home: Program May Be Halted as State, Feds Disagree on Whether Program Rules are Legal," *Times-Picayune*, March 17, 2007; Coleman Warner, "Road Home to Pay Some Lump Sums: Only Applicants without Mortgage Are Affected," *Times-Picayune*, March 23, 2007; Bruce Alpert, "State Yields to Feds: Road Home to Give Cash Upfront," *Times-Picayune*, March 21, 2007.

65. Greater New Orleans Fair Housing Action Center, "What Is the Road Home Program," n.d., http://www.gnofairhousing.org/wp-content/uploads/2012/02/AboutRoadHome.pdf (accessed August 22, 2014); Campbell Robertson, "Settlement Is Reached in Suit over Katrina Grants," *New York Times*, July 6, 2011.

66. David Hammer, "Court Lifts Hold on Road Home: Ruling Goes against Housing Advocates," *Times-Picayune*, April 9, 2011; David Hammer, "Road Home Grantees in Low-Income Areas Aided: $62 Million Push Affects Four Parishes," *Times-Picayune*, May 3, 2011; Katy Reckdahl, "Road Home Gives 1,460 More Help: Settlement Ends Long Legal Battle," *Times-Picayune*, July 7, 2011; Timothy F. Green and Robert B. Olshansky, "Rebuilding Housing in New Orleans: The Road Home Program after the Hurricane Katrina Disaster," *Housing Policy Debate* 22, no. 1 (2012): 75–99.

67. Allison Plyer and Elaine Ortiz, "Benchmarks for Blight: How Much Blight Does New Orleans Have?" Greater New Orleans Community Data Center, August 21, 2012; Gordon Russell "N.O. Blight Ranks Worst in Nation: One in Three Properties Unoccupied, Data Show," *Times-Picayune*, September 20, 2012.

68. City of New Orleans, "Blight Reduction Report," January 2014, http://www.nola.gov/getattachment/Performance-and-Accountability/Initiatives-and-Reports/BlightSTAT/Blight-Report_web.pdf/ (accessed August 23, 2014).

69. Stephanie Grace, "Blight, Displacement Recovery," *Times-Picayune*, August 8, 2010.

70. Ibid.

71. Summarized from City of New Orleans Office of Performance and Accountability, "BlightSTAT: Reporting Period, May 2013," http://new.nola.gov/getattachment/8dc46423-b052–42a2-b427–57b5a51d3085/BlightSTAT-May-2013/ (accessed August 23, 2014).

72. City of New Orleans, "Blight Reduction Report"; "Editorial: Dropping in Blight Ranks," *Times-Picayune*, August 22, 2012; Plyer and Ortiz, "Benchmarks for Blight."

73. City of New Orleans, Mayor Mitchell J. Landrieu, "City Surpasses Blight Reduction Milestone of 10,000 Units by 2014," January 9, 2014; City of New Orleans, Mayor Mitchell J. Landrieu, "Mayor Landrieu, City Council Strengthen City's Enforcement Capabilities on Blighted Properties," August 22, 2013; City of New Orleans, "Blight Reduction Report."

6. Public Safety or an Unsafe Public?

1. This section is based on Mike Wallace, "NOPD Blues: New Orleans Police Department Cited as Most Brutal in Entire United States," *60 Minutes*, October 30, 1994.

2. Leonard N. Moore, *Black Rage in New Orleans: Police Brutality and African American Activism from World War II to Hurricane Katrina* (Baton Rouge: LSU Press, 2010); "New Orleans Racial Tension: Police Resignation, Trial Moved," Associated Press, November 25, 1980; Victoria R. Bowles, "Convictions Seen as Clear Message to New Orleans Police Department," United Press International, March 29, 1983.

3. Moore, *Black Rage*; Lee Mitgang, "Few Minority Gains in Big-City Police Departments since '60s," Associated Press, May 21, 1980; *The Police Association of New Orleans v. The City of New Orleans*, 100 F.3d 1159 (5th Cir. December 9, 1996).

4. Rob Gurwitt, "The Comeback of the Cops," *Governing Magazine*. January 1998, 14.

5. Ibid.

6. Chris Bonura, "Mayor Put Police Department Back on Its Feet, Some Say," *New Orleans CityBusiness*, October 8, 2001.

7. Eric Westervelt and Bob Edwards, "New Orleans Police," National Public Radio, February 4, 1998; Gary Fields, "New Orleans' Crime Fight Started with Police," *USA Today*, February 1, 2000.

8. Gurwitt, "Comeback of the Cops"; Westervelt and Edwards, "New Orleans Police"; Fields, "New Orleans' Crime"; Paul Keegan, "The Thinnest Blue Line," *New York Times*, March 31, 1996.

9. Ernie Suggs, "Q&A with Richard Pennington," *Atlanta Journal-Constitution*, June 2, 2002; Sue Anne Pressley, "The Big Easy Makes Serious Effort to Solve Sobering Crime Problem: Additional Police Officers, Money Aimed at Erasing New Orleans' Tarnished Image," *Washington Post*, July 5, 1997.

10. Fields, "New Orleans' Crime"; Gurwitt, "Comeback of the Cops"; Samuel Walker, Geoffrey P. Alpert, and Dennis J. Kenney, "Early Warning Systems: Responding to the Problem Police Officer," in *NIJ Research in Brief* (Washington, DC: National Institute of Justice, 2001).

11. Daniel Pedersen, "'Go Get the Scumbags,'" *Newsweek*, October 20, 1997, 32.

12. Deon Roberts, "Resignation of New Orleans Police Dept. Superintendent Eddie Compass Creates Concern," *New Orleans CityBusiness*, September 25, 2005; Keith Pandolfi, "New Orleans Police Foundation Works to Reduce Crime Rate," *New Orleans CityBusiness*, November 25, 2002; Carlos Campos and Lyda Longa, "Private Giving to Police? Some Warn of Favoritism," *Atlanta Journal and Constitution*, December 10, 1998; Pressley, "Big Easy Makes Serious Effort."

13. Bonura, "Mayor Put Police"; Janet Plume, "N.O. Police Details Bauerleint to Polish Image, Boost Ranks," *Adweek*, April 28, 1997; "New Orleans Police Foundation Awarded Two Grants for Project Safe," *PR Newswire*, October 10, 2002; "U.S. Attorney Announces Federal Grant Money for New Orleans Area Agencies," *New Orleans CityBusiness*, June 2, 2003; "Landrieu Secures

$367 Million in Projects to Benefit Southeast LA," *States News Service*, March 13, 2009.

14. Fields, "New Orleans' Crime"; Suggs, "Q&A"; "New Orleans Police Dept. Promotions Add $1.4M to Payroll," *New Orleans CityBusiness*, March 14, 2004.

15. Cheryl W. Thompson, "From across U.S., Five Finalists for Job of D.C. Police Chief: Pennington; Scandal-Rife Force Restored in New Orleans," *Washington Post*, March 22, 1998; "New Orleans Murders Up 22 Percent in '02," Associated Press State & Local Wire, January 1, 2003; Deon Roberts, "NOPD Slide Bodes Poorly for Business," *New Orleans CityBusiness*, January 26, 200; Lee Hancock, "Storm Tossed What Was Left of New Orleans' Police Image," *Dallas Morning News*, October 26, 2005.

16. "Police Trying to Move Out Remaining New Orleans Residents," Associated Press, September 5, 2005.

17. Ibid. Approximately 150 officers were saved during search and rescue operations.

18. Jed Horne, *Breach of Faith* (New York: Random House, 2006).

19. Robert Tanner, "New Orleans Mayor Orders Police Back to Streets Amid Looting," Associated Press, September 1, 2005. Examples of police looting can be found in a variety of sources, including Douglas Brinkley, *The Great Deluge* (New York: William Morrow, 2006); and Horne, *Breach of Faith*.

20. "Another Seven New Orleans Police Officers Fired for Being AWOL," Associated Press, November 10, 2005.

21. Michael Perlstein and Trymaine Lee, "The Good and the Bad," *Times-Picayune*, December 18, 2005.

22. Interview with NOPD commander, July 17, 2009.

23. "Exhausted New Orleans Police, Firemen, Getting R&R," Associated Press, September 5, 2005.

24. For example, Brinkley, *The Great Deluge;* and Michael Eric Dyson, *Come Hell or High Water: Hurricane Katrina and the Color of Disaster* (New York: Basic Books, 2006).

25. "Editorial: Where Is the Cavalry?" *Times-Picayune*, September 1, 2005.

26. April Capochino, "Challenged New Orleans Police Department Receives Reprieve from Residency Rule," *New Orleans CityBusiness*, December 26, 2005; Amy Rocbach, "New Orleans Police Department Fires 45 Police Officers and 6 Other Employees for Abandoning Their Posts during Hurricane Katrina," *NBC News Transcripts*, October 29, 2005; Ed Bradley, "Order Out of Chaos: New Orleans Police Department Trying to Hold the Flood-Ravaged City Together," *60 Minutes*, September 11, 2005.

27. Quotations in this paragraph come from "New Orleans Police Officers Cleared of Looting: But Four Suspended for 10 Days for Not Stopping Ransacking of Store," *Associated Press*, March 20, 2006.

28. Moore, *Black Rage*; Michael Peter Wigginton Jr., "The New Orleans Police Emergency Response to Hurricane Katrina: A Case Study" (PhD diss., University of Southern Mississippi, 2007); Horne, *Breach of Faith*.

29. Harry Smith, "Eddie Compass of the New Orleans Police Department Discusses His Force's Evacuation Plans," *The Early Show*, CBS News Transcripts, September 8, 2005.

30. Bradley, "Order Out of Chaos."

31. Hancock, "Storm Tossed What Was Left of New Orleans' Police Image."

32. David Heinzmann. "New Orleans Police Department Challenged by Its Own Instability," *Chicago Tribune*, October 9, 2005.

33. Michelle Krupa, "Guard, Police Plan Storm Tactics," *Times-Picayune*, June 4, 2006; Joe Gyan, "Force of 160 Guardsman, Troopers Arrives in City," *Times-Picayune*, June 21, 2006; Trymaine Lee, "NOPD Triple Weekend Arrest Tally," *Times-Picayune*, June 27, 2006; Michael Perlstein, "Guard, Troopers Flexing Muscles," *Times-Picayune*, July 4, 2006.

34. "Guard Wraps Up Its Time in N.O.," *Times-Picayune*, February 28, 2009.

35. Brendan McCarthy, "City's Murder Rate Drops in 2008—But Riley Says 'There Is No Celebration,'" *Times-Picayune*, January 1, 2009.

36. Brendan McCarthy, "Year Begins with 3 Shooting Deaths," *Times-Picayune*, January 2, 2009.

37. Laura Maggi, Brendan McCarthy, and Brian Thevenot, "New Orleans Is Breeding Bold Killers," *Times-Picayune*, January 25, 2009; "Editorial: Tide of Violence," *Times-Picayune*, February 1, 2009.

38. Laura Maggi, "Crime Count Dips in N.O.—But Killings Remain Stubbornly High," *Times-Picayune*, February 10, 2011; Brendan McCarthy, "Murder Studies Paint Grim Picture," *Times-Picayune*, March 26, 2009.

39. Katy Reckdahl, "City Is Plagued by Spate of Recent Murders," *Times-Picayune*, October 21, 2011.

40. Katie Urbaszewski and Stephen Babcock, "Murder Rate Tops 2010's after Double Homicides," *Times-Picayune*, November 28, 2011; Brendan McCarthy, "Feds to Send N.O. Help to Fight Crime," *Times-Picayune*, March 13, 2012.

41. Quotations in this paragraph are from Michelle Krupa, "Police Chief: No Promises on Murders," *Times-Picayune*, June 29, 2012.

42. John Simerman and Gordon Russell, "In Most Cities, Violent Crime Tracks the Murder Rate," *Times-Picayune*, May 19, 2013; John Simerman, "Classifying a Crime Isn't an Exact Science," *Times-Picayune*, May 19, 2013.

43. Allen Powell, "NOPD Steps Up Traffic Stops," *Times-Picayune*, May 3, 2011; John Simerman, "Community Policing Skills to Be Sharpened," *Times-Picayune*, December 1, 2011; "Editorial: Cooling Down the Hot Spots," *Times-Picayune*, December 3, 2011.

44. Brendan McCarthy, "NOPD Filing Away Mountain of Data from Traffic Stops across City," *Times-Picayune*, July 11, 2012; Andrew Vanacore, "NAACP Leader, Landrieu to Discuss Profiling," *Times-Picayune*, March 20, 2013.

45. See http://metrocrime.org/ (accessed August 23, 2014). The Metropolitan Crime Commission's quarterly reports are listed online, beginning in 2007; see http://metrocrime.org/mcc-programs/research-program/ (accessed August 23, 2014); Laura Maggi, "NOPD Wastes Time on Petty Offenses," *Times-Picayune*, December 20, 2010; John Simerman, "NOPD Is Making Felony Arrests a Top Priority, Report Says," *Times-Picayune*, May 14, 2012.

46. "N.O. Cop Indicted on Rape," *Times-Picayune*, February 24, 2006; Michael Perlstein, "2 Cops Arrested in Theft, Beating Cases," *Times-Picayune*, March 17, 2006; Bruce Eggler, "Increase in Police Brutality in N.O. Alleged," *Times-Picayune*, March 17, 2006; Michael Perlstein, "3 Cops Indicted in Quarter Beating," *Times-Picayune*, March 30, 2006.

47. Bruce Nolan, "Police Probe Alleged Beating," *Times-Picayune*, April 7, 2006; Bruce Eggler, "Independent Monitor Urged for N.O. Police," *Times-Picayune*, April 28, 2006.

48. Brendan McCarthy, "2 N.O. Officers Reassigned in Beating Case," *Times-Picayune*, January 9, 2007; Laura Maggi, "NAACP Asks Feds to Investigate N.O. Police," *Times-Picayune*, January 30, 2007; Brendan McCarthy, "N.O. Police Captain Arrested in Crash," *Times-Picayune*, November 8, 2007; Walt Philbin, "Officer Faces Incest Charge," *Times-Picayune*, February 1, 2007; Laura Maggi, "Former N.O. Cop Enters Guilty Plea," *Times-Picayune*, March 20, 2007; Walt Philbin, "2 N.O. Police Officers Fired for Misconduct, Brutality," *Times-Picayune*, March 29, 2007; Brendan McCarthy, "Police Captain Reassigned amid Fraud Probe," *Times-Picayune*, March 30, 2007; Paul Rioux, "N.O. Cop Is Booked in Bridge Chase Case," *Times-Picayune*, April 7, 2007; Laura Maggi, "Ex-Cop Accused of Aiding Drug Suspect," *Times-Picayune*, April 18, 2008; Laura Maggi, "Cop's Arrest Taints Drug Cases," *Times-Picayune*, May 30, 2008.

49. Laura Maggi, "2 Cops Walk in Beating Burning, Cover-Up," *Times-Picayune*, December 10, 2010; Brendan McCarthy, "Missing Money at NOPD Site Draws FBI Attention," *Times-Picayune*, January 15, 2011; Jarvis DeBerry, "Officer Had the Tools of a Predator," *Times-Picayune*, February 18, 2011; Laura Maggi and Danny Monteverde, "NOPD Looks at Its Officers' Role in Fracas," *Times-Picayune*, March 10, 2011; Brendan McCarthy and Laura Maggi, "2 Officers Convicted in Beating," *Times-Picayune*, April 14, 2011.

50. Laura Maggi, "7 N.O. Cops Indicted in Killings on Bridge," *Times-Picayune*, December 29, 2006; Laura Maggi, "NOPD's Bridge Probe Full of Blanks," *Times-Picayune*, February 18, 2007.

51. "Feds Will Look into Killings on Bridge after Katrina," *Times-Picayune*, October 1, 2008; Brendan McCarthy and Laura Maggi, "Officer's Account Didn't Add Up," *Times-Picayune*, July 31, 2011; Katie Urbaszewski and Brendan McCarthy, "Danziger Evidence Outweighed Chaos Theory," *Times-Picayune*, August 23, 2011; Brendan McCarthy, "Danziger Trial Judge's Speech Scorches," *Times-Picayune*, April 16, 2012; Juliet Linderman, "Danziger Ruling Fallout Spreads," *Times-Picayune*, September 22, 2013.

52. Brendan McCarthy and John Simerman, "Pact Makes NOPD More Transparent, Accountable," *Times-Picayune*, July 25, 2012; Stephanie Grace, "Consent Decree Warrants Superlatives," *Times-Picayune*, July 26, 2012; "Blueprint for Police Reform," *Times-Picayune*, July 26, 2012.

53. "Blueprint for Police Reform"; John Simerman, "Police Group Wants Its Say in Reform," *Times-Picayune*, August 7, 2012; "Judge Rebuffs Group on Consent Decree," *Times-Picayune*, September 1, 2012; Laura Maggi, "Police Monitor's Role Called into Question," *Times-Picayune*, October 14, 2012.

54. John Simerman, "Judge Forces Landrieu's Hand on Consent Decree," *Times-Picayune*, January 13, 2013; Ramon Antonio Vargas, "City Scrambles to Avoid Consent Decree Bills," *Times-Picayune*, February 3, 2013; John Simerman, "Justice Department to City: Quit Stalling on NOPD Reform Deal," *Times-Picayune*, February 8, 2013; John Simerman, "Judge Denies Motion to Halt Consent Decree," *Times-Picayune*, February 10, 2013.

55. John Simerman, "Landrieu Fights Federal Consent Decree," *Times-Picayune*, February 24, 2013; Ramon Antonio Vargas, "Firms Vie to Take on Consent Decree," *Times-Picayune*, April 3, 2013; Naomi Martin, "Bill Would Let NOPD Detail Hours Count," *Times-Picayune*, April 10, 2013; Helen Freund, "Union Battles NOPD Overhaul," *Times-Picayune*, September 11, 2013.

56. Naomi Martin, "New Orleans Mayor Mitch Landrieu Introduces 'Reorganized' NOPD Sex-Crimes Unit, Promises Reform," *Times-Picayune*, December 3, 2014.

57. Andrew Boyd, "NOPD Superintendent Ronal Serpas to Announce Retirement, Source Says," *Times-Picayune*, August 18, 2014.

58. For example, see Vera Institute of Justice, "Proposals for New Orleans' Criminal Justice System: Best Practices to Advance Public Safety and Justice," Report Submitted to the Criminal Justice Committee of the New Orleans City Council, June 2007.

59. David Bayley and Robert Perito, "Police Corruption: What Past Scandals Teach about Current Challenges" (Washington, DC: United States Institute for Peace Special Report, November 2011); Martin Shefter, "The Emergence of the Political Machine: An Alternative View," in *Theoretical Perspectives on Urban Politics*, ed. Willis D. Hawley (Englewood Cliffs, NJ: Prentice-Hall, 1976), 14–42.

60. William K. Muir, *Police: Streetcorner Politicians* (Chicago: University of Chicago Press, 1977).

61. For further information on the neighborhood-level effects of criminal justice policy, see Traci Birch, *Trading Democracy for Justice: Criminal Convictions and the Decline of Neighborhood Political Participation* (Chicago: University of Chicago Press, 2013).

62. Robert Dahl, *Who Governs? Democracy and Power in an American City* (New Haven: Yale University Press, 1961).

63. Lawrence Sherman, *Scandal and Reform: Controlling Police Corruption* (Berkeley: University of California Press, 1978).

Conclusion

1. Testimony of Mayor C. Ray Nagin, *A Vision and Strategy for Rebuilding New Orleans, Hearing before the Subcommittee on Economic Development, Public Buildings and Emergency Management and Subcommittee on Water Resources and Environment of the Committee on Transportation and Infrastructure, United States House of Representatives*, 109th   Cong., 1st sess., October 18, 2005.

2. Testimony of Gregory C. Rigamer, *Five Years Later: Lessons Learned, Progress Made, and Work Remaining from Hurricane Katrina: Hearing before the Ad Hoc Committee on Disaster Recovery of the Committee on Homeland Security and Governmental Affairs*, U.S. Senate, 111th Congress, 2nd sess., August 26, 2010.

3. Kevin Fox Gotham, "From 9/11 to 8/29: Post-Disaster Recovery and Rebuilding in New York and New Orleans," *Social Forces* 87, no. 2 (2008): 1039–62; Cedric Johnson, Chris Russill, and Chad Lavin, *Neoliberal Deluge: Hurricane Katrina, Late Capitalism, and the Remaking of New Orleans* (Minneapolis: University of Minnesota Press, 2011); John Arena, *Driven from New*

Orleans: How Nonprofits Betray Public Housing and Promote Privatization (Minneapolis: University of Minnesota Press, 2012).

4. Peter Eisinger, "Is Detroit Dead?" *Journal of Urban Affairs* 36, no. 1 (2014): 1–12.

5. Peter Burns, "Regime Theory, State Government, and a Takeover of Urban Education," *Journal of Urban Affairs* 25, no. 3 (2003), 285–303; Peter Burns, "The Intergovernmental Regime and Public Policy in Hartford, Connecticut," *Journal of Urban Affairs* 24, no. 1 (2002): 55–73; Peter F. Burns and Matthew O. Thomas, "Governors and the Development Regime in New Orleans," *Urban Affairs Review* 39, no. 6 (2004): 791–812.

6. Building Resilient Regions, "New Book on a Resilient New Orleans Six Years after Katrina," http://brr.berkeley.edu/2011/09/new-book-on-a-resilient-new-orleans-six-years-after-katrina/. (accessed August 24, 2014); The words are those of Amy Liu, one of the editors of Resilience and Opportunity.

7. Frederick D. Weil, "Rise of Community Organizations, Citizen Engagement, and New Institutions," in *Resilience and Opportunity: Lessons from the U.S. Gulf Coast after Katrina and Rita*, ed. Amy Liu et al. (Washington, DC: Brookings Institution Press, 2011), 217; Daniel P. Aldrich and Kevin Crook, "Strong Civil Society as a Double-Edged Sword: Siting Trailers in Post-Katrina New Orleans," *Political Research Quarterly* 61, no. 3 (2008): 379–89; Min Hee Go, "The Power of Participation Explaining the Issuance of Building Permits in Post-Katrina New Orleans," *Urban Affairs Review* 50, no. 1 (2014): 34–62.

8. Nancy Burns and Gerald Gamm, "Creatures of the State: State Politics and Local Government, 1871–1921," *Urban Affairs Review* 33, no. 1 (1997): 59–96.

9. Vincent Sylvain, "Will New Orleans Have 5–2 African American–White City Council Ratio?" Bayoubuzz.com, December 10, 2013, http://www.bayoubuzz.com/buzz/latest-buzz/item/562315-will-new-orleans-have-5–2-african-american-white-city-council-ratio (accessed August 23, 2014); Frank Donze, "New Orleans City Council Runoff May Be Test of Trends in the City's Racial Politics," *Times-Picayune*, April 19, 2012.

10. University of New Orleans, "'Keeping People: The 2007 Quality of Life Survey in Orleans and Jefferson Parishes," May 2007; University of New Orleans, "2010 Quality of Life Study," November 30, 2010.

11. William Paul Simmons and Monica J. Casper, "Culpability, Social Triage, and Structural Violence in the Aftermath of Katrina," *Perspectives on Politics* 10, no. 3 (2012): 681.

Bibliography

Ahlers, Douglas, and Rebecca Hummel. "Lessons from Katrina." Harvard University Belfer Center, 2007. http://belfercenter.ksg.harvard.edu/publication/17815/lessons_from_katrina.html?breadcrumb=%2Fproject%2F54%2F broadmoor_project (accessed August 8, 2014).

Airiess, Christopher A., Wei Li, Karen J. Leong, Angela Chia-Chen Chen, and Verna M. Keith. "Church-Based Social Capital, Networks and Geographical Scale: Katrina Evacuation, Relocation, and Recovery in New Orleans Vietnamese American Community." *Geoforum* 39, no. 3 (2008): 1333–46.

Albala-Bertrand, J. M. *Political Economy of Large Natural Disasters: With Special Reference to Developing Countries.* Oxford: Oxford University Press, 1993.

Aldrich, Daniel P. "Fixing Recovery: Social Capital in Post-Crisis Resilience." *Journal of Homeland Security* 6 (2010): 1–10.

Aldrich, Daniel P., and Kevin Crook. "Strong Civil Society as a Double-Edged Sword: Siting Trailers in Post-Katrina New Orleans." *Political Research Quarterly* 61, no. 3 (2008): 379–89.

Al-Marhubi, Fahim A. "Corruption and Inflation." *Economics Letters* 66 (2000): 199–202.

Among Brothers: Politics in New Orleans. VHS. Directed by Paul Stekler. New Orleans: Deep South Productions, 1987.

Arena, John. *Driven from New Orleans: How Nonprofits Betray Public Housing and Promote Privatization.* Minneapolis: University of Minnesota Press, 2012.

Atlas, John. *Seeds of Change: The Story of ACORN, America's Most Controversial Anti-Poverty Community Organizing Group.* Nashville: Vanderbilt University Press, 2010.

Baker, Liva. *The Second Battle of New Orleans: The Hundred-Year Struggle to Integrate the Schools.* New York: HarperCollins, 1996.

Barry, John M. *Rising Tide: The Great Mississippi Flood of 1927 and How It Changed America*. New York: Simon and Schuster, 1997.

Bates, Lisa K. "Post-Katrina Housing: Problems, Policies, and Prospects for African-Americans in New Orleans." *The Black Scholar* 36, no. 4 (2006): 13–31.

Baumbach, Richard O., and William E. Borah. *The Second Battle of New Orleans: A History of the Vieux Carré Riverfront Expressway Controversy*. Tuscaloosa: Published for the Preservation Press, National Trust for Historic Preservation in the United States by University of Alabama Press, 1981.

Bayley, David, and Robert Perito. *Police Corruption: What Past Scandals Teach about Current Challenges*. Washington, DC: United States Institute for Peace Special Report, November 2011.

Berke, Philip R., Jack Kartez, and Dennis Wenger. "Recovery after Disaster: Achieving Sustainable Development, Mitigation, and Equity." *Disasters* 17, no. 2 (1993): 93–109.

Berube, Alan, and Bruce Katz. *Katrina's Window: Confronting Poverty across America*. Washington, DC: Brookings Institution, October 2005.

Birch, Traci. *Trading Democracy for Justice: Criminal Convictions and the Decline of Neighborhood Political Participation*. Chicago: University of Chicago Press, 2013.

Birkmann, J., P. Buckle, J. Jaeger, M. Pelling, N. Setiadi, M. Garschagen, N. Fernando, and J. Kropp. "Extreme Events and Disasters: A Window of Opportunity for Change? Analysis of Organizational, Institutional, and Political Changes, Formal and Informal Responses after Mega-Disasters." *Natural Hazards* 55 (2010): 637–55.

Blakely, Edward J. *My Storm: Managing the Recovery of New Orleans in the Wake of Katrina*. Philadelphia: University of Pennsylvania Press, 2011.

Bolin, Robert. *Household and Community Recovery after Earthquakes*. Boulder: Institute of Behavioral Science, University of Colorado, 1993.

Bolin, Robert, and Patricia A. Bolton. *Race, Religion, and Ethnicity in Disaster Recovery*. Boulder: Institute of Behavioral Science, University of Colorado, 1986.

Bolin, Robert, and Lois Stanford. "Shelter, Housing, and Recovery: A Comparison of U.S. Disasters," *Disasters* 15, no. 1 (1991): 24–34.

BondGraham, Darwin. "Building the New New Orleans: Foundation and NGO Power." *Review of Black Political Economy* 38, no. 4 (2011): 279–309.

Brandt, James, and Robert K. Whelan. "New Orleans: Metropolis against Itself." In *Metropolitan Governance without Metropolitan Government?*, edited by Donald Phares, 135–53. Burlington, VT: Ashgate Publishing Company, 2004.

Bridges, Amy. *Morning Glories: Municipal Reform in the Southwest*. Princeton: Princeton University Press, 1997.

Bring New Orleans Back Commission, Government Effectiveness Committee. "Recommendations." March 20, 2006. https://repository.library.brown.edu/studio/item/bdr:65564 (accessed August 8, 2014).

Bring New Orleans Back Commission, Urban Planning Committee. "Action Plan for New Orleans: The New American City." Washington, DC: Urban Land Institute, 2006. http://uli.org/wp-content/uploads/2012/11/NewOrleans-LA-05-v5.pdf (accessed August 9, 2014).

Brinkley, Douglas. *The Great Deluge*. New York: William Morrow, 2006.

Brooks, Fred. "One Hypothesis about the Decline and Fall of ACORN." *Social Work* 58, no. 2 (2013): 177–80.

Brooks, Jane S., and Alma H. Young. "Revitalising the Central Business District in the Face of Decline: The Case of New Orleans." *Town Planning Review* 64, no. 3 (1993): 251–71.

Brox, Brian J. "Elections and Voting in Post-Katrina New Orleans." *Southern Studies* 16, no. 2 (2009): 1–23.

Brunsma, David L., David Overfelt, and J. Steven Picou. *The Sociology of Katrina: Perspectives on a Modern Catastrophe*. New York: Rowman & Littlefield, 2010.

Buras, Kristen L. "Race, Charter Schools, and Conscious Capitalism: On the Spatial Politics of Whiteness as Property (and the Unconscionable Assault on Black New Orleans)." *Harvard Educational Review* 81, no. 2 (2011): 296–331.

Bureau of Governmental Research. "On the Right Track? New Orleans Economic Development Investment in Perspective." New Orleans, November 2004. http://www.bgr.org/files/reports/EconomicDevelopmentReport11–04.pdf (accessed August 9, 2014).

———. "Wanted: A Realistic Development Strategy." New Orleans, December 22, 2005. http://www.bgr.org/files/news/BGR_Reports_Realistic_Development_Strategy_12_22_05.pdf (accessed August 9, 2014).

"History of BGR." New Orleans, n.d. www.bgr.org/about/history (accessed August 9, 2014).

———. "Profile." New Orleans, n.d. www.bgr.org/about/ (accessed August 9, 2014).

Burns, Ashley Brown. "New Communities in Old Spaces: Evidence from HOPE VI." PhD diss., Duke University, 2013.

Burns, Nancy, and Gerald Gamm. "Creatures of the State: State Politics and Local Government, 1871–1921." *Urban Affairs Review* 33, no. 1 (1997): 59–96.

Burns, Peter. "The Intergovernmental Regime and Public Policy in Hartford, Connecticut." *Journal of Urban Affairs* 24, no. 1 (2002): 55–73.

———. "Regime Theory, State Government, and a Takeover of Urban Education." *Journal of Urban Affairs* 25, no. 3 (2003): 285–303.

———. "Race and Support for State Takeovers of Local School Districts." *Urban Education* 45, no. 3 (2010): 274–92.

Burns, Peter F. "Community Organizations in a Non-Regime City: The New Orleans Experience." In *Transforming the City: Community Organizing and the Challenge of Political Change*, edited by Marion Orr, 56–83. Lawrence: University Press of Kansas, 2007.

Burns, Peter F., and Matthew O. Thomas. "Governors and the Development Regime in New Orleans." *Urban Affairs Review* 39, no. 6 (2004): 791–812.

———. "The Failure of the Nonregime: How Katrina Exposed New Orleans as a Regimeless City." *Urban Affairs Review* 41, no. 4 (2006): 517–27.

———. "A New New Orleans? Understanding the Role of History and the State-Local Relationship in the Recovery Process." *Journal of Urban Affairs* 30, no. 3 (2008): 259–71.

Burton, Ian, Robert W. Kates, and Gilbert F. White. *The Environment as Hazard*. New York: Guilford Press, 1993.

Campanella, Richard. *Time and Place in New Orleans: Past Geographies in the Present Day*. Gretna, LA: Pelican Publishing, 2002.

————. *Geographies of New Orleans: Urban Fabrics before the Storm.* Lafayette, LA: Center for Louisiana Studies, 2006.

————. *Bienville's Dilemma: A Historical Geography of New Orleans.* Lafayette, LA: Center for Louisiana Studies, 2008.

Carr, Sarah. *Hope Against Hope: Three Schools, One City, and the Struggle to Educate America's Children.* New York: Bloomsbury Publishing USA, 2014.

Chamlee-Wright, Emily, and Virgil Henry Storr. "Club Goods and Post-Disaster Community Return." *Rationality and Society* 21, no. 4 (2009): 429–58.

Chaskin, Robert J., and Mark L. Joseph. "Building 'Community' in Mixed-Income Developments: Assumptions, Approaches, and Early Experiences." *Urban Affairs Review* 45, no. 3 (2010): 299–335.

————. "Social Interaction in Mixed-Income Developments: Relational Expectations and Emerging Reality." *Journal of Urban Affairs* 33, no. 2 (2011): 209–37.

Clarke, Caroline L., and Mohan Munasinghe. "Economic Aspects of Disasters and Sustainable Development: An Introduction." In *Disaster Prevention for Sustainable Development: Economic and Policy Issues,* edited by Caroline L. Clark and Mohan Munasinghe, 1–10. Washington, DC: The World Bank, 1995.

Cole, Richard, Robert K. Whelan, Lori Moon, and Nadine Jarmon. "Housing Authority of New Orleans: Pre-Katrina Resident Survey." Paper presented at the Annual Meeting of the Urban Affairs Association, Baltimore, April 23–26, 2008.

Collins, Robert A. 2011. "No More 'Planning by Surprise': Post-Katrina Land Use Planning in New Orleans." In *Resilience and Opportunity: Lessons from the U.S. Gulf Coast after Katrina and Rita,* edited by Amy Liu, Roland V. Anglin, Richard Mizelle, and Allison Plyer, 161–72. Washington, DC: Brookings Institution Press, 2011.

Cook, Christine C., and Mickey Lauria. "Urban Regeneration and Public Housing in New Orleans." *Urban Affairs Review* 30, no. 4 (1995): 538–57.

Cook, Daniella A. "Voices Crying Out from the Wilderness: The Story of Black Educators on School Reform in Post Katrina New Orleans." PhD diss., University of North Carolina, 2008.

Cooper, F., and L. Laughy. "Managing Hazards in a Changing Multinational World." Unpublished paper (1994).

Council for a Better Louisiana (CABL). "New Orleans Voter Survey." Baton Rouge, August 26, 2009. http://www.cabl.org/pdfs/CABL_Katrina_Poll_FINAL.pdf (accessed August 9, 2014).

Crain, Robert. *The Politics of School Desegregation.* Chicago: Aldine Publishing Company, 1968.

Curtis, Wayne, "The Cost of Progress? Razing Entire Blocks for a Massive Hospital Complex in New Orleans Divided Residents and Decimated Parts of a Historic Neighborhood." *Preservation,* May–June 2011.

Dahl, Robert Alan. *Who Governs? Democracy and Power in an American City.* New Haven: Yale University Press, 2005.

Darcy, Michael. "De-Concentration of Disadvantage and Mixed Income Housing: A Critical Discourse Approach." *Housing, Theory and Society* 27, no. 1 (2010): 1–22.

Davis, Diane E. "Reverberations: Mexico City's 1985 Earthquake and the Transformation of the Capital." In *The Resilient City: How Modern Cities Recovery from Disaster*, edited by Lawrence J. Vale and Thomas J. Campanella, 255–80. New York: Oxford University Press, 2005.

Day, Christine L. "Katrina Seven Years On: The Politics of Race and Recovery—Notes on a Roundtable Organized for the 2012 APSA Annual Meeting." *PS: Political Science & Politics* 46, no. 4 (2013): 748–52.

Diaz, Manny. *Miami Transformed: Rebuilding America One Neighborhood, One City at a Time*. Philadelphia: University of Pennsylvania Press, 2012.

Dingerson, Leigh. "Dismantling a Community Timeline." *High School Journal* 90, no. 2 (2006), 8–15.

Dreher, Rod. "Big Sleazy Sobers Up." *National Review*, July 31, 2002.

Duke, Joanna. "Mixed Income Housing Policy and Public Housing Residents' 'Right to the City.'" *Critical Social Policy* 29, no. 1 (2009): 100–120.

Dynes, Russell R., and E. L. Quarantelli, "A Brief Note on Disaster Restoration, Reconstruction, and Recovery: A Comparative Note Using Post-Earthquake Observations." University of Delaware, Preliminary Paper no. 259 (2008).

Dyson, Michael Eric. *Come Hell or High Water: Hurricane Katrina and the Color of Disaster*. New York: Basic Books, 2006.

Edgington, David W. *Reconstructing Kobe: The Geography of Crisis and Opportunity*. Vancouver: University of British Columbia Press, 2010.

Eisinger, Peter. "Is Detroit Dead?" *Journal of Urban Affairs* 36, no. 1 (2014): 1–12.

Ellickson, Robert C. "The False Promise of the Mixed-Income Housing Project." *UCLA Law Review* 57 (2009): 983.

Elliott, James R., and Jeremy Pais. "Race, Class, and Hurricane Katrina: Social Differences in Human Responses to Disaster." *Social Science Research* 35, no. 2 (2006): 295–321.

Erie, Steven P., Vladimir Kogan, and Scott A. MacKenzie. *Paradise Plundered: Fiscal Crisis and Governance Failures in San Diego*. Stanford: Stanford University Press, 2011.

Evans, Pat, and Sarah Lewis, "A Reciprocity of Tears: Civic Engagement after a Disaster." In *Civic Engagement in the Wake of Katrina*, edited by Amy Koritz and George J. Sanchez, 44–58. Ann Arbor: University of Michigan Press, 2009.

Farquhar, Stephanie, and Noelle Dobson. "Community and University Participation in Disaster-Relief Recovery." *Journal of Community Practice* 12, no. 3–4 (2005): 203–17.

Finch, Christina, Christopher T. Emrich, and Susan L. Cutter. "Disaster Disparities and Differential Recovery in New Orleans." *Population and Environment* 31, no. 4 (2010): 179–202.

Flaherty, Jordan. "Floodlines: Preserving Public Housing in New Orleans." *Race, Poverty & the Environment* 17, no. 2 (2010): 61–65.

Ford, Kristina. *The Trouble with City Planning: What New Orleans Can Teach Us*. New Haven: Yale University Press, 2010.

Forward New Orleans. "Fourth Progress Report." New Orleans, September 2013. http://bcno.org/wp-content/uploads/2009/04/FNO-4th-Progress-Report-2013-September.pdf (accessed August 9, 2014).

Fothergil, Alice, Enrique G. M. Maestas, and JoAnne DeRouen Darlington. "Race, Ethnicity, and Disasters in the United States: A Review of the Literature." *Disasters* 23, no. 2 (1999): 156–73.

Fradkin, Philip L. *The Great Earthquake and Firestorms of 1906: How San Francisco Nearly Destroyed Itself.* Berkeley: University of California Press, 2005.

Francaviglia, Richard. "Xenia Rebuilds: Effects of Pre-Disaster Conditioning on Post-Disaster Redevelopment." *Journal of the American Institute of Planners* 44 (1978): 13–24.

Fraser, James C., and Edward L. Kick. "The Role of Public, Private, Non-Profit and Community Sectors in Shaping Mixed-Income Housing Outcomes in the U.S." *Urban Studies* 44, no. 12 (2007): 2357–77.

Fraser, James Curtis, Ashley Brown Burns, Joshua Theodore Bazuin, and Deirdre Aine Oakley. "HOPE VI, Colonization, and the Production of Difference." *Urban Affairs Review* 49, no. 4 (2013): 525–56.

Fussell, Elizabeth, Narayan Sastry, and Mark VanLandingham. "Race, Socioeconomic Status, and Return Migration to New Orleans after Hurricane Katrina," *Population & Environment* 31, no. 1–3 (2010): 20–42.

Gajewski, Stephanie, Holly Bell, Laura Lein, and Ronald J. Angel. "Complexity and Instability: The Response of Nongovernmental Organizations to the Recovery of Hurricane Katrina Survivors in a Host Community." *Nonprofit and Voluntary Sector Quarterly* 40, no. 2 (2011): 389–403.

Garda, Robert. "The Politics of Education Reform: Lessons from New Orleans." *Journal of Law & Education* 40, no. 1 (January 2011): 57–150.

Garvey, Joan B., and Mary Lou Widmer. *Beautiful Crescent: A History of New Orleans.* 10th ed. New Orleans: Garmer Press, 2011.

Gelinas, Nicole. "The Big Easy Rebuilds, Bottom Up." *City Journal* 18, no. 2 (2008) (accessed August 9, 2014).

Germany, Kent B. *New Orleans after the Promises: Poverty, Citizenship, and the Search for the Great Society.* Athens: University of Georgia Press, 2007.

Gewertz, Catherine, Erik W. Robelen, and Michelle R. Davis. "Crescent Wrench." *Teacher Magazine* 17, no. 3 (November–December 2005): 20.

Gill, James. *Lords of Misrule: Mardi Gras and the Politics of Race in New Orleans.* Jackson: University Press of Mississippi, 1997.

Go, Min Hee. "The Power of Participation Explaining the Issuance of Building Permits in Post-Katrina New Orleans." *Urban Affairs Review* 50, no. 1 (2014): 34-62.

Goetz, Edward G. "The Politics of Poverty Deconcentration and Housing Demolition." *Journal of Urban Affairs* 22, no. 2 (2000): 157–73.

———. "The Transformation of Public Housing Policy, 1985–2011." *Journal of the American Planning Association* 78, no. 4 (2012): 452–63.

Gotham, Kevin Fox. "Tourism Gentrification: The Case of New Orleans' Vieux Carre (French Quarter)." *Urban Studies* 42 (2005): 1099–1121.

———. "From 9/11 to 8/29: Post-Disaster Recovery and Rebuilding in New York and New Orleans." *Social Forces* 87, no. 2 (2008): 1039–62.

———. "Disaster, Inc.: Privatization and Post-Katrina Rebuilding in New Orleans." *Perspectives on Politics* 10, no. 3 (2012): 633–46.

Gotham, Kevin Fox, and Richard Campanella. "Toward a Research Agenda on Transformative Resilience: Challenges and Opportunities for Post-Trauma Urban Ecosystems." *Critical Planning* 17 (2010): 9–23.

Graves, Erin M. "The Structuring of Urban Life in a Mixed-Income Housing 'Community.'" *City & Community* 9, no. 1 (2010): 109–31.

————. "Mixed Outcome Developments: Comparing Policy Goals to Resident Outcomes in Mixed-Income Housing." *Journal of the American Planning Association* 77, no. 2 (2011): 143–53.

Greater New Orleans Fair Housing Action Center. "What Is the Road Home Program," n.d., http://www.gnofairhousing.org/wp-content/uploads/2012/02/AboutRoadHome.pdf (accessed August 9, 2014).

Green, Rebekah, Lisa K. Bates, and Andrew Smyth. "Impediments to Recovery in New Orleans' Upper and Lower Ninth Ward: One Year after Hurricane Katrina." *Disasters* 31, no. 4 (2007): 311–35.

Green, Rodney D., Marie Kouassi, and Belinda Mambo. "Housing, Race, and Recovery from Hurricane Katrina." *Review of Black Political Economy* 40, no. 2 (2013): 145–63.

Green, Timothy F., and Robert B. Olshansky. "Rebuilding Housing in New Orleans: The Road Home Program after the Hurricane Katrina Disaster." *Housing Policy Debate* 22, no. 1 (2012): 75–99.

Grube, Laura, and Virgil Henry Storr. "The Capacity for Self-Governance and Post-Disaster Resiliency." *Review of Austrian Economics* 27, no. 3 (2013): 301–24.

Gurwitt, Rob. "The Comeback of the Cops." *Governing Magazine*, January 1998, 14.

————. "Charter Changeover." *Governing Magazine*, September 2006, 28.

Haas, Edward F. *DeLesseps S. Morrison and the Image of Reform: New Orleans Politics, 1946–1961*. Baton Rouge: Louisiana State University Press, 1974.

————. "Political Continuity in the Crescent City: Toward an Interpretation of New Orleans Politics, 1874–1986." *Louisiana History: The Journal of the Louisiana Historical Association* 39, no. 1 (1988): 5–18.

Hanger, Kimberly S. "Patronage, Property, and Persistence: The Emergence of a Free Black Elite in Spanish New Orleans." Special issue. *Slavery & Abolition: A Journal of Slave and Post-Slave Studies* 17, no. 1 (1996): 44–64.

Hankins, Katherine B. "Regime Politics in Geography." *Urban Affairs Review*, first published November 28, 2014, as doi: 10.1177/1078087414559606.

Henig, Jeffrey R., Richard C. Hula, Marion Orr, and Desiree S. Pedescleaux. *The Color of School Reform*. Princeton: Princeton University Press, 1999.

Hill, Paul T., Christine Campbell, and James Harvey. *It Takes a City: Getting Serious about Urban School Reform*. Washington, DC: Brookings Institution Press, 2000.

Hill, Paul T., and Jane Hannaway. "The Future of Public Education in New Orleans." After Katrina: Rebuilding Opportunity and Equity into the *New* New Orleans Series. Washington, DC: The Urban Institute, 2006.

Hirayama, Yosuke. "Collapse and Reconstruction: Housing Recovery Policy in Kobe after the Hanshin Great Earthquake." *Housing Studies* 15, no. 1 (2000): 111–28.

Hirsch, Arnold. "Simply a Matter of Black and White: The Transformation of Race and Politics in Twentieth-Century New Orleans." In *Creole New Orleans: Race and Americanization,* edited by Arnold Hirsch and Joseph Logsdon, 262–319. Baton Rouge: Louisiana State University Press, 1992.

Holli, Melvin G., and Peter d'Alroy Jones. *Biographical Dictionary of American Mayors, 1820–1980*. Westport, CT: Greenwood Press, 1981.

Horne, Jed. *Breach of Faith: Hurricane Katrina and the Near Death of a Great American City*. New York: Random House, 2006.

Inger, Morton. *Politics and Reality*. New York: Center for Urban Education, 1969.

Ishiwata, Eric. "'We Are Seeing People We Didn't Know Exist': Katrina and the Neoliberal Erasure of Race." In *The Neoliberal Deluge: Hurricane Katrina, Late Capitalism, and the Remaking of New Orleans*, edited by Cedric Johnson, 32–59. Minneapolis: University of Minnesota Press, 2011.

Jones-Correa, Michael, and Diane Young. "Whose Politics? Reflections on Clarence Stone's *Regime Politics*." *Urban Affairs Review*, first published November 27, 2014, as doi: 10.1177/1078087414558949.

Joseph, Mark, and Robert Chaskin. "Living in a Mixed-Income Development: Resident Perceptions of the Benefits and Disadvantages of Two Developments in Chicago." *Urban Studies* 47, no. 11 (2010): 2347–66.

Joseph, Mark L. "Is Mixed-Income Development an Antidote to Urban Poverty?" *Housing Policy Debate* 17, no. 2 (2006): 209–34.

Kates, Robert William, C. E. Colten, S. Laska, and S. P. Leatherman. "Reconstruction of New Orleans after Hurricane Katrina: A Research Perspective." *Proceedings of the National Academy of Sciences* 103, no. 40 (2006): 14653–60.

Katz, Bruce. "Concentrated Poverty in New Orleans and Other American Cities." Washington, DC: Brookings Institution, August 4, 2006. http://www.brookings.edu/opinions/2006/0804cities_katz.aspx (accessed August 9, 2014).

Katz, Bruce, Matt Fellowes, and Mia Mabanta, "Katrina Index: Tracking Variables of Post-Katrina Reconstruction." Washington, DC: The Brookings Institution's Metropolitan Policy Program, May 3, 2006. http://www.brookings.edu/metro/pubs/200605_KatrinaIndex.pdf (accessed August 9, 2014).

Keith, Verna M., and Cedric Herring. "Skin Tone and Stratification in the Black Community." *American Journal of Sociology* 97, no. 3 (1991): 760–78.

Kendall, John. *History of New Orleans*. Chicago: Lewis Publishing Company, 1922.

Kiel, Daniel. "It Takes a Hurricane: Might Karma Deliver for New Orleans Students What *Brown* Once Promised," *Journal of Law & Education* 40, no. 1 (January 2011), 105–50.

Klein, Naomi. *Shock Doctrine: The Rise of Disaster Capitalism*. New York: Picador, 2007.

Klinenberg, Eric. *Heat Wave: A Social Autopsy of Disaster in Chicago*. Chicago: University of Chicago Press, 2003.

———. Letter to the editor. "Review of *Heat Wave: Social Autopsy of Disaster in Chicago*." *New England Journal of Medicine* 348, no. 7 (2003): 666–67.

Lay, J. Celeste. "Race, Retrospective Voting, and Disasters: The Re-Election of C. Ray Nagin after Hurricane Katrina." *Urban Affairs Review* 44, no. 5 (2009): 645–62.

Lewis, Peirce F. *New Orleans: The Making of an Urban Landscape*. 2nd ed. Santa Fe, NM: Center for American Places, 2003.

Lindell, Michael K., and Carla S. Prater. "Assessing Community Impacts of Natural Disasters." *Natural Hazards Review* 4, no. 4 (2003): 176–85.

Lipman, Pauline. "Mixed-Income Schools and Housing: Advancing the Neoliberal Urban Agenda." *Journal of Education Policy* 23, no. 2 (2008): 119–34.

Liu, Amy, Roland V. Anglin, Richard Mizelle, and Allison Plyer, eds. *Resilience and Opportunity: Lessons from the U.S. Gulf Coast after Katrina and Rita*. Washington, DC: Brookings Institution Press, 2011.

Liu, Amy, Matthew Fellowes, and Mia Mabanta. *Special Edition of the Katrina Index: A One Year Review of Key Indicators of Recovery in Post-Storm New Orleans*. Washington, DC: Brookings Institution, 2006.

Liu, Baodong, and James M. Vanderleeuw. *Race Rules: Electoral Politics in New Orleans, 1965–2006*. Lanham, MD: Rowman & Littlefield, 2007.

Logan, John R. "The Impact of Katrina: Race and Class in Storm-Damaged Neighborhoods," n.d. www.s4.brown.edu/katrina/report.pdf.

Longoria, Thomas, Jr. "School Politics in Houston: The Impact of Business Involvement." In *Changing Urban Education*, edited by Clarence N. Stone, 184–98. Lawrence: University Press of Kansas, 1988.

Louisiana Recovery Authority. "The Road Home Housing Programs Action Plan Amendment for Disaster Recovery Funds," n.d. http://archives.hud.gov/news/2006/pr06–058.pdf.

Louisiana Recovery School District. "Information at a Glance: Louisiana Recovery School District." n.d. www.rsdla.net/resources.aspx.

Luft, Rachel E. "Beyond Disaster Exceptionalism: Social Movement Developments in New Orleans after Hurricane Katrina." *American Quarterly* 61, no. 3 (2009): 499–527.

Luft, Rachel E., and Shana Griffin. "A Status Report on Housing in New Orleans after Katrina: An Intersectional Analysis." In *Katrina and the Women of New Orleans*, 50–53. New Orleans: Newcomb College Center for Research on Women, 2008.

Lumpkins, Charles L. *American Pogrom: The East St. Louis Race Riot and Black Politics*. Athens: Ohio University Press, 2008.

Machiavelli, Niccolò. *The Prince*. Translated by Peter Bondanella. Oxford: Oxford University Press, 2005.

Mack, Vicki, and Elaine Ortiz. "Who Lives in New Orleans and the Metro Now?" The Data Center, New Orleans, September 26, 2013. http://www.datacenterresearch.org/data-resources/who-lives-in-new-orleans-now/ (accessed August 9, 2014).

Marcello, David A. 2011. "Systemic Ethics Reform in Katrina's Aftermath." In *Resilience and Opportunity: Lessons from the U.S. Gulf Coast after Katrina and Rita*, edited by Amy Liu, Roland V. Anglin, Richard Mizelle, and Allison Plyer, 82–98. Washington, DC: Brookings Institution Press, 2011.

Masozera, Michel, Melissa Bailey, and Charles Kerchner. "Distribution of Impacts of Natural Disasters across Income Groups: A Case Study of New Orleans." *Ecological Economics* 63, no. 2 (2007): 299–306.

Mauro, Paolo. "Corruption and Growth." *Quarterly Journal of Economics* 110, no. 3 (1995): 681–712.

McBride, Allan, and Joseph B. Parker. "'Chocolate City' Politics: Race and Empowerment in the First Post-Katrina New Orleans Mayoral Election." *Politics & Policy* 36, no. 3 (2008): 350–74.

Menes, Rebecca. "Limiting the Reach of the Grabbing Hand: Graft and Growth in American Cities, 1880 to 1930." In *Corruption and Reform: Lessons from America's Economic History*, edited by Edward L. Glaeser and Claudia Goldin, 63–94. Chicago: University of Chicago Press, 2006.

Merton, Robert K. Foreword to *Communities in Disaster: A Sociological Analysis of Collective Stress Situations*, by Allen H. Barton, vii–xxxvii. New York: Doubleday, 1969.

Mezzacappa, Dale. "The Vallas Effect: The Supersized Superintendent Moves to the Superdome City." *Education Next* 8, no. 2 (Spring 2008): 30–37.

Mirón, Luis. "Corporate Ideology and the Politics of Entrepreneurism in New Orleans." *Antipode* 24, no. 4 (1992): 263–88.

———. "Introduction: Education in Post-Katrina New Orleans: Where are We Now and Where Might Imagination Take Us?" *Policy Futures in Education* 12, no. 8 (2014): 975–80.

Moore, Harry Estill. *Tornadoes over Texas: A Study of Waco and San Angelo in Disaster.* Austin: University of Texas Press, 1958.

Moore, Leonard N. *Black Rage in New Orleans: Police Brutality and African American Activism from World War II to Hurricane Katrina.* Baton Rouge: Louisiana State University Press, 2010.

Montinola, Gabriella R., and Robert W. Jackman. "Sources of Corruption: A Cross-Country Study." *British Journal of Political Science* 32, no. 1 (2002): 147–70.

Montjoy, Robert S., and Edward E. Chervenak. "Race, Performance, and Change in Post-Katrina New Orleans." Paper presented at the Annual Meeting of the Southern Political Science Association, Orlando, January 3–5, 2013.

Morello-Frosch, Rachel, Phil Brown, Mercedes Lyson, Alison Cohen, and Kimberly Krupa. "Community Voice, Vision, and Resilience in Post-Hurricane Katrina Recovery." *Environmental Justice* 4, no. 1 (2011): 71–80.

Morris, Christopher. "Impenetrable but Easy: The French Transformation of the Lower Mississippi Valley and the Founding of New Orleans." In *Centuries of Change: Human Transformation of the Lower Mississippi*, edited by Craig E. Colten, 22–42. Pittsburgh: University of Pittsburgh Press, 2000.

Muir, William K., Jr. *Police: Streetcorner Politicians.* Chicago: University of Chicago Press, 1977.

Mumphrey, Anthony J., and Pamela H. Moomau. "New Orleans: An Island in the Sunbelt." *Public Administration Quarterly* 8, no. 1 (1984), 91–111.

Nelson, Marla, Renia Ehrenfeucht, and Shirley Laska. "Planning, Plans, and People: Professional Expertise, Local Knowledge, and Governmental Action in Post–Hurricane Katrina New Orleans." *Cityscape* 9, no. 3 (2007): 23–52.

Nigg, Joanne M. "Disaster Recovery as a Social Process." University of Delaware Research Center, Preliminary Paper no. 219 (1995).

Oliver-Smith, Anthony. "Post-Disaster Housing Reconstruction and Social Inequality: A Challenge to Policy and Practice." *Disasters* 14, no. 1 (1990): 7–19.

Olshansky, Robert B. "How Do Communities Recover from Disaster? A Review of Current Knowledge and an Agenda for Future Research." Forty-Sixth Annual Conference of the Association of Collegiate Schools of Planning, Kansas City, 2005.

Olshansky, Robert B., Laurie A. Johnson, Jedidiah Horne, and Brendan Nee. "Planning for the Rebuilding of New Orleans." *Journal of the American Planning Association* 74, no. 3 (2008): 273–87.

Olson, Richard Stuart. "Toward a Politics of Disaster: Losses, Values, Agendas, and Blame." *International Journal of Mass Emergencies and Disasters* 18, no. 2 (2000): 265–87.

Orr, Marion. *Black Social Capital: The Politics of School Reform in Baltimore, 1986–1998*. Lawrence: University Press of Kansas, 1999.

Pais, Jeremy, and James R. Elliott. "Places as Recovery Machines: Vulnerability and Neighborhood Change after Major Hurricanes." *Social Forces* 86, no. 4 (2008): 1415–53.

Parent, Wayne. *Inside the Carnival: Unmasking Louisiana Politics*. Baton Rouge: Louisiana State University Press, 2006.

Parker, Joseph B. *The Morrison Era: Reform Politics in New Orleans*. Gretna, LA: Pelican Publishing Company, 1974.

Peck, Jamie. *Constructions of Neoliberal Reason*. New York: Oxford University Press, 2010.

Pelling, Mark, and Kathleen Dill. "Disaster Politics: From Social Control to Human Security." Environment, Politics and Development Working Paper Series, Department of Geography, King's College London, 2008.

———. "Disaster Politics: Tipping Points for Change in the Adaptation of Socio-political Regimes." *Progress in Human Geography.* 34, no. 1 (2010): 21–37.

Perkins, Lyle Kenneth. "Failing the Race: A Historical Assessment of New Orleans Mayor Sidney Barthelemy, 1986–1994." MA thesis, Louisiana State University Agricultural and Mechanical College, 2005.

Perry, Huey L. "The Reelection of Sidney Barthelemy as Mayor of New Orleans." *PS: Political Science and Politics* 23, no. 2 (1990): 156–57.

Phillips, Brenda D. "Cultural Diversity in Disasters: Sheltering, Housing, and Long-Term Recovery." *International Journal of Mass Emergencies and Disasters* 11, no. 1 (1993): 99–110.

Piliawsky, Monte. "The Impact of Black Mayors on the Black Community: The Case of New Orleans' Ernest Morial," *Review of Black Political Economy* 13, no. 4 (1985): 5–23.

Plyer, Allison, Richard M. Mizelle Jr., and Roland V. Anglin, eds. *Resilience and Opportunity: Lessons from the U.S. Gulf Coast after Katrina and Rita*. Washington, D.C.: Brookings Institution, 2009.

Plyer, Allison, and Elaine Ortiz. "Benchmarks for Blight: How Much Blight Does New Orleans Have?" Greater New Orleans Community Data Center, August 21, 2012.

The Police Association of New Orleans v. The City of New Orleans, 100 F.3d 1159 (5th Cir. December 9, 1996).

Popkin, Susan J. *The Hidden War: Crime and the Tragedy of Public Housing in Chicago*. New Brunswick, NJ: Rutgers University Press, 2000.

Popkin, Susan J., Larry Buron, Diane Levy, and Mary Cunningham. "The *Gautreaux* Legacy: What Might Mixed-Income and Dispersal Strategies Mean for the Poorest Public Housing Tenants?" *Housing Policy Debate* 11, no. 4 (2000): 911–42.

Popkin, Susan J., Bruce Katz, Mary K. Cunningham, Karen D. Brown, Jeremy Gustafson, and Margery Austin Turner. "A Decade of HOPE VI: Research Findings and Policy Challenges." Washington, DC: The Urban Institute, 2004. http://www.urban.org/UploadedPDF/411002_HOPEVI.pdf (accessed August 22, 2014).

Popkin, Susan J., Margery A. Turner, and Martha Burt. "Rebuilding Affordable Housing in New Orleans: The Challenge of Creating Inclusive Communities." After Katrina series. Washington, DC: The Urban Institute, 2006.

Poumadere, Marc, Claire Mays, Sophie Le Mer, and Russell Blong. "The 2003 Heat Wave in France: Dangerous Climate Change Here and Now." *Risk Analysis* 25, no. 6 (2005): 1483–94.

Powell, Lawrence N. *The Accidental City: Improvising New Orleans*. Cambridge: Harvard University Press, 2012.

Provenzo, Eugene F., and Sandra H. Fradd. *Hurricane Andrew, the Public Schools, and the Rebuilding of Community,* Albany: State University of New York Press, 1995.

Putnam, Robert D., Robert Leonardi, and Raffaella Y. Nanetti. *Making Democracy Work: Civic Traditions in Modern Italy*. Princeton: Princeton University Press, 1994.

Pyles, Loretta. "Neoliberalism, INGO Practices, and Sustainable Disaster Recovery: A Post-Katrina Case Study." *Community Development Journal* 46, no. 2 (2011): 168–80.

Quarantelli, Enrico L. "Patterns of Sheltering and Housing in U.S. Disasters." *Disaster Prevention and Management* 4, no. 3 (1995): 43–53.

Quigley, William P. "Obstacle to Opportunity: Housing That Working and Poor People Can Afford in New Orleans since Katrina." *Wake Forest Law Review*. 42 (2007): 393.

Rast, Joel. "Urban Regime Theory and the Problem of Change." *Urban Affairs Review*, first published November 27, 2014 as doi: 10.1177/1078087414559056.

Rathke, Wade, and Beulah Laboistrie. "The Role of Local Organizing: House to House with Boots on the Ground." In *There Is No Such Thing as a Natural Disaster: Race, Class, and Hurricane Katrina,* edited by Gregory Squires and Chester Hartman, 255–70. New York: Routledge, 2006.

Reed, Adolph, Jr. "Class Inequality, Liberal Bad Faith, and Neoliberalism." In *Neoliberal Strategies in Disaster Reconstruction*, edited by Nandini Gunewardena and Mark Schuller, 147–54. Lanham, MD: Rowman AltaMira, 2008.

Reichl, Alexander J. "Learning from St. Thomas: Community, Capital, and the Redevelopment of Public Housing in New Orleans." *Journal of Urban Affairs* 21, no. 2 (1999): 173–74.

Renwick, Edward F., T. Wayne Parent, and Jack Wardlaw. "Louisiana: Still *Sui Generis* Like Huey." In *Southern Politics in the 1990s*, edited by A. P. Lamis, 281. Baton Rouge: Louisiana State University Press, 1999.

Reynolds, George M. *Machine Politics in New Orleans, 1897–1926*. New York: Columbia University Press, 1968.

Rich, Wilbur C. *Black Mayors and School Politics: The Failure of Reform in Detroit, Gary, and Newark*. New York: Garland Publishing, 1996.

Rose, Kalima. "Community, Faith, and Nonprofit-Driven Housing Recovery." In *Resilience and Opportunity: Lessons from the U.S. Gulf Coast after Katrina and Rita*, edited by Amy Liu, Roland V. Anglin, Richard Mizelle, and Allison Plyer, 99–119. Washington, DC: Brookings Institution Press, 2011.

Rosenbaum, James E., Linda K. Stroh, and Cathy A. Flynn. "Lake Parc Place: A Study of Mixed-Income Housing." *Housing Policy Debate* 9, no. 4 (1998): 703–40.

Saltman, Kenneth J. "Schooling in Disaster Capitalism: How the Political Right Is Using Disaster to Privatize Public Schooling." *Teacher Education Quarterly* (Spring 2007): 131–56.

Sanders, Heywood. "The Politics of Development in Middle-Sized Cities: Getting from New Haven to Kalamazoo." In *The Politics of Urban Development*, edited by Clarence Stone and Heywood Sanders, 182–98. Lawrence: University Press of Kansas, 1987.

Sakakeeny, Matt. "Privatization, Marketization, and Neoliberalism: The Political Dynamics of Post-Katrina New Orleans." *Perspectives on Politics* 10, no. 3 (2012): 709–47.

Savitch, Harold V., and Paul Kantor. *Cities in the International Marketplace: The Political Economy of Urban Development in North America and Western Europe*. Princeton: Princeton University Press, 2002.

Schneider, Aaron. "Privatization, Marketization, and Neoliberalism: The Political Dynamics of Post-Katrina New Orleans." *Perspectives on Politics* 10, no. 3 (2012): 718–20.

Schott, Matthew J. "The New Orleans Machine and Progressivism." *Louisiana History: The Journal of the Louisiana Historical Association* 24, no. 2 (1983): 141–53.

Seligson, Mitchell A. "The Measurement and Impact of Corruption Victimization: Survey Evidence from Latin America." *World Development* 34, no. 2 (2006): 381–404.

Shefter, Martin. "The Emergence of the Political Machine: An Alternative View." In *Theoretical Perspectives on Urban Politics*, edited by Willis D. Hawley, 14–42. Englewood Cliffs, NJ: Prentice-Hall, 1976.

Shipps, Dorothy. Corporate Influence on Chicago School Reform. In *Changing Urban Education*, edited by Clarence N. Stone, 161–83. Lawrence: University Press of Kansas, 1998.

———. "Pulling Together: Civic Capacity and Urban School Reform. *American Educational Research Journal* 40, no. 4 (2003): 841–78.

Sherman, Lawrence. *Scandal and Reform: Controlling Police Corruption*. Berkeley: University of California Press, 1978.

Simmons, William Paul, and Monica J. Casper. "Culpability, Social Triage, and Structural Violence in the Aftermath of Katrina." *Perspectives on Politics* 10, no. 3 (2012): 675–86.

Simpson, Dick, James Nowlan, Thomas J. Gradel, Melissa Mouritsen Zmuda, David Sterrett, and Douglas Cantor. "Chicago and Illinois, Leading the Pack in Corruption." University of Illinois at Chicago and the Illinois Integrity Initiative of the University of Illinois' Institute for Government and Public Affairs, February 15, 2012. http://cbschicago.files.wordpress.com/2012/02/leadingthepack.pdf (accessed August 24, 2014).

Smith, Michael Peter, and Marlene Keller. "'Managed Growth' and the Politics of Uneven Development in New Orleans." In *Restructuring the City: The Political Economy of Urban Development*, rev. ed., edited by Susan S. Fainstein, Norman I. Fainstein, Richard Child Hill, Dennis R. Judd, and Michael Peter Smith, 126–66. New York: Longman, 1986.

Sosna, Morton. Review of *Leander Perez: Boss of the Delta*, by Glen Jeansonne. *American Historical Review* 83, no. 3 (June 1978): 840–41.

Stone, Clarence N. *Regime Politics: Governing Atlanta, 1946–1988*. Lawrence: University Press of Kansas, 1989.

————. "Introduction: Urban Education in Political Context." In *Changing Urban Education*, edited by Clarence N. Stone, 1–22. Lawrence: University Press of Kansas, 1998.

————. "Reflections on *Regime Politics*: From Governing Coalition to Urban Political Order." *Urban Affairs Review*, first published November 23, 2014, as doi: 10.1177/1078087414558948.

Stone, Clarence N., Robert Stoker, et al. *Urban Neighborhoods in a New Era: Revitalization Politics in the Post-Industrial City*. Chicago: University of Chicago Press, 2015.

Stone, Clarence Nathan, and Heywood T. Sanders. *The Politics of Urban Development*. Lawrence: University Press of Kansas, 1987.

Stringfield, Jonathan D. "Higher Ground: An Exploratory Analysis of Characteristics Affecting Returning Populations after Hurricane Katrina." *Population and Environment* 31, nos. 1–3 (2010): 43–63.

Torregano, Michelle Early. "Clean State: Making Sense of Public Education in the 'New' New Orleans." PhD diss., Pennsylvania State University, 2010.

Torregano, Michelle Early, and Patrick Shannon. "Educational Greenfield: A Critical Policy Analysis of Plans to Transform New Orleans Public Schools." *Journal for Critical Education Policy Studies* 7, no. 1 (2009): 320–40.

Tracy, James. "Hope VI: Mixed-Income Housing Projects Displace Poor People." *Race, Poverty & the Environment* 15, no. 1 (2008): 26–29.

Travers, Eva. "Philadelphia School Reform: Historical Roots and Reflections on the 2002–2003 School Year under State Takeover." *Perspectives on Urban Education* 2, no. 2 (2003). http://www.urbanedjournal.org/archive/volume-2-issue-2-fall-2003/philadelphia-school-reform-historical-roots-and-reflections-2002- (accessed August 8, 2014).

Trounstine, Jessica. *Political Monopolies in American Cities: The Rise and Fall of Bosses and Reformers*. Chicago: University of Chicago Press, 2009.

Unter, Kevin A. "The New Orleans Police Department: Melding Police and Policy to Dramatically Reduce Crime in the City of New Orleans." MA thesis, University of New Orleans, 2007.

Useem, Elizabeth. "Big City Superintendent as Powerful CEO: Paul Vallas in Philadelphia." *Peabody Journal of Education: Issues of Leadership, Policy, and Organizations* 84, no. 3 (2009): 300–317.

Vale, Lawrence J., and Thomas J. Campanella. "Conclusion: Axioms of Resilience." In *The Resilient City: How Modern Cities Recovery from Disaster*, edited by Lawrence J. Vale and Thomas J. Campanella, 335–55. New York: Oxford University Press, 2005.

————. "Introduction: The Cities Rise Again." In *The Resilient City: How Modern Cities Recovery from Disaster*, edited by Lawrence J. Vale and Thomas J. Campanella, 3–26. New York: Oxford University Press, 2005.

Van Zandt, Sharon, Walter Gillis Peacock, Dustin W. Henry, Himanshu Grover, Wesley E. Highfield, and Samuel D. Brody. "Mapping Social Vulnerability to Enhance Housing and Neighborhood Resilience." *Housing Policy Debate* 22, no. 1 (2012): 29–55.

Viuker, Steve. "Special Report: Rebuilding New Orleans." *Multi-Housing News*. September 2007.

Walker, Samuel, Geoffrey P. Alpert, and Dennis J. Kenney. "Early Warning Systems: Responding to the Problem Police Officer." In *NIJ Research in Brief.* Washington, DC: National Institute of Justice, 2001.

Wallace, Nicole. "Blueprint for Rebuilding." *Chronicle of Philanthropy* 19, no. 21 (2007): 32.

———. "Fight for Survival Revives New Orleans." *Chronicle of Philanthropy* 20, no. 14 (2008): 30.

———. "Rebuilding Block by Block." *Chronicle of Philanthropy* 20, no. 14 (2008): 27.

Weems, John Edward. "The Galveston Storm of 1900." *Southwestern Historical Quarterly* 61, no. 4 (1958): 494–507.

Weible, Christopher M., Paul A. Sabatier, and Kelly McQueen. "Themes and Variations: Taking Stock of the Advocacy Coalition Framework." *Policy Studies Journal* 37, no. 1 (2009): 121–40.

Weil, Frederick D. "Rise of Community Organizations, Citizen Engagement, and New Institutions." In *Resilience and Opportunity: Lessons from the U.S. Gulf Coast after Katrina and Rita,* edited by Amy Liu, Roland V. Anglin, Richard Mizelle, and Allison Plyer, 201–19. Washington, DC: Brookings Institution Press, 2011.

———. "Can Citizens Affect Urban Policy? Blight Reduction in Post-Katrina New Orleans." Paper prepared for presentation at the Annual Meeting of the American Political Science Association, New Orleans, August 30–September 2, 2012. http://www.rickweil.com/Writings/Weil2012APSACanCitizensAffect UrbanPolicy.pdf (accessed August 8, 2014).

Whelan, Robert K. "New Orleans: Mayoral Politics and Economic-Development Policies in the Postwar Years, 1945–1986." In *The Politics of Urban Development,* edited by Clarence Stone and Heywood Sanders, 216–29. Lawrence: University Press of Kansas, 1987.

———. "New Orleans: Public-Private Partnerships and Uneven Development. In *Unequal Partnerships: The Political Economy of Urban Redevelopment in Postwar America,*" edited by Gregory D. Squires, 222–39. New Brunswick, NJ: Rutgers University Press, 1991.

———. "An Old Economy for the 'New' New Orleans? Post-Katrina Economic Development Efforts." In *There Is No Such Thing as a Natural Disaster: Race, Class, and Hurricane Katrina,* edited by Chester W. Hartman and Gregory D. Squires, 215–31. New York: Routledge, 2006.

Whelan, Robert K., and Alma Young. "New Orleans: The Ambivalent City." In *Big City Politics in Transition,* edited by Hank V. Savitch and John Clayton Thomas, 132–48. Newbury Park, CA: Sage Publications, 1991.

Whitehall, Geoffrey, and Cedric Johnson. "Making Citizens in Magnaville: Katrina Refugees and Neoliberal Self-Governance." In *The Neoliberal Deluge: Hurricane Katrina, Late Capitalism, and the Remaking of New Orleans,* ed. Cedric Johnson, 60–84. Minneapolis: University of Minnesota Press, 2011.

Wieder, Alan. "The New Orleans School Crisis of 1960: Causes and Consequences." *Phylon* 48, no. 2 (1987): 122–31.

Wigginton, Michael Peter, Jr.. "The New Orleans Police Emergency Response to Hurricane Katrina: A Case Study." PhD diss., University of Southern Mississippi, 2007.

Wolensky, Robert P., and Kenneth C. Wolensky. "Local Government's Problem with Disaster Management: A Literature Review and Structural Analysis." *Review of Policy Research* 9, no. 4 (1990): 703–25.

Woods, Clyde. "Les Misérables of New Orleans: Trap Economics and the Asset Stripping Blues, Part I." *American Quarterly* 61, no. 3 (2009): 769–96.

Wu, Jie Ying, and Michael K. Lindell. "Housing Reconstruction after Two Major Earthquakes: The 1994 Northridge Earthquake in the United States and the 1999 Chi-Chi Earthquake in Taiwan." *Disasters* 28, no. 1 (2004): 63–81.

Zhang, Yang. "Will Natural Disasters Accelerate Neighborhood Decline? A Discrete-Time Hazard Analysis of Residential Property Vacancy and Abandonment Before and After Hurricane Andrew in Miami-Dade County (1991–2000)." *Environment and Planning, Part B: Planning and Design* 39, no. 6 (2012): 1084–1104.

Zhang, Yang, and Walter Gillis Peacock. "Planning for Housing Recovery? Lessons Learned from Hurricane Andrew." *Journal of the American Planning Association* 76, no. 1 (2009): 5–24.

Zhang, Yue. *The Fragmented Politics of Urban Preservation: Beijing, Chicago, and Paris*. Minneapolis: University of Minnesota Press, 2013.

Index

Page numbers in *italics* indicate illustrations; those with a *t* indicate tables.

New Orleans Police Foundation (NOPF), 129, 134, 143, 145, 146
New Orleans Recreation Department (NORD), 37–38, 58t
New Schools for New Orleans, 86–88, 101, 102
New Teacher Project, 86
No Child Left Behind policy, 68. *See also* public education
NOPD. *See* New Orleans Police Department

Office of Community Development (OCD), 117, 120, 121, 123
Office of Inspector General (OIG), 36–37, 57, 58t
Office of Recovery Management (ORM), 42
Office of Supplier Diversity, 53
Old Regulars (political organization), 13, 14
Oprah (TV show), 132–133
Orticke, Joseph, 126

Paige, Rod, 83
Palmer, Kristin Gisleson, 56
Pastorek, Paul, 63, 87–94
patronage, 9, 12–13, 15, 147, 153; among local boards and commissions, 17, 22–23, 33; in public education, 62; with Superdome, 27
Peel, Robert, 145
Pennington, Richard, 17, 41, 127–129, 143–146
Perez, Leander, 21–22
Picard, Cecil, 71–73, 81, 88
Piltch, Stuart, 65–67
Pitt, Brad, 48
police. *See* New Orleans Police Department
political arrangements, 4–7, 4t, 5, 6, 148t, 150–162; dysfunctional, 9, 10, 12, 150, 161; for economic development, 57–61; for educational reform, 75–78, 101–103; for housing after Katrina, 112–125, 156; for housing before Katrina, 104–112; machine-style, 13, 143, 147–148, 151, 157, 160–161; for police reform, 129–130, 141–146, 160
Pollitt, Jeff, 65
Port of New Orleans, 28
Powell, Donald, 118, 123
Pratt, Renee Gill, 158
Preservation Resource Center, 107
Project FOCUS, 72–73
Provenzo, Eugene F., 79

public education, 24, 79–80; corruption in, 11, 62, 64–68, 71; desegregation of, 9–10, 20, 66–67; disabled students and, 82, 95, 162; performance of, 63, 67, 68, 89–90, 97–101, 99t, 100t; political arrangements for, 75–78, 101–103; post-Katrina reforms of, 80–103, 152–154; pre-Katrina reforms of, 62–78, 154–156; private schools versus, 10, 24, 45, 84, 103; Quick Start schools and, 45; school violence and, 71; state takeover of, 21, 69–70, 84–85, 84t, 92; teachers' unions and, 69, 71–74, 77, 81–86, 94–95; two-tier, 94–96, 160–162; voter attitudes toward, 82t, 86t, 92–94, 92t, 93t, 94–97; voucher programs and, 96–97. *See also* charter schools
public-private partnerships, 148–153, 148t, 160; for economic development, 38, 40, 43–46, 49–54, 59; for education, 103; for public housing, 107, 111, 115, 122–123, 157
public safety. *See* New Orleans Police Department
Putnam, Robert D., 15, 155

Quality Housing and Work Responsibility Act, 104–105
Quick Start schools, 45
Quigley, Bill, 113

Rathke, Dale, 49
Rathke, Wade, 10, 49
Reagan, Ronald, 28
recovery agenda, 42–45; fidelity to, 4–6, 4t, 149; master plan for, 38–39, 56, 58t; setting of, 47, 150–154. *See also* disaster recovery
Recovery School District (RSD), 80–85, 89, 92–103
red-lining practices, 41. *See also* housing
Reichl, Alexander J., 106–107
Reilly, Robert, 63
Reiss, Jimmy, 71
Renwick, Edward F., 10, 20
Richmond, Cedric, 35–36, 54, 118, 155
Rigamer, Gregory, 151
Riley, Warren, 131, 134, 136, 137, 143, 144
Road Home program, 45, 117–121, 123, 124, 157
Roberti, Bill, 74–75, 83
Robinette, Garland, 133
Rockefeller Foundation, 42, 43
Roemer, Buddy, 30